Working with Families

An Integrative Model by Level of Need

THIRD EDITION

Allie C. Kilpatrick

Professor Emerita, the University of Georgia

Thomas P. Holland

The University of Georgia

Boston   New York   San Francisco
Mexico City   Montreal   Toronto   London   Madrid   Munich   Paris
Hong Kong   Singapore   Tokyo   Cape Town   Sydney

To our grandchildren, who remind us of the
exuberance and joy of living

Allie's grandchildren:

Nicholas Jacob Smith
and
Jessica Rose Smith

Tom's grandchildren:

Trevor Davis Bolton
and
Zachary Tyler Bolton

Series Editor, Social Work and Family Therapy: Patricia Quinlin
Series Editorial Assistant: Annemarie Kennedy
Marketing Manager: Taryn Wahlquist
Composition and Prepress Buyer: Linda Cox
Manufacturing Buyer: JoAnne Sweeney
Cover Administrator: Kristina Mose-Libon
Production Administrator: Deborah Brown
Editorial-Production Service: P. M. Gordon Associates, Inc.

Library of Congress Cataloging-in-Publication Data

Kilpatrick, Allie C.
    Working with families : an integrative model by level of need / Allie C. Kilpatrick, Thomas P. Holland.—3rd ed.
        p.   cm.
    Includes bibliographical references and index.
    ISBN 0-205-36008-4 (paperbound)
    1. Family psychotherapy.   2. Family social work.   I. Holland, Thomas P.

RC488.5 .K55 2002
616.89'156—dc21

2002020063

Printed in the United States of America

10   9   8   7   6   5   4   3   RRDVA   06   05   04

Contents

PART TWO • *First Level of Family Need: Basic Survival   69*

5 *Interventions to Meet Basic Needs in High-Risk Families with Children   69*

R. Kevin Grigsby, D.S.W.

6 *A Family Case Management Approach for Level I Needs   85*

Roberta R. Greene, Ph.D., and Nancy P. Kropf, Ph.D.

PART FOUR • *Third Level of Family Need:*
Boundaries and Control 131

Foreword

As both a family practitioner and an educator for almost 40 years, I have been aware of the need to formulate a theoretical base for family practice that explains family dynamics and provides clear guidelines for effective interventions. In this book, the goal of bringing together family levels of need and practice models is accomplished in a manner that is both comprehensive and easy to grasp.

For me, some of the most valuable material in this book relates to the use of the practitioner's self in the helping process. Clearly, as in all helping endeavors, the person of the practitioner is the vital factor for facilitating change. Murray Bowen, in my opinion, accurately addressed the essence of family practice in his insistence that practitioners can progress with a family only as far as they have progressed in their own family relationships. Linking the maturity level of the practitioner to the overall conditions of the problem context captures a powerful dynamic in the helping process.

In this edition of *Working with Families,* Kilpatrick and Holland outline ways to approach the diversity of family dynamics, family need levels and lifestyles, and the many commonalities shared by all human aggregates throughout the life cycle. In this text, the emphasis on diversity and difference has not obscured the common human needs, capacities, and coping styles of people. There are four entirely new chapters dealing with various strategies to meet different levels of need, written by national and international experts in the field. The ethics cases and commentaries are valuable teaching tools.

Some of the most cogent and thought-provoking parts of *Working with Families* are to be found in the constant emphasis on family strengths and coping capacities. While the authors assert that no single theory is adequate to deal with all family styles, the theories presented here all contain a basic strategy that focuses on levels of need rather than on levels of pathology.

The expanded attention to the domains of family spirituality and professional ethics is especially relevant for the present period of rapid cultural change. The importance of the spiritual dimension cuts across all levels of family need. For many families, the spiritual dimension is crucial for their moral and behavioral guidelines. How can family practitioners understand family needs if they are unaware of the specific moral underpinnings for a particular family?

Family spiritual considerations and professional ethics form a critical part of the ecology of the treatment process for each family with whom we work. The attention *Working with Families* gives to spiritual and ethical considerations deserves careful reading.

Finally, this book directs attention to the specific needs of each specific family and to the interventions needed to address the uniqueness of the family. The content of this book provides the basis for reflective consideration of the meaning of the spiritual and ethical dimensions of family work.

D. Ray Bardill
Professor, School of Social Work
Florida State University
Past President, American Association for Marriage
and Family Therapy

Preface

Working with Families: An Integrative Model by Level of Need was written especially for use as a text for students in social work, marriage and family therapy, counseling, psychology, and human service courses. Faculties in over 100 colleges and universities nationally and internationally are using this text in both undergraduate and graduate courses. This book is especially geared toward applications with families that are usually seen in social service and family agencies, ones that students would typically be working with in their internships and practicum experiences. However, it also addresses family needs at higher levels. Practitioners in the various disciplines have also found it to be useful in their practices.

The purpose of *Working with Families* is to fill the need in social work and family therapy literature for an appropriately relevant textbook on family interventions, addressing the needs of families that students and practitioners typically see. Previous texts have focused on overviews of different models of family therapy, emphasizing primarily one model, a special population, or a problem group. Some have been geared toward middle-class, private-practice clients. Most have presented the therapist as the expert within a family systems context. What is needed is an integrative model for practice, one based on an assessment of the level of need in the family and the particular problems clients are facing within a wider ecological context. Once this assessment is done, then different interventions can be selected that are appropriate for that family's particular level of need at that point in time, around their specific problem area. The authors' goal was to meet the need for such a selective approach.

When students are given a broad overview of all the different models of working with families, they often come away from the course not knowing which specific approach to use in which particular situation. On the other hand, when only one model is taught, students are tempted to use that model with every family, even when it may not be suitable. When the focus is on a special population or problem group, students have difficulty generalizing appropriately to other populations or problem groups. Many family therapy texts are geared toward middle-class, walking-wounded, private-practice clients. These are *not* the families that students or practitioners typically see in agency settings.

This book presents an integrative model to help students and practitioners make the fit between therapeutic style and family need. An overall ecosystems–social constructionism metatheory serves as the philosophical and theoretical base for working with families on four levels of family need. Examples are given of specific approaches to intervention that would be relevant to use on each level of family need.

This third edition of *Working with Families* is revised and updated in order to contain current content and methods. There are four entirely new chapters on practice methods written by internationally known experts in the field. Other chapters have been revised extensively. With the increasing need for professional practitioners to work cross-culturally, even within national boundaries, new vignettes and case studies have been added that are more current and that contribute to examples of client diversity and ethnic-sensitive practice. There is a greater emphasis on diversity, both in a specific chapter and throughout the practice methods sections.

An increased student and client interest in spirituality has led us to emphasize this area of sensitive practice in a specific chapter as well as in various chapters devoted to practice. This added emphasis reflects the current state of knowledge, interest, and attention surrounding this subject area. The concepts of resilience and family strengths are emphasized as the base on which to build. Ethically informed practice is a current issue. For this reason, we have added an appendix that contains the NASW Code of Ethics and seven ethics cases with commentaries from experts in the field, along with references to specific standards of the code of ethics relevant to that particular case. The Glossary has been expanded to include terms used in the new chapters.

Part One of *Working with Families* covers the theory base and contextual and practice concerns that are useful with families at any level of need. Chapter 1, by Kilpatrick, presents a framework of the four levels of needs of families. This framework serves as a priority-setting guide that enables students and practitioners to determine which methods approach one would use with a specific family. As such, the chapter is a beginning assessment tool grounded in the therapeutic assumption that interventions must start addressing the level of the most basic need before moving on to higher levels of needs and interventions. In Chapter 2, the theory that undergirds this integrative approach is discussed by Holland and Kilpatrick. The metatheories of ecosystems and social constructionism form the philosophical and theoretical foundations for the needs of families and for the methods used to meet these needs as presented in this book.

In Chapter 3, Hopps and Kilpatrick discuss the importance of the helping relationship/therapeutic alliance and the contexts of client diversities that must be addressed on any level of need. The focus on human diversity and ethnic-sensitive practice gives a global perspective to students and practitioners, and requires the practitioner to think in terms of a multisystem, interactive, international approach. Whether practiced in the United States or elsewhere, this perspective on diversity is crucial as our world becomes one community. A cross-cultural practice model is presented, and client diversity in terms of gender, power, and family structures is discussed. Although the focus is on diversity issues, the emphasis is on commonalities that unite us rather than on differences that divide us.

In the last chapter in Part One, Chapter 4, Kilpatrick, Becvar, and Holland provide suggestions for creating a practice that is well informed relative to ethical decision making and sensitive to the role of spirituality in the lives of both practitioners and clients. Guides for ethical decision making are presented and relevant codes of ethics discussed. The appendix added to this third edition of *Working with Families* is to be used in connection with this chapter. The discussion on spirituality has been greatly enlarged and emphasized. A Framework for Spiritual Assessment that students and practitioners should find very helpful is included. Specific examples of spiritually oriented helping activities that students and practitioners could utilize with their clients are also presented.

Parts Two through Five focus on interventions that are appropriate for families on each of the four levels of family need. Each chapter includes examples of interventions that would be relevant but that are not the only ones that could be used on that level. With a shift in emphasis, some of the approaches could be used on more than one level of family need. Each chapter discusses how a specific approach could be applied to families that have needs on levels other than the one that we focus on in that chapter.

Each chapter in Parts Two through Five follows a similar format, addressing the following subjects:

- Needs presented by the family.
- Assessment, especially determining the level of need of the family.
- Goals of the intervention.
- Intervention approach used, including the basic tenets of the approach, application to a family, specific interventions, and how the interventions are evaluated for effectiveness.
- Application to families on other levels of need.
- Summary.
- Discussion questions.
- Suggested readings.
- References.

Page numbers indicating where each of these subjects can be found in each chapter are given in the Outline of Approaches on p. xx.

In Part Two, the first level of family need is addressed. This first level deals with basic survival issues. The chapters in this part present two approaches to family practice that are appropriate for families on the first level of need. Chapter 5, by Grigsby, presents the family-centered approach, which is designed to address basic needs in high-risk families with children. Greene and Kropf, in Chapter 6, present the case management approach, which is a process for assisting families who have multiple service needs.

The second level of family need is presented in Part Three. This level is concerned with structure, limits, and safety. In a new Chapter 7, Aponte, internationally known as one of the founders and developers of structural family therapy, presents this systems-based model that places a special focus on the internal organization of relationships within families. In Chapter 8, Horne and Sayger present the social learning family interventions approach to families. This approach deals with both internal and external, or environmental, factors that affect family needs and focuses on learning more effective social skills.

Part Four deals with the third level of family need, which is concerned with boundaries and control. Both chapters presenting approaches to intervention are new. In Chapter 9, Koob discusses solution-focused interventions, one of the brief intervention approaches that are appropriate for families at this level of need. The emphasis on health and strengths makes it an especially useful model for families at this level of need. In Chapter 10, Walsh presents family systems interventions, a widely utilized approach to family assessment and intervention. It provides a comprehensive conceptual framework for understanding how *emotional ties* within families of origin influence the lives of individuals and pays attention to multigenerational family processes and interventions.

Part Five addresses interventions at the fourth level of family need: family and personal growth. This higher level of need is represented by a focus on inner richness and quality of life. In Chapter 11, a new chapter, Williams and Kurtz discuss narrative family interventions. This approach emphasizes the *meaning* that families make of their experiences instead of the cause of the problem. It makes use of a collaborative, co-learning therapeutic relationship. The second approach, presented in Chapter 12 by Kilpatrick and Trawick, is object relations family interventions (ORFI). ORFI is a bridge between working with individuals and working with families and is essentially interactional in its intervention processes. It gives primacy to the need for a human relationship, even at birth.

In Part Six, the final chapter looks at the larger issues of the family in the community context. Chapter 13, by Turner and MacNair, discusses the ecosystem implications of working with families at the macrosystem level, thus integrating the previous intervention approaches with the theoretical and philosophical foundations presented earlier.

Acknowledgments

Our great appreciation goes to all the contributors to this third edition. They are experts in their fields, and we are grateful for the time and energy they have given.

The reviewers of the first and second editions made some very valuable suggestions that made the book more relevant, readable, and user friendly. These suggestions and ideas were helpful and have been incorporated into later editions.

Dr. Ray Bardill kindly agreed to write the Foreword for this edition. Many thanks go to him for taking time out of his busy schedule, and also for the many contributions and insights as well as the inspiration he has provided the senior author in working with families. He has been a role model in having the courage to write and speak about spirituality when it was not popular to do so.

Thanks are due to the reviewers of this third edition: Joseph Walsh, Virginia Commonwealth University; Thomas E. Smith, Florida State University; and Jean M. Granger, California State University. We are very grateful to Patricia Quinlin and the editorial staff of Allyn and Bacon. They have been most supportive and cooperative even while gently pushing to get this new edition into production. Their contributions have been helpful, timely, and professional. Thank you!

A final and most heartfelt note of appreciation goes to our families. They have been very patient and loving during this process, and contributed in unique ways to our ideas about families. Allie would like to pay special tribute to her sisters, Martha Jo Paxson, Wynelle Ruark, and Myra Folsom, for the special "sister" relationship we have and for their special abilities to laugh, love, and serve their God, their Church, and others, and to her brother Marshall Callaway, for his love of nature, his good-natured teasing, and his patience with his four younger sisters.

Authors

Allie C. Kilpatrick, M.S.W., M.C.E., Ph.D., is Professor Emerita of the University of Georgia School of Social Work, where she taught for almost 25 years. She has published extensively in areas of family and social work practice and was instrumental in the development of the interdisciplinary certificate program in Marriage and Family Therapy (MFT) at the University of Georgia, where she served as its coordinator. She is a Diplomate in Clinical Social Work, member of the Academy of Certified Social Workers, and Clinical Member and Approved Supervisor for AAMFT, and is licensed in Georgia as a Clinical Social Worker and as a Marriage and Family Therapist.

Thomas P. Holland, Ph.D., is Professor and Director of the Institute for Nonprofit Organizations, University of Georgia. He also has been Associate Dean and Chairman of the doctoral program at the Mandel School of Applied Social Sciences, Case Western Reserve University, Cleveland, Ohio. Dr. Holland has published extensively on management and governance of nonprofit organizations. He was recently recognized by the University of Georgia as Outstanding Teacher of the Year and by his school as Outstanding Scholar of the Year.

Contributors

Harry J. Aponte, M.S.W., L.C.S.W., currently directs the Family Therapy Training Program of Philadelphia and trains therapists in a variety of locations within and outside of the United States. He has an appointment as Clinical Associate Professor at MCP Hahnemann University in Philadelphia. He is advisory editor on a variety of professional journals in this country and abroad, including *Family Process.* Mr. Aponte was a teacher of family therapy at the Menninger Clinic and Director of the Philadelphia Child Guidance Clinic. He has published *Bread & Spirit* through Norton, a book that speaks to therapy with today's poor in the context of ethnicity, culture, and spirituality.

Dorothy S. Becvar, Ph.D., is a Licensed Marital and Family Therapist, a Licensed Clinical Social Worker in private practice in St. Louis, Missouri, and President and CEO of the Haelan Centersä. She has authored *In the Presence of Grief: Helping Family Members Resolve Death, Dying, and Bereavement Issues* (Guilford Press, 2001); and *Soul Healing: A Spiritual Orientation in Counseling and Therapy* (Basic Books, 1997) and is editor of *The Family, Spirituality, and Social Work* (Haworth, 1997). She has served on the faculties of the University of Missouri, St. Louis; St. Louis University; Texas Technical University; Washington University; and Radford University.

Roberta R. Greene, M.S.W., Ph.D., is Professor of Social Work at the University of Indiana, Indianapolis. She is the former Dean of this School and also served as Associate Dean of the University of Georgia School of Social Work. She is a leading author in the areas of social work literature, multicultural issues, gerontology, and geriatric social work. Her books include *Social Work Case Management* (with B. S. Vourlekis), *Human Behavior Theory: A Diversity Framework,* and *Human Behavior Theory and Social Work Practice* (with P. Ephross).

R. Kevin Grigsby, D.S.W., L.C.S.W., is Vice Dean for Faculty and Administrative Affairs and Professor of Behavioral Science at Pennsylvania State College of

Medicine in Hershey, Pennsylvania. Dr. Grigsby has an extensive history of program planning, implementation, and evaluation in the area of innovative home- and community-based health and mental health services. His practice experience has been primarily in underserved rural and inner-city areas. His areas of practice expertise include children at imminent risk of out-of-home placement, perinatal intervention with substance-abusing women, children and adolescents in shelter care, home-based services to parents and children with HIV-related illnesses, and the use of advanced telecommunications technology in health services delivery.

June G. Hopps, Ph.D., is Professor and Dean Emerita, Graduate School of Social Work, Boston College. Currently she is Visiting Professor at the University of Georgia, School of Social Work, and Chair, Board of Trustees, Spelman College. She is former editor-in-chief of the journal *Social Work* and associate editor-in-chief for the *Encyclopedia of Social Work,* 19th ed. She is the coauthor of two books and coeditor of one other published by the Free Press: *The Power to Care, Group Work with Overwhelmed Clients,* and *Social Work at the Millennium.* She is also coeditor of two other books: *Evaluation of Human Service Programs* (Schenkeman Press) and *Privatization in Central and Eastern Europe* (Praeger). She is the author of more than 50 articles and editorials.

Arthur M. Horne, Ph.D., is Professor in the Counseling Psychology Program and a faculty member of the certificate program in Marriage and Family Therapy at the University of Georgia. Dr. Horne is coauthor or coeditor of *Troubled Families, Family Counseling and Therapy, Group Counseling and Group Psychotherapy, Handbook of Counseling Boys and Adolescent Males, Treating Conduct and Oppositional Defiant Disordered Children,* and *Bully Busters.* He is the Principal Investigator of the Middle School Violence Prevention Program and the Coprincipal Investigator of ACT Early: Identifying and Assisting Youth at Risk.

Jeffrey J. Koob, M.S.W., L.C.S.W., Ph.D., is an Assistant Professor at California State University, Long Beach, Department of Social Work. He originally interned at the Brief Family Therapy Center in Milwaukee, Wisconsin, in 1985, when Steve de Shazer and Insoo Berg were writing and developing Solution-focused Brief Therapy (SFBT). His research, teaching, and service are directed toward the application of SFBT to different populations and treatment settings.

Nancy P. Kropf, M.S.W., Ph.D., is Associate Professor of Social Work and former Associate Dean at the University of Georgia. Her areas of research include caregiving relationships of older families and older people who have lifelong disabilities. She is currently President of the Association for Gerontology Education–Social Work (AGE–SW) and is a Hartford Geriatric Social Work Scholar. Her extensive publications include *Developmental Disabilities: Handbook of Interdisciplinary Practice* (with B. A. Thyer) and *Gerontological Social Work: Knowledge, Service Settings, and Special Populations* (with R. L. Schneider).

P. David Kurtz, Ph.D., is retired from the University of Georgia, where he served as a full Professor in the School of Social Work for 20 years. He also served as Director of the Social Work Doctoral Program and Coordinator of the Pre-Professional Certificate Program in Marriage and Family Therapy. Prior to coming to the University of Georgia, he was on the faculties at The Pennsylvania State University and the University of Tennessee. His teaching and research interests include troubled children and adolescents, family violence, school social work, family counseling, social justice, and spirituality.

Ray H. MacNair, M.A., M.S.W., Ph.D., is Director of M.S.W. Admissions at the University of Georgia School of Social Work. His practice specialties are community development, neighborhood organizing, affordable housing, social movement organizing, community-based research, and collaborative systems. His publications include analysis of collaborative system styles, citizen participation, agency boundary maintenance, research on human service planning groups, the ecological theory of community practice, analysis of various forms of community practice research, and the impact of identities on social movement organizing.

Thomas V. Sayger, Ph.D., is a Professor and Co-Director of Training in Counseling Psychology at the University of Memphis. He is a licensed psychologist, member of the Division of Family Psychology of the American Psychological Association, and member of the Executive Board of the Council of Counseling Psychology Training Programs. Dr. Sayger's research and clinical practice focus on prevention, early intervention, and family–school collaborative programs for behavior-disordered children and their families.

Elizabeth O. Trawick, M.D., is a psychoanalyst in private practice in Beverly Hills, California. She has been interested in Object Relation/Kleinian theory for many years and treats children, adults, and families using these formulations. She is an Assistant Clinical Professor of Psychiatry at the University of California, Los Angeles. She is on the faculty of two psychoanalytic institutes and is the current president of the Los Angeles Psychoanalytic Society.

John B. Turner, D.S.W., is Dean and Professor Emeritus, School of Social Work, University of North Carolina, Chapel Hill. He has also been Dean and Professor at the Mandel School of Applied Social Sciences, Case Western Reserve University, Cleveland, Ohio. He taught at Atlanta University School of Social Work; the University of Georgia School of Social Work; Smith College, McGill University, and the University of Toronto Schools of Social Work; and also taught at schools of social work in Egypt. His practice and research interests include minority poor families and children, group work, community organization, and policy.

Joseph Walsh, L.C.S.W., Ph.D., is an Associate Professor of Social Work at Virginia Commonwealth University. He has been a clinical practitioner in the field of mental health since 1974, specializing in work with persons having mental illness and their families. He is the author of *Clinical Case Management with Persons Having Mental Illness: A Relationship-based Perspective* and coauthor (with Kia Bentley) of *The Social Worker and Psychotropic Medication.*

Nancy R. Williams, Ph.D., is an Assistant Professor of Social Work in the University of Georgia's School of Social Work. She received her doctorate in Marriage and the Family from Florida State University and is licensed as both a Clinical Social Worker and Marriage and Family Therapist. She has over 25 years of direct practice experience in the mental health/human services field, working with individuals, groups, couples, and families. Her current research areas include resilience development in trauma survivors, conflict resolution skill development, and integrative psychoeducational groups for couples.

Outline of Approaches

Level of Need	I	I	II	II	III	III	IV	IV
Authors	Grigsby	Greene & Kropf	Aponte	Horne & Sayger	Koob	Walsh	Williams & Kurtz	Kilpatrick & Trawick
Approach	Family Preservation	Case Management	Structural Family Interventions	Social Learning Family Interventions	Solution-focused Interventions	Family Systems Interventions	Narrative Family Interventions	Object Relations Family Interventions
Need(s)	70	85	104	116	132	152	176	197
Assessments	70	86	105	119	133	152	177	200
Goals	73	88	107	119	136	158	178	204
Intervention approach	74	89	108	121	143	158	178	204
Basic tenets	74	89	108	121	134	158	178	204
Application	75	94	108	122	138	161	183	208
Interventions	76	95	108	122	143	163	183	209
Evaluation	79	97	111	127	146	167	189	211
Other levels	80	99	112	128	148	169	190	213
Summary	81	99	112	128	148	169	191	214
Discussion questions	81	100	113	129	148	170	191	214
Suggested readings	82	100	113	129	148	171	192	215
References	83	101	114	130	149	171	193	215

Note: Numbers in the table body are page references.

1

Levels of Family Need

Allie C. Kilpatrick, Ph.D.

Helping professionals see families who are on many different levels of need. Their circumstances, problems, and skills are varied. For a practitioner to use only one model of assessment and intervention is like the saying "If the only tool you have is a hammer, everything looks like a nail." The situation is required to fit the helper's model even when there is no workable fit. Thus the helper's need is met, rather than the clients' needs. This chapter describes four levels of family need and explores various methods of assessment and interventions that are relevant at each level.

In her 1945 social work classic, *Common Human Needs*, Charlotte Towle wrote about needs in relation to factors that affect human development. She contended that the following elements are essential if persons are to develop into maturity and be motivated toward social goals: physical welfare, such as food, shelter, and health care; opportunity for emotional and intellectual growth; relationships with others; and provision for spiritual needs. She points out that needs are relative to a person's age and life situation. Most human needs are typically met within a family structure or in relationship with others.

Abraham Maslow (1970) developed a hierarchy of needs that supports Towle's thinking and expands our understanding of human development. According to his hierarchy, a person must satisfy primary physiological needs before social needs can be considered. He included five levels of need: physical and life-sustaining needs (the need for food, water, air, warmth, sexual gratification, elimination of bodily wastes, and so on); physical safety (the need for protection from physical attack and disease); love (the need to be cherished, supported, and aided by others); self-esteem (the need to have a sense of personal worth and value, to respect and value one's self); and self-actualization (the need to be creative and productive, and to attain worthwhile objectives). We must remember, however, that often a lower-level need cannot be satisfied without a relationship with another person, as, for example, a young child's need for food.

Building on these two formulations of needs, family problems encountered in helping situations may be seen as clustered around various levels of need based on the primary need at that time. These range from the basic survival needs to concerns about the self-actualization of family members and spiritual needs. Weltner (1985, 1986) views functional levels of families' needs from the analogy of building a house, which draws our attention to the necessity of addressing the most basic level of needs before moving to higher levels of need. Figure 1.1 illustrates the four levels of family need that will be utilized in this book.

Level I

The most basic level of family need has to do with the essential requisites for survival and well-being. These include the family's needs for food, shelter, protection from danger, health care, and minimums of nurturance. Referring to the house analogy, Level I would be the basement and refers to life and death issues (see Figure 1.1).

Some families experience crises, such as a job loss or major illness that leaves them destitute. Other families who do not adequately meet these challenges are often considered neglectful and underorganized. These families lack a leadership and control structure that is needed in order to meet basic nurturing and protection needs of members. In other words, there is insufficient parenting capacity. According to the Beavers Family Competence Scale (Beavers, Hulgus, & Hampson, 1988), these families are leaderless; no one has enough power to structure interactions. This situation was more descriptive of neglectful families in lower socioeconomic circumstances than of nonneglectful families in similar circumstances (Gaudin, Polansky, Kilpatrick, & Shilton, 1991).

Sometimes, families struggling with Level I problems show evidence that the parental coalition is weakened or undermined by a parent–child coalition; family closeness is amorphous and vague, with indistinct boundaries among members. Faced with such basic resource deprivations as food, shelter, protection, education, clothing, transportation, and medical care, these families are rarely able to provide one another with the necessary emotional nurturance (Epstein, Bishop, & Baldwin, 1982). Examples of typical problems may include an overwhelmed single mother (as is the case in most neglectful families); the incapacitation or dysfunction of the strongest family member by illness, alcohol, or drugs; and natural or emotional catastrophes and pervasive life stresses that have depleted physical and emotional resources.

Work with these families must build on basic strengths and resiliences—as is true at all levels—and focus on resources. For Level I families, Weltner (1985) suggests that the intervention should center on mobilizing support for the ineffective executive or parental system. Intervention could begin with a survey of potential resources from the community, including church groups or extended family (genograms and ecomaps are helpful; see Hartman & Laird, 1983), and then assess and build on family resilience and family strengths. Resilience, or the ability

Level IV
Fine art of living.
Focus on inner conflict,
problems, intimacy,
self-actualization,
insight, and yearnings.

Level III
Space (privacy and
access). Focus on
boundaries (individual,
family, and generational).

Level II
Limits and safety.
Focus on strengths,
controls, patterns
of coping.

Level I
Food, shelter,
protection, medical
care, minimal
nurturance. Focus on
strengths and resources.

IV
Furnishing & Decorations
(Richness & Quality)

III
Placement of Walls & Doors
(Space & Boundaries)

II
Framing and Roof
(Structure and Organization)

I
Basement/Foundation
(Basic Survival)

FIGURE 1.1   *Levels of Family Needs: Issues and Relevant Interventions*
Source: Kilpatrick & Cleveland, 1993.

to withstand and rebound from crises and adversities, can be strengthened. Helping families to discover positive meanings in stress and distress is an important ingredient in strength-based interventions. Wolin and Wolin (1993), for example, highlight the "survivor's pride" (p. 8). This help could be offered to families demonstrating resilience in some area. Case management and referral to medical, income maintenance, and legal resources; protective services and family preservation programs; and hospitalization in crises may be necessary. Advocacy and guidance may be indicated, depending on the situation. Guidance on the use of respite care, referral to substance-abuse counseling, child development and child care information, and budget and time management may be necessary. Often, an advocacy role with school, welfare, and correctional or juvenile justice systems is necessary. Table 1.1 illustrates some of the issues, relevant intervention strategies, and possible intervention techniques that could be applicable on this level.

The following brief case study is illustrative of a family with needs on Level I and typical interventions that could be used. The case study demonstrates the mobilization of resources through case management skills and building on strengths to meet family needs.

> Mrs. M. came to the attention of Family Services after she called the hotline. She had not been feeling well for some time and had lost her job. After she was diagnosed with AIDS, which was given to her by her husband, he had left her. She had no source of income and was being evicted from her apartment in the housing project. She had two daughters, ages two and four, and they were without food. Family Services was able to meet her immediate needs by helping with food and paying the rent. They then referred her to Family Support Services. The worker there, using case management, helped her to obtain treatment for AIDS. After assessing her potential resources and strengths, and with some encouragement from the worker, Mrs. M. agreed to contact some family members for help with the children. In the meantime, with education and support from the worker, the mother was able to provide more security, nurturing, and support for the children. With Mrs. M's approval and cooperation, the worker helped to locate her husband. After counseling with them both, he agreed to obtain medical treatment and to return home.

Level II

With Level II families, the basic needs of minimal safety, stability, and nurturance have been met, and maintaining authority and setting limits are the prominent issues. In the house analogy in Figure 1.1, Level II refers to the framing and roof of the house, and represents the family's structure and organization. The parental system is unable to set and maintain sufficient limits for one or more family members, and this inability threatens the stability of the whole family system. This failure could involve either a lack of clear expectations or a lack of power to enforce the expectations.

Other examples could include families where the children are out of control, acting-out teenagers and parents are involved in substance abuse or excessive gambling, or are otherwise failing to maintain key structures for the family. Marital conflict may appear to be out of control and threaten dissolution of the family

TABLE 1.1 Family Assessment and Intervention

Level	Issue	Intervention Strategy	Intervention Technique

I	• Is executive capacity sufficient to manage all basic nurturant needs?
	• Food, shelter, protection, medical care, minimal nurturance.
	• Resilience of individual and family.
		• Focus on strengths, not problems.
		• Survey and mobilize available support to bolster executive capacity.
		• Family resilience building.
		• Positive response to stress.
			• Family preservation.
			• Case management.
			• Marshal more troops from:
			    Nuclear family.
			    Extended family.
			    Community.
			• Professional as convener, advocate, teacher, role model.

II	• Is there sufficient authority to provide minimal structure, limits, and safety?	• Focus on strengths.
		• Develop a coalition of those in charge against those needing control.
		• Increase clarity of expectation.
			• Parental coalitions.
			• Set limits.
			• Clear communication.
			• Social learning skills.
			    Written contracts.
			    Behavioral reinforcers.
			    Task assignments.

III	• Are there clear and appropriate boundaries?
	    Family
	    Individual
	    Generational
		• Focus on problems.
		• Clarify the "ideal" family structure in conformity with ethnic or family expectations.
		• Generational clarity.
			• Defend family and individual boundaries.
			• Balance triangles.
			• Rebuild alliances.
			• Develop generational boundaries.
			• Communication skills.

IV	• Are there problems of inner conflict or problems with intimacy? • Are family members self-actualizing?	• Focus on problems. • Clarification and resolution of legacies and historical trauma. • Insight. • Focus on yearnings and spiritual needs.	• Narrative interventions. • Family sculpture. • Object relations interventions. • Resolution of three-generational issues. • Spiritual growth.

Source: Adapted from Weltner, 1985, p. 49.

unit. Violence in the family may be a threat, but members are not seen as needing immediate protection.

    Again, interventions would begin with a survey of strengths, resiliences, and resources. In order to have the authority to deal with the situation and to offer sufficient hope, the practitioner must be in charge of structuring the sessions. Structural interventions enable the spouses to develop a coalition strong enough to demonstrate sufficient authority for the family to gain control of threatening or destructive behaviors.

Weltner (1986) points out that the focus of treatment in such situations must be to "develop a coalition of those in charge against those needing control" (p. 53). Family mapping of coalitions (Minuchin, 1974; Hartman & Laird, 1983) could be helpful with these families. Social learning and behavioral techniques with structural considerations may prove empowering to family members. Paquin and Bushorn (1991) show how behavioral techniques can help clarify the family's expectations for the behavior of each of its members and help them recognize their potential for modifying the behaviors of other family members.

The case study given below is typical of Level II family needs. As in Level I, interventions would begin with a survey of strengths, resilence, and resources.

> Jose, age ten, was referred to the school social worker for disrupting the classroom, fighting with the other boys, and failing to do homework. His father was the head of household in this single-parent, Hispanic family. His mother had died of cancer when Jose was seven. He had two older sisters in high school who were going through turbulent teenage years.
>
> After talking with Jose, his teachers, and then his father, the social worker began working with the teachers on some social learning and behavior techniques to modify Jose's behavior in the classroom. Jose's father was unable to come to the school during the day because he could not get off from work. The worker talked with him by phone in the evening and found that Jose was alone at home after school, with little or no supervision or structure from his sisters. His father worked long hours and was so tired at night that he just wanted to sit and drink beer. The children usually ate junk food for dinner on their own.
>
> The worker scheduled an appointment to see all of them together in the evening. The mother's sister who lived nearby was also there. After discussing the concerns all of them were seeing in the family, they agreed that the aunt would work with the girls to help them take more responsibility for supervising Jose and helping him with his homework. She would also help them to prepare more nourishing meals at night. The father agreed to spend more time with Jose, especially on weekends. They related that they had all become more disorganized since the mother had died. Jose in particular had gradually become more aggressive and less interested in school. The worker suggested a referral to the mental health clinic so that Jose, as well as the rest of the family, could do their grief work concerning the mother. They all agreed to go. Within a few months, Jose's behavior and grades improved and he was taking more interest in school.

Although a wide variety of techniques may be used, both Level I and Level II interventions are essentially structural (Weltner, 1985) and ecosystems oriented. The goal is to mobilize all of the resources available, to modify the organizational patterns of the family, and to increase and test the strength of the parental or executive system. It is important to remember that children such as Jose have a readiness to fall in line. They are often aware of how much their own and their family's lives suffer as a result of their lack of discipline and control.

Level III

Level III focuses on space, with privacy and access as the issues. Using the house analogy in Figure 1.1, this level is concerned with the inner architecture. Although the foundation, walls, and roof are satisfactory, the arrangements of inner space, or the placement of walls and doors, are not. Level III families are complicated, and they have a structure and style that is often perceived as working. They may draw on and express a three-generational legacy, not a set of inherited deficiencies (Weltner, 1985). As pointed out by Aponte (1976), underorganized families (Levels I and II) generally do not transmit adequate patterns of coping. By contrast, Level III and IV families have a rich mixture of coping mechanisms. Weltner (1985) describes these coping mechanisms as their characteristic defenses, the culture to which they are committed and which they attempt to pass on to and through their children.

If work with such families involves changing ingrained patterns, we can anticipate some struggle. Therefore, our techniques need to encompass and adapt to such struggles. The Beavers Interactional Competence Scale (Beavers et al., 1988) rates these families as having marked or moderate dominance (control is close to absolute, with little or no negotiation; dominance and submission are the rule) while family members are isolated and distanced from one another.

Level III interventions involve processes of reshaping the internal architecture of the family so that everyone has appropriate space, access, and privacy. Interventions with these families must challenge the existing family structure and confront the family's tendency to remain in current patterns of behavior. Examination of the communication and power structures around the presenting problem may be useful. Differentiation and individuation of family members from each other and the emotional system, flexibility, and clear generational boundaries are essential.

The following case study summarizes a case presented by Pippin & Callaway (1999) and is illustrative of the needs of families in Level III. Although a family systems approach is taken in this case, other Level III families' needs could be approached through solution-focused family interventions.

Bill, Sr., and Carmen have two children, Bill, Jr., age 14, and Sonia, age 12. Bill, Jr., has always been difficult to manage. At this time he is sullen and negative at home, his school grades are low, and his parents fear that he is involved with alcohol and marijuana. Sonia seems to be a model child. Carmen is quiet, has an overinvolved relationship with Sonia, but appears to be bonded with Bill, Jr. Bill, Sr., is a successful surgeon. At home he exerts absolute authoritarian control. Both parents describe their own parents' relationships as conflictual and their own relationship as conflictual.

There are three significant intergenerational triangles. First, Bill, Jr., and his mother are allied against his father. Next, Carmen and her mother have an overinvolved relationship which is repeated in Carmen's relationship with her own daughter. The third significant triangle is that of Bill, Sr., Carmen, and Bill, Jr., which is the same as Bill, Sr., had in his family of origin. The significance of these triangles is the degree of fusion. Members in this three-generational family are so deeply enmeshed that inevitable growth and change with age is viewed with terror.

The overarching goal of treatment with this Level III family is realignment of the family system and establishment of boundaries. A second overall goal is to identify and ameliorate the sources of chronic anxiety within the family system that undermine individual growth and autonomy. The parental subsystem must be strengthened to become a supporting team in the management of the children.

Level IV

In Level IV families, basic needs are met, and structural boundaries are relatively clear and satisfactory. Presenting problems often focus on a desire for greater intimacy, greater sense of self, or more autonomy. The concern of Level IV families is the fine art of living fully and growing toward actualization of each member's potential. In relation to the house analogy, this level of functioning represents decorations, pictures, rugs, and lamps. Here the richness and quality of individuals and family life become the focus of interventions. Although some of these issues may have been discussed at earlier levels, it is on Level IV that such issues as inner conflicts, intimacy, self-realization, insight, and spiritual yearnings become the primary focus and are explored in depth.

Genograms extending over three or four or more generations are useful on this level in showing transgenerational patterns. Family sculpting may also be used. A focus on narrative interventions and rewriting one's own story are especially applicable on this level of family functioning. Object relations family interventions may be particularly helpful with these families, who desire insight into patterns and intergenerational functioning. Some families or individuals may want to focus on clarifying personal values, meanings, and spirituality, or they may wish to deal with existential issues. Helping professionals must be open to pursuing such issues, be comfortable in discussing them, and be able to assist families in clarifying their values and discovering the transcendent aspects of their being without imposing personal conclusions on them. Referrals to church-related counseling centers may be indicated.

Following is a family situation that may be a typical example for Level IV families:

> A middle-class couple with several children entered treatment with the complaint by the wife of vague feelings of depression and loneliness. She and her husband began to do extended family work with some emphasis on object relations. Working through some of their earlier relationships and projection processes and contacts with family made the wife feel more connected and less lonely. The couple was able to weather the terminal illness of her mother in a relatively calm fashion, without the wife's becoming too depressed during the grief-work period. The loss of her mother opened up the desires of both members of the couple to focus more

on inner awareness and spiritual growth. Building on insights gained and ongoing contacts with extended family, both were able to rewrite their own life story to some degree.

Intervention Criteria

Once the primary, current level of need is assessed, then an opening for intervention must be determined. Do you start with the family, the couple, or an individual? Do you deal with what people do, what they think and feel, or what has happened in the past? Do you assume health or pathology? Is the primary need for maintenance of functioning or problem resolution? These questions are addressed by an intervention choice points grid developed by Pinsof (1995, 1991), shown in Figure 1.2.

The "Contexts" columns in the table refer to the people who are involved in the problem maintenance structure. This could be the family (including the extended family and the community), the couple in the same generation (allowing for alternate lifestyles), or an individual. The "Orientations" headings refer to three intervention choices.

The *behavioral/interactional choice* has to do with what people do, their actions, and changing this. It involves surface behavior and is visual. Social learning, strategic, functional, and structural techniques may be used here.

Orientations	Contexts		
	Family/ Community	Couple Dyadic	Individual
Behavioral/Interactional	*Start Here If Fails Go*		
Experiential			
Historical			

FIGURE 1.2 *Intervention Choice Points*

Source: Adapted from Pinsof, 1991.

The *experiential choice* makes use of cognition, affect, communication, and interpersonal relationships—what people think and feel. It involves meaning and uses auditory senses—listening. Both of these first two choices focus on the here and now.

The *historical choice* is the third intervention. It adds the dimension of time and addresses what has happened in the past. Family-of-origin work and psychodynamic or psychoanalytic methods may be used.

This model assumes that the people involved are healthy and that the problem can be resolved at a direct behavioral level. Therefore, in order to choose how to intervene, your decision points should progress from upper left to lower right, as shown in Figure 1.2. In other words, begin with the context of the family and the behavioral orientation. If the approach in this cell does not work, proceed down the cells diagonally to working with the couple experientially. If this approach does not work, then go to the individual and work with historical material. The progression is problem or failure driven in that, if a more direct approach is not successful, you proceed to another, less direct approach. It is also circular in that you continue to deal with meaning and behavior, and link what you are doing to the presenting problem. There is an explicit contract between the practitioner and the family to address the problem, so there must be a link between the presenting problem and what the practitioner does. This helps to keep the practitioner honest.

The essence of the choice framework is that working with families is a process of discovery, a "peeling of the onion." Is the problem simple and superficial or deep and complex? The family is assumed to be healthy and to have a simple, superficial problem that can be addressed at the family-unit level with behavioral interventions until it is proven that the problem exists at deeper levels. Therefore, practice begins with simple, cost-effective interventions. The goal is to teach the family to learn from the practitioner how to solve problems for themselves. This process may involve internalizing the approach of the practitioner so the family can assume what the practitioner would say or do and thus work things out for themselves.

Once a family's basic survival needs are met, this choice framework can provide a guide for work at the four levels of need within the house metaphor. The three orientations of the Pinsof choice points grid are then applicable at the intersection of the levels of the family need, as shown in Figure 1.3. The overlay of these two grids provides a practical guide for choosing the most applicable treatment model and the individual, couple, or family focus based on the assessment of family need.

A caveat is that these guidelines are rough frameworks into which families may not easily fit. There may be characteristics of several levels of need, as well as orientations. Professional judgment is required to decide the more relevant point of entry and intervention. The key question for the family practitioner is: What specific therapeutic intervention produces specific change in specific families under specific conditions?

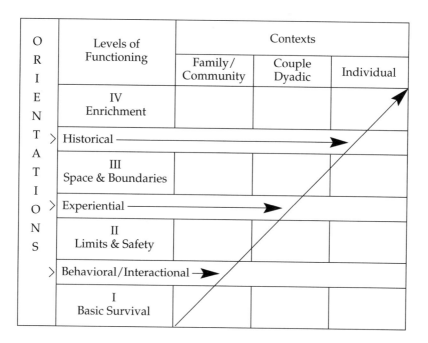

FIGURE 1.3 *Intervention Choice Points by Level of Functioning*

Summary

Needs and problems of families are quite varied. It is helpful to view families through the lenses of their particular level of need in order to assess strengths and resiliences and provide relevant interventions. Problems encountered in practice with families tend to cluster into four levels of need, from very basic to very high. Lower-level needs must be met before higher-level needs are addressed. Four levels of family need are described, ranging from basic survival to self-actualization. An analogy of building a house is used to illustrate the basic assumptions. In the first two levels, strengths are emphasized. On the higher two levels, problem areas are addressed directly. Working with these types of problems requires purposive selection among methods of practice and the application of appropriate interventions according to situation and needs of the specific family. Issues on each level, relevant intervention strategies, and possible techniques are identified.

Remember that these levels are not discrete. Family need is a continuum and rarely shows categorical typologies. Some characteristics are found in several levels. In the assessment process, the level that is most characteristic of the needs experienced by a particular family at that point in time must be assessed. In Levels III and IV particularly, the most crucially felt need of a given family could vary between the two levels, depending on whether there is a specific problem or crisis that needs to be addressed at that time or if the need is more toward growth.

Interventions that are particularly appropriate at a given level may also be used at some other levels, given certain conditions. An intervention choice point grid provides a guide that can be used in connection with the levels of need to decide the context and orientation for intervention. The application of specific methods of interventions with other levels of need is discussed in each chapter in Parts II through V with discussion and caveats.

Discussion Questions

1. Describe the four levels for assessing family needs and give some relevant intervention strategies and techniques that may be useful for each of these levels.

2. On which level would families involved with addiction issues likely be found, and where would be the most likely point for intervention?

3. What are some challenges or obstacles that would keep families' basic needs at a low level? What are some strengths, skills, or actions that would raise families' basic needs to a higher level?

4. What do the decorations in Weltner's "house" represent? At what level of need are the families who are concerned with these decorations? How would a therapist help them?

5. Formulate a case study to illustrate Level IV families.

6. Is the determination of family need level the responsibility of the clinician, or is it a joint effort involving the clients? What happens in the event of a disagreement on levels of need?

7. Apply all concepts discussed in this chapter to the choice point grid (Figure 1.2), utilizing families with whom you are working or know.

8. Select an incident from your childhood. Identify and describe the level of need of your family at that time. Choose a point of intervention in terms of context and orientation, and explain your rationale.

Suggested Readings

Beavers, W. R., & Hampson, R. B. (1990). *Successful families.* New York: W. W. Norton & Co. Family competence is seen as ranging from healthy family functioning to severely dysfunctional and is viewed along a progressive continuum. The approach focuses on assessment and intervention and stems from years of clinical, observational, and empirical work.

Minuchin, S., & Montalvo, B. (1967). Techniques for working with disorganized low socioeconomic families. *American Journal of Orthopsychiatry, 37,* 380–387.

Minuchin, S., Montalvo, B., Guerney, B. G., Rosman, B. L., & Schumer, F. (1967). *Families of the slums.* New York: Basic Books.

These two books focus on the structure and dynamics of poor and disorganized families, and give specific techniques for working with them. They are based on a research study of families with more than one delinquent child and are especially helpful when working with Level I families.

Towle, C. (1945). *Common human needs.* Washington, DC: National Association of Social Workers. This book is one of the classics in social work. It discusses in more detail the human needs that are common to all. It is one of the few books that urge provision for spiritual needs.

Weltner, J. S. (1986). A matchmaker's guide to family therapy. *Family Therapy Networker, 10*(2), 51–55. This is an easy-to-read summary of the levels of functioning as seen by Weltner. It will give more detail than is given in this chapter for those who wish to explore the concept further.

References

Aponte, H. (1976). Underorganization in the poor family. In P. Guerin (Ed.), *Family therapy: Theory and practice.* New York: Gardner Press.

Beavers, W. R., Hulgus, Y. F., & Hampson, R. B. (1988). *Beavers system model of family functioning: Family competence and family style evaluation manual.* Dallas: University of Texas Health Science Center.

Epstein, N. B., Bishop, D. S., & Baldwin, L. M. (1982). McMaster model of family functioning: A view of the normal family. In F. Walsh (Ed.), *Normal family processes.* New York: Guilford.

Gaudin, J., Polansky, N. A., Kilpatrick, A. C., & Shilton, P. (1991). *Structure and functioning in neglectful families.* Paper presented at the Ninth National Conference on Child Abuse and Neglect, Denver, CO.

Hartman, A., & Laird, J. (1983). *Family-centered social work practice.* New York: Free Press.

Kilpatrick, A., & Cleveland, P. (1993). Unpublished course material. University of Georgia School of Social Work.

Maslow, A. (1970). *Motivation and personality.* New York: Harper & Row.

Minuchin, S. (1974). *Families and family therapy.* Cambridge, MA: Harvard University Press.

Paquin, G. W., & Bushorn, R. J. (1991). Family treatment assessment for novices. Milwaukee, WI: Families International, Inc. *Families in Society: The Journal of Contemporary Human Services, 72*(6), 353–359.

Pinsof, W. (1991). An integrated approach to chronic marital conflict. *The Learning Edge Series* (Video). Washington, DC: American Association for Marriage and Family Therapy.

Pinsof, W. (1995). *Integrative problem centered therapy: A synthesis of biological, individual, and family therapies.* New York: Basic Books.

Pippin, J. A., & Callaway, J. (1999). Family systems interventions. In A. C. Kilpatrick & T. P. Holland, *Working with families: An intergrative model by level of need.* Needham Heights, MA: Allyn and Bacon.

Towle, C. (1945). *Common human needs.* Washington, DC: National Association of Social Workers.

Weltner, J. S. (1985). Matchmaking: Choosing the appropriate therapy for families at various levels of pathology. In M. P. Mirkin & S. L. Koman (Eds.), *Handbook of adolescents and family therapy* (pp. 39–50). New York: Gardner Press.

Weltner, J. S. (1986). A matchmaker's guide to family therapy. *Family Therapy Networker, 10*(2), 51–55.

Wolin, S. J., & Wolin, S. (1993) *The resilient self.* New York: Villard Books.

2

An Ecological Systems–Social Constructionism Approach to Family Practice

Thomas P. Holland, Ph.D., and Allie C. Kilpatrick, Ph.D.

This chapter presents an overall framework within which the integrative model to family practice by level of need takes place. For family practice to be more applicable to the families served by helping professionals, we are adapting the comprehensive theories or metatheories of ecological systems and social constructionism for this framework. Each meta- or comprehensive theory offers a way of looking at the world, and each is inclusive of other methods (Breunlin, Schwartz, & Kune-Karrer, 1992; Payne, 1991). The description of these metatheories, their divergences and convergences, and how they blend to form a firm foundation for an integrated approach to family practice is now presented.

Ecological Systems Perspective

The ecological systems (ecosystems) perspective is a framework for assessment and interventions. It has been a dominant theoretical approach for viewing human behavior in the social environment. The environment is all-inclusive of micro- to macro-level systems and resources required for meeting family needs. The interface between people and their environment is seen as bidirectional and interactional, meaning that people affect the environment and in turn the environment affects people. The focus for the practitioner is to assess and intervene in all relevant factors at all levels of systems. This allows the practitioner to view situations holistically in assessment and interventions. It also stimulates the use of a broad repertoire of interventions that are suitable for the varying needs of particular family situations. Because it can encompass any relevant treatment model, the ecosystems approach can serve as a unifying perspective in family practice (Long & Holle, 1997; Meyer, 1988). It makes clear the need to see people and their environments within their historic and cultural contexts, in relationships to each other, and as continually influencing each other.

The Ecological View

The ecological perspective is based in the metaphor of biological organisms that live and adapt in a complex network of environmental forces. Von Bertalanffy (1968) believed that living organisms are organized wholes, not just the sum of their separate parts, and that they are essentially open systems, maintaining themselves with continuous inputs from and outputs to their environments.

The ecological perspective rests on an evolutionary, adaptive view of human beings in continuous transaction with their environment, with both the person and the environment continuously changing and accommodating each other (Brower, 1988). The key assumptions of an ecological perspective emphasize that people and environments are holistic and transactional. This approach makes clear the need to see people and their environments within their historic and cultural contexts, in relationships to one another, and as continually influencing one another, as described by Germain and Gitterman (1995).

Because ecologists were among the first systems thinkers, the perspective is also systemic. Germain and Gitterman give seven major concepts of the ecosystems perspective that are applicable to working with families. These are reciprocal exchanges, life stress, coping, habitat, niche, relatedness, and adaptations.

1. Transactions are understood as continuous **reciprocal exchanges** in the person–environment system. Through these exchanges, each shapes, changes, or otherwise influences the other over time. People's needs and predicaments are viewed as outcomes of person–environment exchanges, not just as the products of personality or environment alone (except in those cases where a specific problem may be an outcome of environmental or societal processes alone).

2. The concept of **life stress** can refer to either a positive or a negative person–environment relationship (Lazarus, 1980). Germain and Gitterman (1987) cite Cox's explanation that stress can be seen as positive when an environmental demand, process, or event is experienced as a challenge and is therefore associated with positive feelings, a higher level of self-esteem, and the anticipation of mastery. Stress can be seen as negative when "actual or perceived environmental demands, harms, losses, or conflicts (or the future threat of any of these) exceed the actual or perceived capacity for dealing with them" (p. 488). They state that life stress and challenge express forms of person–environment relationships because they include both the external demand and the accompanying physiological or emotional stress at a subjective level.

3. The concept of **coping** refers to the special adaptations that are made in response to internal stress. Lazarus (1980) states that two major functions of coping are problem solving and managing negative feelings, and that these are interdependent. Each of these coping adaptations needs personal, familial, and environmental resources and relationships. When coping efforts are working, the demand or threat that causes the stress may be reduced or eliminated, and thus a crisis is avoided. If coping efforts are not successful, disruption in social functioning may result in various areas. Stress and coping are both transactional. Therefore, they help the practitioner to maintain a focus on both people and environments.

4. **Habitat** refers to the place where a person or family lives. Germain (1985) states

> In the case of human beings, the physical and social settings within a cultural context are the habitat. Physical settings such as dwellings, buildings, rural villages and urban layouts must support the social settings of family life, social life, work life, religious life, and so on, in ways that fit with life styles, age, gender, and culture. Habitats that do not support the health and social functioning of individuals and families are likely to produce or to contribute to feelings of isolation, disorientation, and despair. Such stressful feelings may interfere further with the basic functions of family and community life. (p. 41)

Here again, many impoverished rural and urban communities around the world do not have the resources of habitats that support healthy social functioning and overall human well-being.

5. A **niche** is perceived as the result of one's accommodation to the environment. It refers to the status that is occupied by a member of the community. Niches are defined differently in different societies and in different historical eras. In our society today, one aspect of a good niche is a set of rights, including the rights of equal opportunity to educational and economic resources. However, devalued personal or cultural characteristics, such as color, ethnicity, gender, age, affinity/sexual orientation, disability, poverty, and other types of oppression, force millions of people to occupy niches that are incongruent with human needs and well-being (Germain, 1985).

6. The concept of **relatedness,** based on attachment theory (Bowlby, 1973), incorporates ideas about emotional and social loneliness and isolation (Weiss, 1973). Many research studies demonstrate the important influences of supportive networks of relatives, friends, neighbors, work colleagues, and pets in helping people cope with painful life stresses (Cobb, 1976; Gaudin & Polansky, 1986). This aspect of the ecological perspective suggests the entry points in social networks for professionals to help people work out adaptive social arrangements in family, group, community, and institutional life.

7. It is important to remember that **adaptations,** as used in the ecological perspective, are active, dynamic, and often creative processes. People and their environments create an ecosystem in which each shapes the other. Thus people are not mere reactors to environmental forces. Sometimes they change environments to allow themselves to meet their physical and psychological needs. An example is a recent sit-in by handicapped students at a major university for better accessibility to buildings. They must then adapt to the changes they have induced. At other times, people change themselves to conform or adjust to environmental imperatives or to satisfy needs and reach goals (Germain & Gitterman, 1980, 1995).

The Family Systems View

Systems theory was developed to go beyond mechanistic biology to include the interfunctioning of parts that make up whole systems. It goes beyond static concepts to take account of the temporal quality of life and the omnipresence of change. Among the key assumptions of this theory that are particularly relevant to family systems are wholeness, feedback, equifinality, and circular causality (Watzlawick, Beavin, & Jackson, 1967).

Wholeness.   Because systems behave as wholes, change in any one part will cause change in other parts and throughout the entire system. When this assumption is applied to family systems, it means that a family is not simply a collection of individuals, but a coherent composite whose components behave as an irreducible unit. Therefore, the behavior of each individual in the family is related to and dependent on the behavior of all the others. For this reason, improvements or regressions in one family member prompt repercussions—positive and negative—in other family members (Goldenberg & Goldenberg, 1991; Nichols & Schwartz, 1991; Watzlawick et al., 1967).

Feedback.   Open systems are regulated by feedback loops or inputs from family members and from the environment. These inputs are acted on and modified by the family system. Feedback can be either positive or negative. Negative feedback contributes to homeostasis by the process of self-regulation and plays an important role in maintaining the stability of relationships. It reduces the tendency toward deviation from the family norms. On the other hand, positive feedback leads to change when it is used by the family system to amplify a pattern. For learning and growth to occur, families must incorporate positive feedback. All families together must use some degree of both forms of feedback in order to adapt while maintaining their equilibrium in the face of developmental and environmental stresses (Goldenberg & Goldenberg, 1991; Simon, Stierlin, & Wynne, 1985; Watzlawick et al., 1967).

Equifinality.   **Equifinality** means that the same result may be reached from different beginnings (Von Bertalanffy, 1968). In open systems, different initial conditions may lead to the same final result, and different outcomes may be produced from the same causes. The primary principle here is that, in order to understand families, it is more important to consider the ongoing organization of their interactions, not just the genesis or the product of these interactions (Simon et al., 1985; Watzlawick et al., 1967).

Circular Causality.   **Circular causality** means that systems are constantly modified by recursive circular feedback from multiple sources within and outside of the system. Events are related through a series of interacting loops or repeating cycles. In other words, there is no simple, linear cause and effect; events and behaviors interacting with one another over a period of time produce the effects (Nichols & Schwartz, 1991).

Applications to Family Practice

The use of the ecosystems metatheory in working with families supports adherence to certain principles that are consistent with this perspective.

1. This perspective requires professionals to carry out their practice according to the needs of a particular family, rather than viewing all family needs in terms of a single preferred treatment.

2. This perspective supports a variety of practice roles and tasks. It can serve as a base for internal and external changes, legislative advocacy, policy and planning, program development, primary prevention activities, research, and administration.

3. The practitioner's attention must encompass three interdependent realms or contexts in which human growth, development, and social functioning take place. **Life transitions** encompass developmental changes, such as puberty, aging, role changes, loss, or other crisis events faced by families. **Interpersonal processes** include patterns of relationship and communication in dyads, families, groups, social networks, communities or neighborhoods, and organizations. **Environmental properties** include the aspects of social and physical settings—their formal and informal resources and deficits—as they affect families (Germain & Gitterman, 1987). The use of genograms and ecomaps (Hartman & Laird, 1983; Mattaini, 1997) can facilitate the focus on these contents.

4. The focus is on strengths, not deficits, on solutions, not problems, and on the potential for continued family and individual growth and needed social change.

5. Assessment and intervention from an ecological systems perspective require knowledge of the diverse systems involved in interactions between people and their environments (Hefferman, Shuttlesworth, & Ambrosina, 1988). The different levels of systems, shown in Figure 2.1, are helpful in the assessment process around a given problem situation.

• In this model, the **microsystem** represents the individual in family and group settings that incorporate the day-to-day environment.

• The **mesosystem** incorporates the interactions of individuals, families, and groups within the person's microsystem.

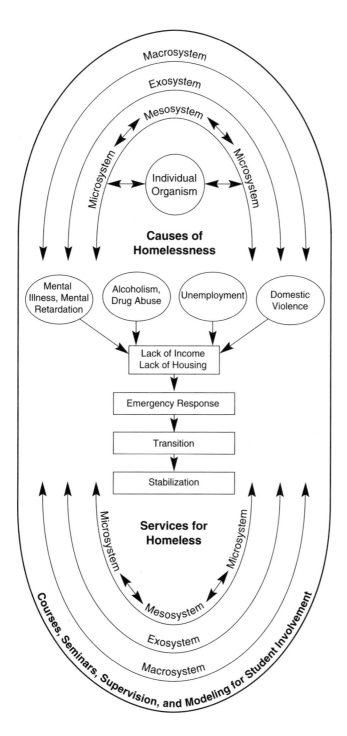

FIGURE 2.1 *An Ecosystems Model for Student Involvement with Homeless Families*

Source: From Cleveland & Kilpatrick, 1990.

- The **exosystem** represents the social structures, both formal and informal, that influence, delimit, or constrain what goes on there. It also includes community-level factors that have an impact on the way the person functions.

- The **macrosystem** involves societal forces and subsumes cultural and societal values, attitudes, and beliefs that influence the micro- and exosystems.

The example of homelessness shown in Figure 2.1 illustrates the use of the figure in helping students learn the ecosystems model. First, we look at the causes of homelessness, which may be apparent in several levels of systems. For example, mental illness, alcoholism, unemployment, and domestic violence may have precipitated the loss of income and housing. Any of these causes could be interrelated at micro-, meso-, exo-, or macrosystem levels. Services for homeless families must also be provided at several system levels. Individual/family counseling at the micro- and mesosystem levels is indicated in the emergency and transition levels. Resources at the exosystem level for temporary shelter and other transition services are needed. Changes in public attitudes and policy concerning employment opportunities, emergency responses, and causes of homelessness may take place at the macrosystem level.

The key assumptions in family systems theory of wholeness, feedback, equifinality, and circular causality are applied at the micro- and mesosystem levels. The ecosystems perspectives of reciprocal exchanges, life stress, coping, habitat, niche, and relatedness are applicable at the exo- and macrosystem levels.

Consideration should be given to the interplay of influences on all four levels during the assessment and intervention processes with families. This interplay helps in understanding the causes of a particular problem situation and also in the provision of services for such problems. Information concerning other problem areas can be used to fill in the blanks in the model to make the ecosystems theory more visible. Effective case management skills are important to applying this framework with some families.

By utilizing knowledge of all levels of the ecosystems perspective, the practitioner is better equipped to assess and provide services for families in accordance with the presenting problems and the family's current level of need. This application requires flexibility, creativity, and mobility outside the office and into the home and community.

A summary of how practitioners can implement this ecosystems perspective in their work is offered by Greene and Ephross (1991, p. 293).

- View the person/family/environment as inseparable.
- See the family practitioner as an equal partner in the helping process.
- Examine transactions between the person/family/environment by assessing all levels of systems affecting adaptiveness.

- Assess life situations and transitions that induce high stress levels.
- Attempt to enhance a person/family's personal and interpersonal competence through positive relationships and life experiences.
- Seek interventions that extend the goodness of fit among the person/family and the environment at all system levels.
- Focus on mutually sought solutions and person/family empowerment.

Caveats in Using the Ecosystems Metatheory

Although ecosystems theory offers a wealth of ideas about families and family practice, the family practitioner must be aware of some possible pitfalls in its use. One issue is that this perspective may lead to a conservative stance of valuing the status quo and avoiding real change. Influences that upset the homeostasis of a system may be framed as problems or forms of deviance, leading to responses that do not assess them on their own merits, but in terms of reducing or limiting their threats to existing relational patterns. Conflict may be seen as a negative influence, disrupting systemic balance; conformity may be assumed to be good. The underlying concern of treatment can be on ways to reduce tensions in the system and return it to stability as soon as possible.

A second issue is that ecosystems theory emphasizes how people adapt to environmental structures that exercise social control. Existing circumstances tend to be accepted as givens, and the focus may become how to adjust participants within those limits, rather than questioning the limits or valuing disruptions positively. Professionals may be in the role of experts in diagnosing sources of tension and in finding ways to enable participants to adapt in order to return to equilibrium. Thus reducing tensions and reestablishing harmony may become goals of intervention. Successful adjustment of individuals within existing social norms may be assumed to be the highest good, and individuality, creativity, and autonomy become subordinate to the needs of the system.

Third, one may conclude that use of this metatheory requires many different interventive skills which practitioners are required to master in order to address the entire range of needs on all system levels. This conclusion, of course, is unrealistic. Metatheories provide a comprehensive theoretical framework within which the domain-specific theories and interventions are integrated and planfully utilized to meet specific needs in a specific situation with specific persons. We support Wakefield's (1996) belief that ecosystems theory is not sufficient in itself and that practitioners should have skills in domain-specific interventions like those presented in this book. We disagree, however, with his contention that an ecosystems theory base is not clinically useful. Myriads of professionals have attested to the usefulness of the metatheory as presented here and supplemented by specific interventive methods to meet varying levels of need.

If family practitioners can avoid such pitfalls and heed these caveats, then effective applications of ecosystems theory may be made to practice. The key points of this section on ecosystems theory are summarized in Table 2.1.

Social Constructionist Perspective

A more recent arrival on the family practice scene, the social constructionist approach, is based on the metaphor of literature. Human actions and relationships are seen in terms of organized efforts to create meaning out of personal experiences. These efforts are like composing narratives, stories that people write about themselves. Experiences of the objective and the subjective realms are selectively arranged on the basis of assumed themes, which organize, structure, and give meaningfulness to the person or family (Berger & Luckmann, 1966; Hoffman, 1988, 1990; Sarbin, 1986; Von Glasersfeld, 1987).

Stories are crucial means that people in every culture use to create meaning and purpose in life. In all communities and families, stories appear in a variety of

---

TABLE 2.1   Key Principles of Ecological Systems Perspective

Ecological View

Transactions are continuous, reciprocal exchanges.
Life stresses are either positive or negative person–environment relationships.
Coping refers to problem solving and managing negative feelings.
Habitat is the physical and social setting within cultural contexts.
Niche is the result of one's accommodation to the environment.
Relatedness involves supportive networks and attachments.

Systems View

Wholeness—change in one part causes changes throughout system.
Feedback—regulates system by inputs from family and environment.
Equifinality—there is more than one way to get to a final goal.
Circular causality—not linear cause and effect, but interactions.

Practice Focus

Recognize diverse needs of families on varying levels.
Explore various practice roles involved in ecosystems dual focus.
Attend to life cycle transitions, interpersonal processes, and environmental settings.
Focus on strengths, not deficits; solutions, not problems.
Assess ecosystems at four levels (micro-, meso-, exo-, macro-).

Pitfalls

Focusing on personal adaptations to the exclusion of social change.
Valuing homeostasis as the goal.
Individuality, creativity, and autonomy becoming subordinate to the system.

---

forms, including anecdotes, myths and fables, plays and movies, novels and poems, histories and biographies, case studies, and others. Much of our development as social beings occurs through listening to and understanding narratives, the stories that people around us tell about their own and others' lives. Reminiscences by the elderly represent important efforts to articulate meanings in their lives, and encouraging such reflections has been recognized as an important component of practice with the aged. Stories constitute the basic structures all persons use in order to make sense of their lives, and hence understanding narratives is fundamental to the practice of social work with families (Goldstein, 1988; Scott, 1989).

The social constructionism perspective on human behavior emphasizes the textual structure of everyday life, especially how people develop meaning in the diverse events of their day-to-day experience. Behavior is seen through the analogy of a story that a person is creating and telling about what that person is doing and how such tasks and experiences are organized into a meaningful whole (Holland, 1991; O'Hanlon & Weiner-Davis, 1988). One's present, dominant story can be empowering, or it can undermine meaningful relationships and effective social functioning (Polkinghorne, 1988).

A fundamental assumption of social constructionism is that reality is constructed or generated by participants, rather than being objective, external, or given. Our efforts to make sense of inner and outer experience involve trying to formulate some coherence and meaning from streams of events (Ricoeur, 1981). In order to create this formulation, we draw on our culture's storehouse of themes and attributions, handed down by our relatives and community leaders. Persons interpret events and experiences on the basis of cultural patterns, preformulated clusters of meaning that serve to enable the person to make sense of perceptions. All of these constructed meanings depend for their existence on the minds of the persons carrying and using them. No one's beliefs or conclusions are more "real" than another's, and all participate in editing, revising, and continuing the stories of meaning that they share.

Such contexts of meaning take on a narrative form, linking past, present, and anticipated future, involving movement toward or away from goals. Or the form may emphasize blockage or no change (Gergen, 1982). Story patterns involving interrupted movement toward a desired goal, followed by an inescapable defeat, constitute the theme of tragedy, whereas patterns involving movement away from a desired goal, followed by unexpected success, constitute the romantic theme. Other themes in many cultures include the use of a journey as a metaphor for life experiences, eventual retribution for injustices, and struggles between light and darkness or hope and despair.

A further component of social constructionism is the assumption that themes and clusters of assumed reality (cultures) cannot be controlled from the outside. They are not amenable to reconstruction through objective or instrumental manipulation by any outside technical expert, because they are formulations of the participants themselves. Participants may observe their own patterns and explore alternatives for themselves, allowing them to understand their experiences in new ways and hence respond differently from the past. All that an outsider can do is to reflect themes in use and offer participants alternative themes for making meaning out of their experiences for their consideration of them. Outsiders (including practitioners) can attempt to create a context that invites participants to pursue such observations, reflections, and developments for themselves, but they cannot directly change the participants' themes or actions.

Applications to Family Practice

The social constructionist metatheory has extensive applicability for practice with families and for the role of the practitioner. In this chapter, the basic overarching principles that are consistent with this perspective are presented. More specific methods and techniques are found in Chapters 9 and 11, where solution-focused and narrative family interventions are discussed.

1. It is assumed that all interpretations and meanings are created by the participants, so there is no outside, "right" standard by which to diagnose or modify. Because everyone, including the professional, is engaged in developing meanings in order to deal with experience, the helping relationship is essentially a process of joint work on the themes brought by the family and the professional. In this shared work, the relationship is between equals and is nonhierarchical, and the power or right to assert interpretations is equally shared (Gergen & McNamee, 1992; Simon et al., 1985; Whitaker & Bumberry, 1988).

2. The professional respects the family's right to make use of its own themes and seeks to understand their origin and application. Together, the family and the professional explore the implications of the assumptions, directions, and anticipated ends of the family's dominant story.

3. We can nurture the development of such supportive, rather than paternalistic, relationships with families by reminding ourselves of the importance of trying to understand what a particular person's experiences seem like from the person's own perspective and by attempting to appreciate life and its problems as they are construed in the person's subjective experience (Goldstein, 1988). What families often need is not so much expert advice, technical fixes, or precise data as a responsive listener to their efforts to make sense out of their experiences and overt, caring encouragement to resume their roles as the capable authors of their own stories (Gergen & McNamee, 1992). The social constructionism approach to family practice emphasizes the client's *strengths*, rather than pathology or deficits; emphasizes *exceptions*, or times when the problem was not present; and builds on those times when something the client tried *did* work effectively. The relationship between family and professional is one of joint exploration and coauthorship, not a hierarchy in which one person has solutions to the other's deficits (Link & Sullivan, 1989).

Caveats in Using the Social Constructionist Metatheory

Social constructionism has prompted a shift in the attention of family practitioners from actions to meanings, from expertise to collaboration, and from diagnosis of problems to mutual creation of solutions. However, the spread of interest in social constructionism ought not be accepted as an unmixed blessing. Implications of its own story about how families and family interventions operate should be examined critically.

The first caveat regarding social constructionism is its assumption of relativism regarding all meanings. The theory holds that there is no reality "out there" and that meanings are strictly constructed by participants. If that is the case, then any interpretation would be as good as any other, from inclusive themes to destructive ones. The theory provides no explicit grounds for precluding various interpretations of experience, including illusions or sadism. Families trying to deny their pain would have a legitimate base for doing so with the maximum possible comfort, a condition about which the theory provides no evident guidance (Becvar & Becvar, 1988; Nichols & Schwartz, 1991). Although social constructionism does not necessarily lead to coauthorship of denials or destructive interpretations, nothing within the theory clearly precludes such possibilities.

A related problem with social constructionism is its inattention to the evident differences in power among family members and between families and communities. Dominant members of a family may impose their preferred interpretations on subordinate members, denying them the legitimacy of their own meanings and undermining their well-being. Likewise, community prejudice and discrimination may lead to denial of basic resources and opportunities for some families, particularly minorities, thus limiting their life chances and well-being regardless of the family's constructions or reconstructions. Again, nothing in social constructionism necessarily supports such abuses of power, but nothing in the theory draws explicit attention to them or provides explicit ways of dealing with them.

Underneath these problems lies a logical dilemma that confronts social constructionism: If there is no external reality, then that principle would preclude the assertion that the components of constructionism itself are true representations of anything, including its descriptions of how people deal with problems, develop meaning, undergo change, or do therapy (Held, 1990). In short, if we cannot know reality, then we cannot assert anything about it. Social constructionism can't have it both ways.

A likely response of advocates of social constructionism to such concerns may be that all of our perceptions of reality are incomplete. The theory is intended to be a metamodel for practice, rather than an assertion about ontological reality. Such defenses are hardly sufficient, because any theory would hasten to take refuge inside such permissiveness. So although social constructionism suggests many useful ideas for family practice, it continues to face difficult challenges in its formulation and refinement. The concern for family practitioners is to emphasize

TABLE 2.2   Key Principles of the Social Constructionist Perspective

Stories and Personal Meaning

Stories transmit meaning.

Their creation formulates coherent sequences.

They shape one's identity.

They organize values and explain choices.

They are organized by plots and themes.

They involve choosing from alternative interpretations.

Family functioning depends on shared meanings.

Meanings cannot be controlled from outside.

Emphasis shifts from actions to meanings, from expertise to collaboration, from diagnosis to problems to mutual creation of solutions.

Practice Focus

Nonhierarchical relationship.

Shared explorations.

Offer new meanings and assumptions.

Bring their themes and values to awareness.

Be coauthor of a living story with them.

Nurture supportive, not paternalistic, relationships.

Pitfalls

Seeing any interpretation as being as good as any other.

Inattention to power differences in family and community regarding interpretations.

Assuming that social constructionism has all the answers and that they are the best.

---

the strengths of this metamodel and avoid its pitfalls. The key points of this section on social constructionism are summarized in Table 2.2.

Comparing and Integrating the Metatheories

Both of these approaches to family practice are comprehensive theories or metatheories, and both offer ways of looking at the world, particularly with regard to individual and social change (Payne, 1991). Each is inclusive in the sense that it accepts perspectives and methods drawn from other theories. We now look at a comparison of the two metatheories.

Both ecosystems and constructionism assume that a family is a group of persons involved in sustained, intimate interaction with one another. The interaction among these members becomes patterned or regularized on the basis of mutually shared expectations, meanings, and responses. Similarity or congruences among the meanings and expectations of members are the basis for stability and satisfaction, whereas incongruences lead to dissatisfaction and conflict. Creative explorations of alternative, more congruent shared meanings are the main concern of practice.

The two metatheories converge on a number of aspects and dimensions of family practice. The time focus of both is on the present and the anticipated future, rather than on the past. The context of each is the family as a group, not individuals. The goals emphasized by both perspectives involve enabling the family to identify and develop creative alternatives to unsatisfying patterns, rather than correcting past deficits. The role of the practitioner called for by both is to be a peer as much as possible in the process of mutual reflection and exploration of alternatives and change, not to be analytical, instructive, or prescriptive. The style of intervention emphasized by each is exploratory, nondirective, less structured, seeking exceptions to problems, and not corrective, analytical, or educational.

Both metatheories interpret experience in symbolic or metaphorical terms, not as literal or as problems to be controlled. Their treatment of "resistance" is one protective of the core meanings and relationships among family members, not one that works in terms of lack of motivation or dysfunction. The criteria for success of intervention emphasized by both are mutual acceptability, satisfaction, and meaningfulness among family members, not logical, objective, or behavioral measures. The key similarities between these perspectives are summarized in Table 2.3.

TABLE 2.3   Convergences in Ecosystems and Constructionism

Dimension	Comment
Time	Both are focused on the present and the anticipated future, rather than on the past.
Goals	Both seek to identify and develop creative alternatives, rather than to correct past deficits.
Style of intervention	Both are exploratory, nondirective, less structured, seek exceptions to problems; not corrective, analytical, or educational.
Context	Both focus on the family as a system, not on individuals.
Role of practitioner	A peer as much as possible in the process of mutual reflection and exploration of alternatives; not analytical, instructive, or prescriptive.
Interpretation of experience	Symbolic or metaphorical; not literal or in terms of problems to be controlled.
Understanding of "resistance"	Protective of the core meanings and relationships among members; not lack of motivation or dysfunction.
Criteria for success	Mutual acceptability, satisfaction, and meaningfulness to participants; not logical, objective, or behavioral.

The two metatheories diverge somewhat in their emphases within the treatment process. The ecosystems perspective focuses attention on breakdowns in family equilibrium needing negotiation to reestablish homeostasis or mutually satisfactory exchanges. Constructionism treats family issues in terms of breakdowns in shared meaning that need reconstruction into new and more satisfying shared meanings.

Both the ecosystems and social constructionism approaches to family practice provide broad perspectives on how to understand and deal with family issues. The ecosystems model focuses primarily on the transactions of the family within the larger social environment, whereas the social constructionist model emphasizes the meanings that families and their members formulate out of those streams of events.

Both approaches are based on specialized bodies of knowledge. The ecosystems theory emphasizes knowledge of the diverse transactions among people and their environments. Means of strengthening the effectiveness of those interactions are major concerns of practice. Social constructionism focuses on how people find meaning in the diverse experiences of their daily lives; treatment involves the development of meanings that are more empowering for families. The key divergences between these perspectives are summarized in Table 2.4.

Although neither approach is a complete practice model in itself, both theories have spawned a variety of specific methods and techniques for application in professional practice with families (Meyer, 1988; Rosen, 1988). For example, the life model of social work practice is based in ecosystems theory (Germain & Gitterman, 1980), as is the family-centered approach (Hartman & Laird, 1983) and the competence approach (Maluccio, 1981). The narrative approach to family practice

TABLE 2.4   Comparisons in Ecosystems and Constructionism

Criteria

1. Explicit knowledge base: How clear and extensive is the grounding of the approach in theory and research?
2. Focus of attention: How are family issues defined?
3. Change process: Does the approach explain how family change occurs?
4. Guidelines for intervention: Does the approach delineate actions of the practitioner?
5. Values: What values are emphasized?

Ecosystems	*Social Constructionism*
1. Moderate	Limited
2. Disruption of equilibrium	Meaninglessness
3. Negotiation of new homeostasis	Construction of new meanings
4. As expert	As coauthor
5. Harmony	Meaningfulness

(White & Epston, 1990) and the solution-focused approach (O'Hanlon & Weiner-Davis, 1988) are based in social constructionism. These and other practice models provide the specificity needed in working directly with families.

Summary

This chapter offers a comprehensive framework for assessing and working with families at each of the four levels of family need presented in the previous chapter. The ecosystems–social constructionism approach to family practice is a combination of two metatheories that complement each other to form a broad theoretical base for family assessment and practice. This approach offers a way of looking at the world and particularly at personal and social change.

The two metatheories each have specific strengths that inform family practice. However, limits of each are discussed. The family practitioner should be aware of these limitations, as they have definite implications for practice. There are areas in which the two theories diverge that supplement each other and fill in particular gaps. There are more similarities that emerge as the theories are analyzed by specific dimensions. These convergences enable the practitioner to draw on the two metatheories in creating a meaningful approach to assessing and working with families.

The following sections of this book provide specific practice methods that can be used in working with families. Each is applied to one of the four levels of family need within the overall framework of the linked ecosystems–social constructionism approach.

Discussion Questions

1. Discuss the key assumptions of the systems view and apply these to a family.

2. Select a presenting problem and design an intervention utilizing the social constructionist perspective on human behavior.

3. Why is it important for practitioners to view a client system holistically?

4. How could the combined ecosystems–social constructionist approach be utilized with lower-functioning clients? Does the use of social constructionist theory imply that clients must be verbally skilled?

5. Discuss how the two metatheories diverge in their emphasis within the treatment process and the ways in which the integration of these two metatheories could be helpful in working with families.

6. Discuss how the theories of social constructionism and ecosystems can be combined to address the problems of families in poverty.

7. Prepare a narrative about your life or an important episode in your life according to the concepts of the social constructionist approach.

8. What biases do you have that would limit your use of social constructionist theory in working with families?

Suggested Readings

Coles, R. (1989). *The call of stories: Teaching and the moral imagination.* Boston: Houghton Mifflin.
The training of child psychiatrists has been immensely enriched by the work of Robert Coles, whose volume leads the reader through the author's experiences of working with the learning from the children in his practice as well as the students in his classes. This book demonstrates the wide applicability of the narrative framework for practice and for education in the helping professions.

Greene, R. R., & Ephross, P. H. (1991). *Human behavior theory and social work practice.* New York: Aldine de Gruyter.
This book gives a good overview of the ecosystems perspective within a human behavior framework. Applications to practice are made.

Hoffman, L. (1990). Constructing realities: An art of lenses. *Family Process, 29*(1), 1–12.
Social construction theory is used to move toward a more collaborative and unconcealed therapeutic stance. This theory plus a second-order view and sensitivity to gender issues are the three "lenses" used for constructing realities.

Polkinghorne, D. E. (1988). *Narrative knowing and the human sciences.* Albany: State University of New York Press.
Using literary criticism, philosophy, history, and recent developments in the social sciences, this volume shows how to use research information organized by the narrative form—such information as clinical case histories, biographies, and personal stories. The relationships between narrative formats and classical empirical research designs are examined, and suggestions for studying human behavior from a narrative framework are set forth.

Sarup, M. (1989). *An introductory guide to poststructuralism and postmodernism.* Athens: University of Georgia Press.
Three of the most influential figures in recent literary criticism—Jacques Lacan, Jacques Derrida, and Michel Foucault—have had extensive influence on the way we think about meaning in our experiences. This book traces the rise of narrative approaches to thought, radically opposed to the Enlightenment tenets of progress and scientific truth, and explores some implications of this perspective for the future of human social life.

Wakefield, J. C. (1988). Psychotherapy, distributive justice, and social work, Parts 1 & 2. *Social Science Review, 62*(2,3), 187–210, 353–382.
Wakefield argues that social work's organizing value is minimal distributive justice, in which all people would have a minimally acceptable level of basic economic, social, and psychological goods. This concept seems to build on an ecosystems framework and then utilize varying methods and interventive skills for meeting specific levels of needs.

References

Becvar, D. S., & Becvar, R. J. (1988). *Family therapy: A systemic integration.* Boston: Allyn and Bacon.

Berger, P., & Luckmann, T. (1966). *The social construction of reality.* Garden City, NY: Doubleday.

Bowlby, J. (1973). Affectional bonds: Their nature and origin. In R. S. Weiss (Ed.), *Loneliness: The experience of emotional and social isolation* (pp. 38–52). Cambridge, MA: MIT Press.

Breunlin, D. C., Schwartz, R. C., & Kune-Karrer, B. M. (1992). *Metaframeworks: Transcending the models of family therapy.* San Francisco: Jossey-Bass.

Brower, A. M. (September 1988). Can the ecological model guide social work practice? *Social Service Review, 62*(3), 411–429.

Cleveland, P. H., & Kilpatrick, A. C. (1990). *Social work students' involvement with the homeless: An international model.* Paper presented at the International Congress of Schools of Social Work, Lima, Peru.

Cobb, S. (1976). Social support as a moderator of life stress. *Psychosomatic Medicine, 38*(5), 300–314.

Gaudin, J. M., Jr., & Polansky, N. A. (1986). Social distancing of the neglectful family: Sex, race and social class differences. *Children and Youth Services Review, 8,* 1–12.

Gergen, K. J. (1982). *Toward transformation in social knowledge.* New York: Springer-Verlag.

Gergen, K. J., & McNamee, S. (1992). *Social constructionism in therapeutic process.* London: Sage.

Germain, C. B. (1985). The place of community within an ecological approach to social work practice. In S. H. Taylor & R. W. Roberts (Eds.), *Theories and practice of community social work* (pp. 30–55). New York: Columbia University Press.

Germain, C. B., & Gitterman, A. (1980). *The life model of social work practice.* New York: Columbia University Press.

Germain, C. B., & Gitterman, A. (1987). Ecological perspective. In A. Minahan et al. (Eds.), *Encyclopedia of social work* (18th ed.) (pp. 488–499). Silver Spring, MD: National Association of Social Workers.

Germain, C. B., & Gitterman, A. (1995). Ecological perspective. In R. L. Edwards et al. (Eds.), *Encyclopedia of social work* (19th ed., pp. 816–824). Silver Spring, MD: National Association of Social Workers.

Goldenberg, I., & Goldenberg, H. (1991). *Family therapy: An overview* (p. 38). Monterey, CA: Brooks-Cole Publishing.

Goldstein, H. (1988). Humanistic alternatives to the limits of scientific knowledge. *Social Thought, 14*(1), 47–58.

Greene, R. R., & Ephross, P. H. (1991). *Human behavior theory and social work practice.* New York: Aldine de Gruyter.

Hartman, A., & Laird, J. (1983). *Family centered social work practice.* New York: Free Press.

Hefferman, J., Shuttlesworth, G., & Ambrosina, R. (1988). A systems/ecological perspective. In *Social work and social welfare: An introduction.* St. Paul, MN: West Publishing.

Held, B. S. (1990). What's in a name: Some confusions and concerns about Constructivism. *Journal of Marital and Family Therapy, 16,* 179–186.

Hoffman, L. (1988). A constructivist position for family therapy. *The Irish Journal of Psychology, 9,* 110–129.

Hoffman, L. (1990). Constructing realities: An art of lenses. *Family Process, 29*(1), 1–12.

Holland, T. P. (1991). Narrative, knowledge, and professional practice. *Social Thought, 17*(1), 32–40.

Lazarus, R. S. (1980). The stress and coping paradigm. In L. A. Bond & J. C. Rosen (Eds.), *Competence and coping during adulthood* (pp. 28–74). Hanover, NH: University Press of New England.

Link, R. J., & Sullivan, M. (1989). Vital connections: Using literature to illustrate social work issues. *Journal of Social Work Education. 25*(3), 192–230.

Long, D. D., & Holle, M. C. (1997). *Macro systems in the social environment.* Itasca, IL: Peacock.

Maluccio, A. N. (1981). *Promoting competence in clients.* New York: Free Press.

Mattaini, M. A. (1997). *Visual ecoscan for clinical practice.* Silver Spring, MD: NASW Press.

Meyer, C. H. (1988). The ecosystems perspective. In R. A. Dorfman (Ed.), *Paradigms of clinical social work.* New York: Brunner/Mazel.

Nichols, M. P., & Schwartz, R. C. (1991). *Family therapy: Concepts and methods* (1st and 2nd eds.). Boston: Allyn and Bacon.

O'Hanlon, W. H., & Weiner-Davis, M. (1988). *In search of solutions: A new direction in psychotherapy.* New York: Norton.

Payne, M. (1991). *Modern social work theory: A critical introduction.* Chicago: Lyceum.

Polkinghorne, D. E. (1988). *Narrative knowing and the human sciences.* Albany: State University of New York Press.

Ricoeur, P. (1981). *Hermeneutics and the human sciences.* Cambridge, UK: Cambridge University Press.

Rosen, H. (1988). The constructivist-developmental paradigm. In R. A. Dorfman (Ed.), *Paradigms of clinical social work* (pp. 317–355). New York: Brunner/Mazel.

Sarbin, T. R. (1986). *Narrative psychology: The storied nature of human conduct.* New York: Praeger.

Scott, D. (1989). Meaning construction and social work practice. *Social Service Review, 63*(1), 39–51.

Simon, F. B., Stierlin, H., & Wynne, L. (1985). *The language of family therapy.* New York: Family Process Press.

Von Bertalanffy, L. (1968). *General systems theory.* New York: Braziller.

Von Glasersfeld, E. (1987). The control of perception and the construction of reality. *Dialectica, 33,* 37–50.

Wakefield, J. C. (1996). Does social work need the ecosystems perspective? Parts 1 & 2. *Social Service Review, 70*(1,2), 1–32, 183–213.

Watzlawick, P., Beavin, J. H., & Jackson, D. D. (1967). *Pragmatics of human communication: A study of interactional patterns, pathologies and paradoxes.* New York: Norton.

Weiss, R. S. (Ed.) (1973). *Loneliness: The experience of emotional and social isolation.* Cambridge, MA: MIT Press.

Whitaker, C. A., & Bumberry, W. M. (1988). *Dancing with the family.* New York: Brunner/Mazel.

White, M., & Epston, D. (1990). *Narrative means to therapeutic ends.* New York: Norton.

3

Contexts of Helping: Commonalities and Human Diversities

June G. Hopps, Ph.D., and Allie C. Kilpatrick, Ph.D.

In assessing and working with families, four levels of family need have been presented. Following the assessment of the primary level of need, intervention procedures are planned based on this information. The metatheories of ecological systems and social constructionism are utilized as comprehensive perspectives within which to undertake the assessment and interventions with each family.

Another important consideration in the context of family practice is the acknowledgment of commonalities and diversity. It is crucial that the family practitioner have knowledge, awareness, and skill in developing the necessary core and common conditions of the helping relationship or therapeutic alliance and in dealing with human diversity.

Practitioners share many more commonalities than differences with families. These commonalities can serve as the foundation for building the therapeutic alliance and also for exploring differences. Errors in professional judgment that should be avoided are the tendencies (1) to see differences or commonalities when they are *not* there or (2) to not see differences or commonalities when they *are* present. This chapter seeks to explore and balance these two concepts of commonalities and differences.

Research supported by Curtis L. Todd, M.S.W., doctoral student, Clark Atlanta University, School of Social Work. Chapter reviewed by Robbie W. Tourse, Ph.D., Boston College, and Ollie Christain, Ph.D., Southern University.

The Helping Relationship/Therapeutic Alliance

The metatheories of ecosystems and social constructionism that provide the basis for the integrative approach to family practice emphasize the principles of respect, responsive listening, caring encouragement, nonhierarchical relationships, shared power, and equality of meanings as commonalities in working with families. Closely related to these principles is the "I–Thou" relationship described by Buber (1958), in which there is an emphasis on what takes place between people—for our purposes, especially between the practitioner and the family. The goal is for each to relate to the other in a way that acknowledges the other's internal life, without any possibility of one being exploited by the other. The interaction is a dialogue. The focus or emphasis is on the interchange between them and the experience of mutual confirmation that can occur.

Historically, the concept of the helping relationship has permeated work with people since the early days of social casework and psychoanalysis. Biestek (1957) traced the development of this concept in social casework from Mary Richmond in 1899 through 1951. He then developed his legendary seven principles of relationship, which started with the client's needs expressed to the practitioner as the first direction of the interaction, the response of the caseworker to the client's needs as the second direction, then the awareness of the client to the caseworker's responsiveness as the third direction. Based on the needs of the client, the seven principles were then articulated as individualization, purposeful expression of feelings, controlled emotional involvement, acceptance, nonjudgmental attitude, self-determination, and confidentiality.

We have adapted Biestek's (1957) formulation to include terms relating his concepts to working with families (see Table 3.1). These principles are relevant today and applicable to the family as the client system, although none are absolute. For example, the principle of confidentiality is limited by rights of other individuals, the practitioner, the community, and society. Such behaviors as abuse are legally required to be reported.

The personal characteristics and behaviors displayed by practitioners are intrinsically related to the formation of working and maintenance relationships. The research of Rogers, Gendlin, Kiesler, and Truax (1969) and Truax and Carkhuff (1967) presented evidence suggesting that therapists' ability to function in three core emotional and interpersonal dimensions has a significant influence on effectiveness. These core characteristics are **empathy,** the ability to accurately perceive what people are experiencing and to communicate that perception to them; **respect,** positive regard and the indication of a deep and honest acceptance of the worth of persons apart from behaviors; and **genuineness,** the ability to be honest with him or herself and with others. Horvath (2000) agrees with this premise and supports the importance of the practitioner's relatedness to the client in the working alliance. An additional core condition of **warmth** (treating people in a way that makes them feel safe, accepted, and understood) was added by Goldstein (1975), who observed that, without warmth, the practitioner may be "technically correct

TABLE 3.1   Seven Principles in the Helping Relationship

First Direction: The Need of the Family	Second Direction: The Response of the Practitioner	Third Direction: The Awareness of the Client/Family	The Name of the Principle
1. To be treated as individuals			1. Individualization
2. To express feelings			2. Purposeful expression of feelings
3. To get empathic responses to problems	The practitioner is sensitive to, understands, and appropriately responds to these needs.	The client/family is somehow aware of the practitioner's sensitivity, understanding, and response.	3. Controlled emotional involvement
4. To be recognized as people of worth			4. Acceptance
5. Not to be judged			5. Nonjudgmental attitude
6. To make own choices and decisions			6. Self-determination
7. To keep secrets about self and family			7. Confidentiality

Source: Adapted from Biestek, 1957, p. 17.

but therapeutically impotent" (p. 31). These four core characteristics are necessary conditions for assuring that no harm is done and for developing a therapeutic climate within which family work may be conducted.

Most family practitioners consider the relationship between the family and the practitioner to be an essential ingredient of the therapeutic process. However, little systematic attention has been given to examining the function of the therapeutic alliance in working with families. Minuchin (1974) has talked about the necessity for the therapist to "join" the family, and Davatz (1981) has emphasized the importance of "connecting" with family members. Pinsof and Catherall (1986) state that the therapeutic alliance may be the primary mediating variable that determines the outcome of discrete interventions. They assert that adding the alliance concept to the theoretical base of family therapy illuminates and brings into focus a critical aspect of therapy that has existed in a theoretical twilight (p. 138). Pinsof (1994) builds on previous definitions to define the alliance.

> The therapeutic alliance consists of those aspects of the relationship between and within the therapist and patient systems that pertains to their capacity to mutually invest in and collaborate on the tasks and goals of therapy. (p. 7)

The major difference between this definition and preceding ones is that it tries to account for the social field in which the alliance occurs. There is an alliance between two systems—not just two people, regardless of the number of people directly involved in the sessions. The client system consists of all the human systems that are or may be involved in the maintenance or resolution of the presenting problem. The therapist system consists of all the people involved in treating the client system. In other words, the systems consist of all the people who can influence the change process. In working with families, the therapeutic alliance exists on at least three levels—the individual alliance with each family member, the subsystem alliance with each of the multiperson subsystems as parents and children, and the whole system alliance with the whole family system (Pinsof, 1995; Pinsof & Catherall, 1986). The alliance the practitioner has with one or two family members influences the alliance with other family members in a circular, reciprocal fashion. Therefore, no single alliance with dyads or triads can be considered in isolation.

Any individual is affected by the way in which relevant members of his or her social field feel about the practitioner or interventions. If a spouse is resentful of the therapeutic process, then this resentment may be a significant mediating factor in the outcome. On the other hand, a supportive spouse or family system may greatly facilitate the outcome of the process.

Horvath (2000) and Florsheim, Shotorbani, Guest-Warnick, Barratt, and Hwang (2000) indicate that studies over time have proven that the therapeutic alliance is an important element in the helping encounter, regardless of the theoretical perspective utilized in treatment. Kivlighan and Shaughnessy (2000) confirmed in their research the importance of the overall strength of the therapeutic alliance. Their study also supported the notion of an alliance rupture's being part of developing a successful working relationship with clients—"perhaps a general pattern of initial engagement followed by conflict and then reengagement characterizes successful treatment" (p. 370).

A significant contribution to understanding the therapeutic alliance has been the development of three systemically oriented scales to measure the alliance in individual, couple, and family work (Pinsof, 1994; Pinsof & Catherall, 1986). Each measures the content dimensions of tasks, goals, and bonds as they relate to the therapeutic alliance. None of this research, however, definitely addresses client diversity and its impact and influence on the therapeutic alliance.

Client Diversity

Diversity among clients and families includes cultures, ethnicity, race, social class, religious affiliations, regional identities, gender, age, disability, affinity orientation, and other factors that may significantly affect and define our lives. Some of those that are most relevant to practice with families are now more specifically addressed. They include issues of ethnic-sensitive practice, gender, power and powerlessness, poverty, and family structures.

Ethnic-Sensitive Practice

Ethnic-sensitive practice must be in tune with the history, values, and perspectives of the family's ethnic group and social class position. An important component is giving attention to the oppression of members of racial and ethnic groups, and choosing relevant practice models for that family's needs at that point in time. Practitioners should know that unwillingness to challenge and address oppression in large societal systems is akin to aiding families to adjust to their oppressors. Oppression can never be accepted as normal. Some assumptions of ethnic-sensitive practice are that (1) history affects the generation and solution of problems; (2) the present is more important than the past or the future; (3) nonconscious phenomena affect family functioning; and (4) although ethnicity can be a source of strain, discordance, and strife, it is also a source of cohesion, identity, and strength (Schlesinger & Devore, 1995).

A second important component of ethnic-sensitive practice is multiculturalism, which is defined as learning to understand, appreciate, and value (not just tolerate) the unique aspects of cultures different from our own. The end product is learning to value others even though they may be different from us. Multiculturalism is learning that "different from" does not mean "less than." It is getting in touch with our cultural conditioning, learning how we view the world through our own particular filters, and working toward inclusion rather than exclusion and conformity (Bennett-Alexander, 1993).

Efforts at problem resolution must be in tune with ethnically distinctive values and community customs. Such practice involves the concept of the "dual perspective"—a conscious and systematic process of perceiving, understanding, and comparing simultaneously the values, attitudes, and behavior of the larger societal system with those of the family's immediate community system. It recognizes that all clients are a part of two systems: the dominant or sustaining system, which is the source of power and economic resources; and the nurturing system, composed of the physical and social environment of the family and community (Norton, 1998). Ethnic and class history and traditions often involve institutional sources of oppression. Therefore, practice with families must pay simultaneous attention to family and community/systemic concerns.

Thus, for example, we find victims of poverty and oppression caught up in a systemic process of powerlessness in which the failure of the larger society system to provide needed resources operates in a circular feedback process that entraps victims and sets in motion a malignant process. The failure of the larger system to provide necessary supports creates powerlessness in communities. And the more powerlessness in a community due to lack of resources and nutritive supplies, the more powerless are the families within, hindered from meeting the needs of their members and in organizing to improve the community so that it can provide them with more support. And the more powerless the families in efforts to protect their members from the stress of community failure and efforts to change its destructiveness, the more powerless are the individual members, blocked in attempts to acquire skills, develop self-esteem, and strengthen the family. And the more powerless the individual in efforts to acquire skills, develop self-esteem, and strengthen the family, the more powerless the community, which is denied their potential for strengthening it at the same time that the community itself becomes a stressor and a creator of even more powerlessness in people (Solomon, 1976).

Certain knowledge and skill areas have been set forth as mandatory for culturally competent work. They include

1. Knowledge of the specific values, beliefs, and cultural practices of clients.
2. The ability to respect and appreciate the values, beliefs, and practices of all clients, including those culturally different, and to perceive such individuals through their own cultural lenses instead of the practitioner's.
3. The ability to be comfortable with difference in others and thus not to be trapped in anxiety about difference or defensive behavior.
4. The ability to control, and even change, false beliefs, assumptions, and stereotypes, which means that one will have less need for defensive behavior to protect oneself.
5. The ability to think flexibly and to recognize that one's own way of thinking and behaving is not the only way.
6. The ability to behave flexibly. This is demonstrated by the readiness to engage in the extra steps required to sort through general knowledge about a cultural group and to see the specific ways in which knowledge applies or does not apply to a given client. These steps take extra time, effort, and energy (Pinderhughes, 1989; Pinderhughes, 1995, p. 266).

A cross-cultural practice model has been developed by Chau (1990) to guide ethnically sensitive practice. The model consists of four quadrants defined by two axes as shown in Figure 3.1. One axis represents the ideological value continuum of ethnocentrism and pluralism. The other axis defines the targets or goals of intervention and is arranged on a continuum of individual change to sociostructural change. The resulting quadrants (A, B, C, D) specify the four practice processes of psychosocial adaptation, ethnic "conscientization," interethnic integration, and ethnic rights advocacy, which are defined in Figure 3.1.

Not only is this perspective applicable to a broad array of needs experienced by diverse populations, but it also accommodates the use of different practice methods. It enables practitioners to learn about and apply ethnic sensitivity in their helping activities throughout the processes of problem identification, assessment, planning, intervention, and evaluation.

Other useful tools for culturally competent family practitioners are the cultural genogram (Hardy, 1995) and the culturagram (Congress, 1997).

Ethnic-sensitive work often requires the practitioner to think in terms of a multisystems, interactive approach as distinct from an isolated, linear approach to intervention. Many client families are challenged by complex, multiple problems (substance abuse, unemployment, underemployment, and language barriers), which demand concurrent, targeted units of intervention. What this means is that

FIGURE 3.1 *A Cross-Cultural Practice Model*
Source: Adapted from Chau, 1990.

practitioners must be knowledgeable not only about clinical/group processes, but also about policies and operations of other resources, such as health care, employment and training, and substance abuse, so that they can help connect families to needed services. When services are not available or not available in a timely fashion, the therapist must assume an advocacy role. Increasing specialization in many agencies can become a barrier to the multisystems, interactive approaches that many families need. This is also the case with managed care, which requires the segmenting of problems (Hopps, Pinderhughes, & Shankar, 1995).

Gender Issues

Family practitioners are challenged by new levels of awareness regarding gender. The subtext is a priority now for the profession, due largely to advances in feminist theory and thought, broader concepts of masculinity, and the triumphant legal, economic, political, and emancipatory achievements of the civil rights movement, the women's movement, and gay liberation. Gender is at the core of an ideological analysis that facilitates examination of assumptions regarding principles of hierarchy, domination, and power of one sex over another (Hooyman, 1995).

Although viewed initially as a protest against patriarchy, the women's movement initiated a social justice agenda that advocated equality, which brought change in the structure and dynamics of family and community life, and the workplace. In the last quarter of the century past, it became clear that some tenets of family practice were out of synch with feminism. Citing the work of Libow, Raskin, and Caust (1982), the areas of dissensus were teased out by Broderick and Schrader (1991, p. 36) and are summarized below.

1. Most family therapists tend to focus on ongoing, reciprocal circular causation, whereas the feminist therapist focuses on the linear causation of historic sexism and structural inequities.
2. Whereas family therapists intervene with the goal of improving relationships and patterns of interaction, the feminist therapist's goal is, rather, "to facilitate the growth of a strong competent woman who has enhanced control over resources" and "to increase the ability of women to work together politically to change society and its institutions" (Libow, Raskin, & Caust, 1982, p. 8).
3. The family therapist is seen as utilizing expert power, whereas feminists are committed to utilizing referent power (which highlights the commonality of all women's experiences).
4. The family therapist works within the ethnic, social, and religious values of the client family, whereas the feminist therapist challenges those norms and values that directly or indirectly support sexism and patriarchy.

Even with their power and authority attenuated, many men continued to resist new sex role definitions, clinging to traditional perspectives of manhood. But time marched forward, and with women gaining economic and political power which translated into new status arrangements, men began adapting to change and examined opportunities to get in touch with their own masculine potential. Women proffered that patriarchy diminishes feminine characteristics in all: tenderness, love, and relatedness. Men, too, challenged patriarchy and stunted, insecure masculinity, which, they argued, contributes to problems related to inhibited intimacy, homophobia, need to dominate or be dominated, and violence directed toward men and women (Chestang, 1995; Lichtenberg, 1995).

The task ahead: Both men and women should move beyond old barriers and hostilities, seek ways to explore their fullness and maturity, and relate to their common humanity (Keen, 1991). Stories and narratives of failed expectations, tolerance and intolerance, and growth should be shared in the safe zone of mutual respect, appreciation for personal struggle, and empathy. Given new growth, they should also join with other worldwide organizations in fighting servitude, sexism, and homophobia. There is much work to do on the road to personal and community empowerment.

Another development to which therapists must be prepared to relate is the growing, increasingly open, politically and economically significant population of not only gays and lesbians, but also transgenderists and bisexuals (although less is known about the latter two). The gay movement commenced with the Stonewall rebellion in 1969 and paralleled both the black power and women's movements. Hostility to this population originated with rampant and strongly held belief systems in heterocentrism, heterosexism, and homophobia, which throughout history oppressed those who could not or did not "own" a heterosexual identity. Such belief systems provided the undergirding for sociological, economic, political, and psychological factors that affected the development, sexual identity, resilience and coping resources of this population. Victimized in colonial times, when sodomy was a crime punishable by death, and today, when gay people constitute the largest victim group of hate crimes, beatings, torture and death, they also suffer discrimination in employment, access to housing, social service, and health care (Appleby, Colon, & Hamilton, 2001).

Although diverse, gays and lesbians are thought to experience similar affirmative processes, namely,

> identification and confrontation of sexual difference; socialization in the gay and lesbian communities; self-identification or coming out to self and others; sexual experimentation; development of a sexual identity; nurturance of sexual and intimate relationships; formation of families . . . and life long contribution to profession and communities while under psychological and social duress. (Appleby et al., 2001, p. 149)

Indeed, practitioners must be able to work with families as a member transitions through these phases. They must be prepared to help them find coping energy and perseverance when one (or more) of their members is confronted by and must work through internalized homophobia, a normative aspect of affirmative psychology, which can occur at an early age with the incorporation of unavoidable noxious, negative attitudes and societal stigma into one's self-image.

It is not unusual for lesbians and gays to defend against internalized homophobia by denying who they are, distrusting and expressing anger and contempt for those who elect to be open and visible about their sexuality, becoming fearful, and withdrawing from families and associates. Many experience difficulties with intimacy, affectional relationships, and sexual functioning. They may avoid managing alcoholism, drug use, safe sex, and AIDS, and may also become overwhelmed with fragmentation in their lives and exhibit borderline personality features (Appleby et al., 2001).

Coping with stigma, discrimination, abuse, acts of violence, and internalized self-hatred as they do, suicide is no stranger to those who are sexually diverse. Family therapists must be at the forefront of efforts to minimize the influence of heterosexism, heterocentrism, homophobia, and other sexist attitudes in their practice, and take the lead in helping to eradicate these "-isms" in social services where health and mental health services may be denied to the client and family. Therapists must also be mindful that families dealing with sexual diversity suffer trauma, stigma, isolation, and discrimination, but that these forces are even greater in families of color.

Power, Powerlessness, and Power Needs of the Practitioner

Some groups in society are oppressed because of their race and ethnicity, gender, sexual orientation, income, age, or a combination of these. Other client groups with mental, developmental, or physical disabilities may also experience powerlessness.

Power is defined as the capacity to gain whatever resources are necessary to remove oneself from a condition of oppression, to guarantee one's ability to perform, and to affect not only one's own circumstances, but also more general circumstances outside one's intimate surroundings (Goodrich, 1991, p. 10). Power thus involves the capacity to influence for one's own benefit the forces that affect one's life space; powerlessness is the inability to exert such influence (Pinderhughes, 1995).

Power as a construct is useful in understanding the relationship between the majority group and people of color and other ethnic groups, women, gays, and lesbians, as well as their interaction and role in the maintenance of majority–minority status, including discrimination, racism, and sexism. A dominant group requires and holds onto its resources and power by excluding and marginalizing low-status or different groups, making it difficult for them to access and acquire what they need; and by developing expectations that influence opportunities and outcomes for life chances of both the dominant group and those bestowed with less power (Hopps et al., 1995; Pinderhughes, 1995).

Indeed, overwhelmed and less powerful people may react to their role, status, and position by means that are truly unhealthy, unsafe, and unproductive. Pinderhughes (1995, pp. 290–291), states

> For example, as individuals, minority people of color react to being tension relievers, anxiety reducers, and victims in the social system by behaviors that aim to provide them a sense of power. Many of them struggle not to accept the projections of the powerful that they are incompetent, dumb, crazy, a stud, sexual, or dependent. Considerable effort is expended to ward off a sense of powerlessness. People adopt behaviors in which they identify with the aggressor (which leads to feelings of self-hatred); are guarded (seen by the powerful as being paranoid); strike out (seen by the powerful as being violent); and are oppositional, passive-aggressive, or autonomous (seen by the powerful as being stubborn). It is important to consider that the dependency response to conditions of powerlessness does not mean ethnic minorities and people of color desire it; instead, they may adopt dependency to get a sense of power or to be close to persons who actually have power (McClelland, 1975). They may also try to get a sense of power by assuming the negative attributions of the dominant society in an exaggerated way, for example, by being a super-stud, super dumb, or super-dependent. Although reactive, these behaviors, which Chestang (1976) identified as paradoxical mechanisms, also have meaning because they facilitate a feeling that one is the initiator.

These reactive behaviors often inhibit individuals and families from taking proactive steps to improve their social functioning, social standing and rejection of designated, assigned positions. Just as not being able to exercise influence over life's chances can be painful, having such influence can be rewarding. Even so, those with power can exhibit fear of losing status and control, and become fearful of those with little power. They may also experience guilt over their own privileged position; exhibit control needs; demonstrate a lack of tolerance, respect, and compassion for those who are different; and express affinity for those like themselves. Although guilty because of the reality of power, some might be willing to give a little, but few would give it up. Thus this power conundrum is at the crux of the struggle faced by people of color, women (though they have moved well ahead of people of color), new immigrants, gays, and lesbians in relation to the dominant group (Hopps et al., 1995; Pinderhughes, 1995).

Therapists must know that power is embodied in the professional role, which is endowed with knowledge and skills and emboldened by license to assess, intervene, and evaluate family functioning. Thus there is a power differential between the practitioner and the family. The realistic needs of some poor, diverse families are so great and resources so slim that therapists may easily become overwhelmed and anxious, and fall prey to self-comforting behaviors in efforts to reduce their stress and anxiety (Hopps et al., 1995). Therapists must assess and be realistic about their personal needs and never think of manipulating the helping/treatment encounter to meet their own status and power needs.

Poverty, Children, and Persistent Poverty

Poverty is a matter of the differentiated distribution of goods and privileges. In the preface to *The Power to Care,* Wilson states

> In an industrial society groups are stratified in terms of the material assets or resources they control, the benefits and privileges they receive from these resources, the culture experiences they have accumulated from historical and existing economic and political arrangement and the influence they yield because of those arrangements. Accordingly, group variation in resources, lifestyles and life chances is related to these variations. (Hopps et al., 1995, p. vii)

Poverty is a major factor in the lives of too many families. It is not only the lack of sufficient income, but rather an inclusive lifestyle. The government defines the poverty level. Factors used to determine poverty include income before taxes, excluding capital gains and noncash benefits, and family composition and size. The poverty threshold for a family of four was $11,611 in 1987, $12,674 in 1989, $13,359 in 1990, and $17,761 in 2000 (U.S. Bureau of the Census, 2001). These families also depend heavily on other benefits, such as food stamps, rent supplements, and public housing. There is a strong correlation between poverty and single-parent households, which are mostly female; more than 50 percent of families in poverty are headed by females, whereas 22 percent are male headed, and 10 percent have two parents. Regarding children, one in five is poor; under six years of age, one in four; and for African Americans, one in two. Persistent poverty is a problem faced by families impoverished for 8 out of 10 years. In this cohort, African Americans and female-headed families are dominant (Hopps et al., 1995).

Poverty is a diversity issue that directly affects many families. Poverty and lack of housing have given rise to unprecedented rates of homelessness. Families with children are the fastest-growing homeless population. Practitioners must be acutely aware that these families in poverty have needs that are at Levels I and II of family functioning. These needs must be addressed before needs at Levels III and IV can be given adequate attention.

Family Structures

The family, society's most basic institution, has changed. Hopps and Morris state

> The two-parent family in which the husband is the breadwinner and the wife the homemaker is not only no longer the norm but for many, neither a hope nor an ideal. "Alternative" styles now dominate, including the two-parent home, two-earner family, the single-parent family (due to divorce or out-of-wedlock births), the blended family, the gay or lesbian family, and the common-law marriage with family. Even though the rate of increase in these pluralistic styles has slowed, their members indicate that people are significantly less affected either by traditional norms or by social stigma, and create family structures that suit their individual needs. Many others now simply defer marriage or remain single. (2000. p. 7)

Changes in the role and function of the family have occurred, with much less time and energy allocated for nurturance and caregiving. Women are no longer as available for these roles as in the past, although they are in the paid labor force as disproportionately low-wage workers (and are expected to constitute nearly 65 percent of the labor force at the middle of this decade). Groups that are particularly vulnerable because of the shifting economy and its impact on families are the young, the elderly, and single parents (Hopps & Morris, 2000).

Those racial and ethnic families who have been marginalized have experienced a drastically sharp transition from the two-parent to the one-parent family, and a most devastating challenge for them is poverty, as noted earlier. In instances in which a single mother heads a family with children, the potential for poverty becomes substantial: one in two versus one in four, if the head of the family is a male. Practitioners must be knowledgeable about contraception, abstention, and sex education, placing before families options for delayed births, because the birthrate for unmarried African-American women has arguably been viewed as a main cause of poverty. Now that rate is at its lowest in 40 years; currently, the increase in the rate of children born to unmarried white women resembles what occurred three to four decades earlier to African-American women.

If therapists are to help families address and overcome the shift in family structure, they must find a way to incorporate resources relevant to education, including English, job training, work preparation, day care, transportation, and health care in their repertoire of referral services, and be prepared for assertiveness in connecting families to these resources. Families learn to model practitioners who advocate on their behalf, thus becoming empowered.

Summary

Within an ecosystems–social constructionism perspective, there exist many commonalities and differences of which we must be aware as we work with families who are functioning at various levels. Our common humanness unites us and is a foundation on which to build a therapeutic alliance. Differences and diversity issues must be recognized, with the goal of developing mutual respect and appreciation for differences. Thus the focus is on commonalities that unite us, not differences that divide us. The *helping relationship* or *therapeutic alliance* is a necessary condition for assuming that no harm is done and for developing a climate within which work can be done on problems that families bring to practitioners. The core needs of clients and the core conditions of the professional relationship of empathy, respect, genuineness, and warmth are commonalities for all our work with families. The therapeutic alliance consisting of the practitioner and client systems accounts for the social field in which the alliance occurs. *Diversity issues* include valuing multiculturalism and engaging in ethnically sensitive practice. A cross-cultural practice model and a cultural competence continuum are aides to developing ethnic sensitivity in a practitioner. Ways that diversity issues interfere with the provision of social justice and contribute to oppression must be addressed.

Research addresses various dimensions of the therapeutic alliance but has not focused on diversity as a significant variable in the helping relationship. Given the growing presence of people of color and the many cultural differences that exist, attention must be given to this topic.

In the forefront of family practice today are issues of gender, not just women's issues. Consciousness raising over the past few decades has served to focus our attention more on the oppressiveness of patriarchy, thus precipitating changes in both genders. However, oppression is felt by other groups as well, because of race, ethnicity, sexual preference, income, age, and the like. A major factor in oppression is access to the basic economic resources that are necessary for the well-being of any family. Practitioners must be especially sensitive to those families who are functioning at Levels I and II. Closely tied in with oppression is poverty, which is an especially crucial issue for minorities and single-parent families with children. These varying family structures—such as single-parent families but including also blended, childless, same-sex, multigenerational families, and others—may be especially vulnerable. Family practitioners must be sensitive to the different family structures and also realize the impact of ecosystem factors upon them.

Discussion Questions

1. How does the addition of the concept "alliance" alter the previous understanding of the helping relationship?

2. How can new levels of awareness regarding gender and sexual diversity influence the therapeutic alliance on the three levels of individual, subsystem (parents or children), and whole family system?

3. Using a family from your practice, assess the manner in which you engaged or joined the client. Extend this discussion of the therapeutic alliance through all the contexts of helping.

4. What efforts can be made to show value and appreciation of the diverse culture of the families with whom we work?

5. Explain and discuss issues of power, powerlessness, and empowerment in a family from your practice. Identify any power needs that you might have experienced and how you managed them.

Suggested Readings

Biestek, F. P. (1957). *The casework relationship.* Chicago: Loyola University Press.
    This is a classic on the therapeutic relationship and should be required reading for all helping professionals. A chapter is devoted to each of the seven principles of the helping relationship.

Boyd-Franklin, N. (1989). *Black families in therapy: A multisystems approach.* New York: Guilford Press.
    The author dispels myths, focuses on strengths, and sets African-American families in context. She gives major treatment interventions in a multisystemic approach and discusses diversity of family structures.

Brown, L. S., & Ballou, M. (Eds.) (1992). *Personality and psychopathology: Feminist reappraisals.* New York: Guilford Press.
    Synthesizing over 20 years of feminist thinking, this book gives original critiques of primary psychological theories and their accompanying definitions of pathology. The authors challenge previous theories of how healthy personalities develop and point out the need to keep any theory of personality relevant to women's lives.

Edwards, R. L. (Ed. in Chief), 1995. *Encyclopedia of social work* (19th ed., Vols. I, II, & III). Washington, DC: National Association of Social Workers.
    This most recent encyclopedia provides an objective overview of social work in the United States. It contains 10 articles specifically on the family, another on marriage and partners, and many others on methods of practice and diversity issues. It is highly recommended as a state-of-the-art reference book.

Hopps, J. G., Pinderhughes, E., & Shankar, R. (1995). *The power to care: Clinical practice effectiveness with overwhelmed clients.* New York: Free Press.
    This book contains important discussions on diversity, power, powerlessness and oppression, poverty, and clinical practice with overwhelmed clients.

Jordan, J. V., Kaplan, A. G., Miller, J. B., Stiver, I. P., & Surrey, J. L. (1991). *Women's growth in connection.* New York: Guilford Press.

This book offers a new perspective on women's development and women's ways of being in the world. The authors are clinicians, supervisors, and teachers who have been searching for therapeutic models that are based on and reflect the lives of women rather than male models. It discusses women's meaning systems, values, and organization of experiences.

Pinsof, W. F., & Catherall, D. R. (1986). The integrative psychotherapy alliance: Family, couple and individual therapy scales. *Journal of Marital and Family Therapy, 12*(2), 137–151.

This article introduces the therapeutic alliance concept into the family and marital therapy domain. It conceptualizes individual, couple, and family therapy as occurring within the same systemic framework. Three new scales that measure the alliance in individual, couple, and family therapy are discussed.

References

Appleby, G. A., Colon, E., & Hamilton, J. (2001). *Diversity, oppression and social functioning: Person-in-environment assessment and intervention.* Boston: Allyn and Bacon.

Bennett-Alexander, D. (1993). Preparing for the reality of multiculturalism. *The University of Georgia Columns, 20*(13), 5.

Biestek, F. P. (1957). *The casework relationship.* Chicago: Loyola University Press.

Broderick, C. B., & Schrader, S. S. (1991). *The history of professional marriage and family therapy.* In A. S. Gurman & D. P. Kniskern (Eds.), *Handbook of family therapy* (Vol. II, pp. 3–40). New York: Brunner/Mazel.

Buber, M. (1958). *I and thou* (2nd rev. ed.). New York: Charles Scribner's Sons.

Chau, K. L. (1990). A model for teaching cross-cultural practice in social work. *Journal of Social Work Education, (2),* 124–133.

Chestang, L. (1976). *The diverse society.* Washington, DC: National Association of Social Workers.

Chestang, L. (1995). Men: Direct practice. *Encyclopedia of social work.* Washington, DC: National Association of Social Work.

Congress, E. P. (Ed.). (1997). *Multicultural perspectives in working with families.* New York: Springer.

Davatz, U. (1981). Establishing a therapeutic alliance in family systems therapy. In A. S. Gurman (Ed.), *Questions and answers in the practice of family therapy.* New York: Brunner/Mazel.

Florsheim, P., Shotorbani, S., Guest-Warnick, G., Barratt, T., & Hwang, W-C. (2000). Role of the working alliance in the treatment of delinquent boys in community-based programs. *Journal of Clinical Child Psychology, 29*(1), 94–107.

Goldstein, A. (1975). Relationship enhancement methods. In F. Kanfer & A. Goldstein (Eds.),

Helping people change: A textbook of methods. New York: Pergamon Press.

Goodrich, T. J., (Ed.). (1991). *Women and power.* (p. 10). New York: Norton.

Hardy, K. V. (1995). The cultural genogram: Key to training culturally competent family therapists. *Journal of Marital and Family Therapists, 21*(3), 227–237.

Hardy, K. V. (1997). Steps toward becoming culturally competent. *Family Therapy News, 28*(2), 13, 19.

Hoffman, L. (1990). Constructing realities: An art of lenses. *Family Process, 29*(1), 1–12.

Hooyman, N. (1995). Diversity and population at risk: Women. In F. Reamer (Ed.). *The foundation of social work knowledge.* New York: Columbia University Press.

Hopps, J. G., Pinderhughes, E., & Shankar, R. (1995). *The power to care: Clinical practice effectiveness with overwhelmed clients.* New York: Free Press.

Hopps, J. G., & Morris, R. (Eds.). (2000). *Social work at the millennium: Critical reflections on the future of social work.* New York: Free Press.

Hopps, J. G., & Pinderhughes, E. R. (1999). *How the Power of Groups Can Help People Transform Their Lives.* New York: Free Press.

Horvath, A. O. (2000). The therapeutic relationship: From transference to alliance. *Journal of Clinical Psychology: Millenium Issue: The Therapeutic Alliance, 56*(2), 163–173.

Keen, S. (1991). *Fire in the belly: On being a man.* New York: Bantam Books.

Kivlighan, Jr., D. M., & Shaughnessy, P. (2000). Patterns of working alliance development: A typology of client's working alliance ratings. *Journal of Counseling Psychology, 47*(3), 362–371.

Libow, J. A., Raskin, P. A., & Caust, B. L. (1982). Feminist and family systems therapy: Are they irreconcilable? *American Journal of Family Therapy, 10*, 3–12.

Lichtenberg, P. (1995). Men: Overview. *Encyclopedia of social work.* Washington, DC: National Association of Social Work.

McClelland, D. (1975). Wrong, power. *Power, the inner experience.* New York: Wiley.

McGoldrick, M., Giordano, J., & Pearce, J. K. (1996). *Ethnicity and family therapy* (2nd ed., pp. 45–46). New York: Guilford Press.

McGoldrick, M., Pearce, J. K., & Giordano, J. (1982). *Ethnicity and family therapy* (pp. 45–46). New York: Guilford Press.

McGoldrick, M., Preto, N. G., Hines, P. M., & Lee, E. (1991). Ethnicity and family therapy. In A. S. Gurman & D. P. Kniskern (Eds.), *Handbook of family therapy* (Vol. II, pp. 546–582). New York: Brunner/Mazel.

Minuchin, S. (1974). *Families and family therapy.* Cambridge, MA: Harvard University Press.

Moore, R., & Gillette, D. (1990). *King, warrior, magician, lover: Rediscovering the archetypes of the mature masculine.* San Francisco: Harper San Francisco.

National Opinion Research Project (1991). *Speaking of kids: A national survey of children and parents.* Washington, DC: National Commission on Children.

Norton, D. (1998). *The dual perspective.* New York: Council on Social Work Education.

Ooms, T. (1992). *Families in poverty: Patterns, contexts, and implications for policy.* Washington, DC: American Association for Marriage and Family Therapy Family Impact Seminar.

People of Color Leadership Institute. (Jan/Feb 1993). Cultural competence continuum, *NRCCSA News.* Washington, DC: POCLI.

Pinderhughes, E. (1989). *Understanding race, ethnicity and power.* New York: Free Press.

Pinderhughes, E. (1995). Diversity and population at risk: Ethnic minorities and people of color. In F.

Reamer (Ed)., *The foundation of social work knowledge.* New York: Columbia University Press.

Pinsof, W. F. (1994). An integrative systems perspective on the therapeutic alliance: Theoretical, clinical and research implications. In A. Horvath & L. Greenberg (Eds.), *The working alliance: Theory, research and practice.* New York: Wiley.

Pinsof, W. F. (1995). *Integrative problem-centered therapy: A synthesis of family, individual, and biological therapies.* New York: Basic Books.

Pinsof, W. F., & Catherall, D. R. (1986). The integrative psychotherapy alliance: Family, couple and individual therapy scales. *Journal of Marital and Family Therapy, 12*(2), 137–151.

Rogers, C., Gendlin, E. T., Kiesler, D. L., & Truax, C. B. (1969). *The therapeutic relationship and its impact.* Madison: University of Wisconsin Press.

Sawhill, I. V., & Condon, M. (1992). Is U.S. income inequality really growing? Sorting out the fairness question. In *Policy Bites,* No. 13. Washington, DC: Urban Institute.

Schlesinger, E. G., & Devore, W. (1995). Ethnic-sensitive practice. In R. L. Edwards (Ed. in Chief), *Encyclopedia of social work* (19th ed., pp. 902–908). Silver Spring, MD: National Association of Social Workers.

Shulman, L. (1991). *Interactional social work practice: Toward an empirical theory.* Itasca, IL: Peacock.

Solomon, B. (1976). Social work in a multi-ethnic society. In M. Solemeyer (Ed.), *Cross-cultural perspectives in social work practice and evaluation* (pp. 167–176). New York: Council on Social Work Education.

Truax, C. B., & Carkhuff, R. R. (1967). *Toward effective counseling and psychotherapy: Training and practice.* Chicago: Aldine.

U.S. Census Bureau. (2001). http://blue.census.gov/hhes/www/poverty.html

4

Ethically Informed and Spiritually Sensitive Practice

Allie C. Kilpatrick, Ph.D., Dorothy S. Becvar, Ph.D., and Thomas P. Holland, Ph.D.

The entire therapeutic venture is fundamentally an exercise in ethics, involving the inventing, shaping, and reformulating of codes for living together (Efran, Lukens, & Lukens, 1988). Thus, in addition to the need for adherence to professional codes of ethics, there also must be recognition that family interventions constitute a dialogue whose goal is the creation of a context in which accommodation of the needs and desires of all the participants is facilitated. Fundamental to this context is the dimension of spirituality. Indeed, although often little recognized, some form of spirituality is a commonality in humanity (Becvar, in press). At varying times in a person's life, this aspect of being may seek expression and, even when implicit, inevitably influences beliefs and behaviors. This chapter provides suggestions for creating a practice that is well informed relative to ethical issues and is sensitive to the role of spirituality in the lives of both professionals and clients.

Ethically Informed Practice

Most professional groups that work with families have their own codes of ethics by which members are expected to abide. It is essential that practitioners know and practice these codes. Ethical issues discussed in the following section include those that involve some of the larger difficulties that we confront in family practice, as well as several models for dealing with such issues.

Ethical Practice

Working with families requires awareness of several important considerations and challenges in the ethical realm. These involve tensions related to separating interventions from the larger ecosystems, focusing on individual or family welfare, using informed consent, using confidentiality, and avoiding deception and manipulation.

1. *Separating Interventions from the Larger Social, Cultural and Political Ecosystems.* For many years, family therapists have spoken of problems as symptoms of family system dysfunction, rather than as manifestations of individual illness. Interventions have been focused on first-order change (individual behavior change within an unchanged system) or second-order change (changes within the system itself and the rules governing it) (Watzlwick, Weakland, & Fisch, 1974). However, as noted by Doherty and Boss (1991), we do not always consider the wider implications of the community, social, cultural, and political systems in the creation of problems or the ripples our interventions may produce in this wider pond on either level of change.

An illustration of how both society and the practitioner's interventions may play roles in exacerbating problems for clients can be seen in work with abusive families. For many years, society tolerated abusive behavior toward women and children. Now, society has changed, and practitioners label such behaviors as "bad" or "mad." If abusive behavior is part of a family's heritage, however, then their forebears also now may be seen as "bad." Further, if practitioners tell them that the negative consequences of the abuse will likely remain with them all their lives, then they probably will, inasmuch as people create their own reality based, at least in part, on perceptions such as these shared by professionals (Becvar & Becvar, 2000; Becvar, in press).

Society does evolve appropriate rules of conduct, and practitioners contribute to defining acceptable and unacceptable behaviors and problems. We also define what constitutes an ethical issue. Perhaps the ethical imperatives here are to avoid narrowing the range of focus to the point where there is little we see that is not illness, thus limiting preventive interventions (Becvar & Becvar, 2000; Becvar, Becvar & Bender, 1982), and ensuring that we do no harm. We must be careful that our interventions do not create more problems than they solve. We also must be careful that we do not ignore ethical dilemmas that arise in our practice concerning such other social justice issues as institutional racism, societal gender bias, or accessibility to resources.

2. *Individual or Family Welfare.* In a survey of members of the American Association for Marriage and Family Therapy (Green & Hansen, 1989), the ethical dilemma rated as the second most frequently encountered and the second most important was the tension between "family versus individual needs" (second only to "reporting child abuse"). Practitioners are concerned with protecting the rights and promoting the welfare of all clients. When there are multiple clients, an intervention that serves one person's best interests may be counterproductive for another person. The ethical imperative here is to attempt to balance therapeutic responsibility toward individuals and the family as a unit (Doherty & Boss, 1991).

The basic philosophy of Western medicine and the medical code of ethics imply that a clinician's primary loyalty is to the patient as an individual; broader issues of public welfare are relegated to public health. By contrast, in the Eastern European tradition, the clinician's first obligation is to the community and second to the individual. At the same time, another aspect of this dilemma emerges from the fact that society also defines the roles of men and women. Practitioners have been guilty of subordinating rights of women and children to the family good, even when it is to their detriment. It is not surprising that the issue of individual versus family rights was first raised by feminists, who have argued convincingly that balancing individual and family welfare requires practitioners to see beyond the therapy room to the family context (Doherty & Boss, 1991).

3. *Informed Consent.* The idea of informed consent involves "a knowledgeable decision based on adequate information about the therapy, the available alternatives, and the collateral risks" (Bray, Shepherd, & Hays, 1985, p. 53). State laws and professional association codes of ethics have made informed consent procedures standard practice. Disclosure documents are often read by family members before they see the practitioner (Huber & Baruth, 1987). The information that clients should have in order to make informed choices includes the procedures, goals, and possible side effects of interventions; the qualifications, policies, and practices of the practitioner; and other available sources of help. Ethical issues arise around the coercion of reluctant adults or children in the family, especially when it violates the autonomy of a skeptical family member. Refusing to see the family unless all members are present could also be coercive to willing members, who may feel obligated to make successful efforts to engage the other members. Doherty and Boss (1991) assert that refusing treatment if all the family does not participate would be unethical in public mental health centers, which are often the last resort for troubled families.

4. *Confidentiality.* The client has the right to be protected from the disclosure of information discussed in sessions, unless permission, usually written, is given for this disclosure (Huber & Baruth, 1987). However, judicial decisions, as in the case of incest, child abuse, or other clear dangers to a client (such as that addressed by the Tarasoff decision) and third parties such as family courts and insurance companies, have compromised the ideal of full confidentiality for clients (Doherty & Boss, 1991).

A further issue of which to be aware when working with families is the inability to reveal information unless all parties to the therapy have given their consent. In other words, even if one member of the family gives written permission to share information with a third party, the practitioner may not do so unless everyone who participated also gives written permission. The exception, of course, is when parents or legal guardians sign for children who are minors.

Another ethical challenge also may arise relative to the relationships of family members with one another and how to deal with secrets. Whether the practitioner keeps full confidentiality of private revelations, no confidentiality among family members, or a balance between the two, the practitioner's position must be clearly communicated to the family as early as possible in the therapeutic encounter. The ethical imperative is to disclose the practitioner's policy on confidentiality as part of initial informed consent for treatment (Doherty & Boss, 1991).

5. *Avoiding Deception and Manipulation.* According to Doherty and Boss (1991), the issue of deception is, along with gender bias, a central ethical issue in contemporary family treatment. According to some theories, manipulation should be avoided at all costs. Others state that manipulation is unavoidable (Watzlwick et al., 1974). For example, all practitioners influence clients by sharing or withholding information about the practitioner's thoughts and feelings concerning the client.

Given the universality of the influence of practitioners on clients and the continual decisions made by the practitioner about what to disclose, the issue is not whether the intervention is paradoxical or straightforward (because neither is inherently deceptive), but whether any concealment involved is ethical and whether the therapist remains trustworthy (Doherty & Boss, 1991). The ethical imperative is that the practitioner does not deceive the family about the practitioner's beliefs or intentions or conceal family realities about which the family deserves to know.

Handling the ethical issues we have discussed builds on the principles of relationship, ecosystems, and social constructionism that were discussed in earlier chapters. These principles consistently focus on the integrity of practitioners in respectful, genuine, and caring relationships with families and with themselves. We now turn to guides for understanding dimensions of ethical judgment and elements of intervention decisions. Codes of ethics are also considered in the following section.

Guides for Decision Making

The variety of ethical issues faced by family practitioners may be examined in terms of several underlying dimensions. Woody (1990, p.135) proposes a pragmatic approach to dealing with ethical concerns in family practice, drawing on theories of ethics, codes of professional conduct, practice theories, sociological context, and the professional identity. These components serve as five decision bases for practitioners to use for a comprehensive analysis aimed at preventing ethical problems and reaching defensible ethical decisions. The assumption is that practitioners draw from several bases in the process of weighing competing values and coming to a decision, and use both intuitive and critical thinking.

Another perspective on the ways in which family practitioners deal with ethical issues was drawn from qualitative research by Holland and Kilpatrick (1991). They developed a three-dimensional framework based on their findings from a grounded theory study of practitioners and how they defined and made ethical decisions. Their model of clinical judgment consists of three bipolar dimensions:

the focus of decisions, ranging from means to ends; the interpersonal orientation, ranging from autonomy to mutuality; and the locus of authority, ranging from internalized to externalized.

The first dimension focuses directly on the practitioner's decisions and identifies a tension between pursuing solutions that maximize benefits regardless of risk versus complying with principles and procedures that are seen to reflect the values of the profession. The issue of deception and manipulation may be involved here.

The second dimension examines the interpersonal orientation in the decision-making process. It reflects practitioners' struggles between the protection of individual freedom and self-determination, and the responsibility of mutual caring which urges active intervention in the service of protection and improvement for the good of all. Here, the issues of separating interventions from the larger ecosystem and focusing on individual family welfare come into play.

The third dimension involves the source of authority in the decision-making process. It focuses on the grounds for making these decisions, and represents the conflict of allegiance to values that lie within the individual or the client/worker relationship and the obligation to comply with external sources such as agency policy or existing norms. Issues of informed consent and confidentiality are applicable here (see Figure 4.1).

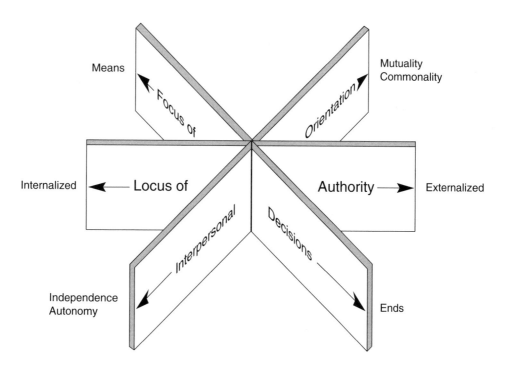

FIGURE 4.1 *Dimensions of Ethical Judgment*

Crossing these three dimensions permits examination of each area in relation to the other two, which yields a comprehensive look at one's ethical orientation. Such a perspective suggests looking for interactions across these three dimensions in specific practice situations. A professional or a family may have a pattern of dealing with ethical problems that emphasizes following standard policies and procedures, exercising centralized control, and protecting the security of his or her position or the internal stability of the family. Another's approach to ethical dilemmas may emphasize a pattern that seeks to distribute power more broadly, to emphasize attainment of ends at the expense of following standard procedural rules, and to advance individual autonomy. Posing these dimensions in terms of polar extremes does not entail their opposition or mutual exclusion. One may attempt to balance them by seeking both group stability and individual flexibility, by encouraging both productivity and cohesiveness, and by being both nurturing and powerful. The importance of balance along each of the dimensions may be highlighted by the extreme forms that any of these values can take if unchecked.

In addressing ethical problems, dimensions such as these should be thoughtfully considered. Before trying to apply them to a decision or dilemma in practice, it is important to be aware of one's own values, prior socialization, and influences from others involved in the situation. Stereotypes and biases can influence judgment, especially if they are not explicitly recognized. In addition, the professional must take into consideration the cultural perspectives of the clients, which may vary from his or her own. If circumstances allow, one should not take up complex problems when fatigued, ill, or unduly influenced by pressures from others. If the professional has a personal stake in the outcome of the decision, a trusted but disinterested outside party should be invited into the deliberations to guard against self-interest bias.

Understanding the facts of the situation is essential, even though one cannot know everything about it. Reasonably complete information bearing on the case should be known and considered. Likewise, the professional is responsible for identifying the relevant technical and professional issues present and possible choices available, including what options are feasible and what the relevant research indicates about them. Codes of professional ethics provide important guidance regarding choices and principles to follow.

The ethical dimensions of the situation must be identified explicitly and weighed reflectively. The decision maker specifies, evaluates, and measures the possible courses of action and the potential consequences of each. Who is involved, and what is at stake for each of them? Identify the duties, obligations, and interests of each party in the situation. What are the alternative courses of action (including doing nothing)? Then one weighs the principles involved in each alternative and their probable results. This includes consideration of the costs and benefits of alternatives, their long- and short-term effects, resources required and limitations on them, prior commitments and other constraints, justice and fairness for all parties involved, and possible need for reparations for those who may suffer losses.

Based on such considerations, it is often possible to identify one or two main courses of action. These should be examined for universality and consistency: Would it be appropriate for anyone in a similar situation to apply these principles and come to the same conclusion? If no alternative passes these tests, then one may select the option that results in the least undesirable net consequences. If others have not already been engaged in the deliberations, it is often helpful to test out conclusions and check for biases (remembering to safeguard the confidentiality of clients). These steps of ethical decision making are illustrated in Figures 4.2 and 4.3. Examples of cases involving ethical dilemmas are offered in Appendix B: Ethics Cases and Commentaries.

Codes of Ethics

Any profession has the responsibility to articulate its basic values and ethics through principles and standards that are relevant to all professional functions, settings, and populations served. These codes of ethics, to which we now turn our attention, serve to guide decision making and conduct relative to practice in general and more specifically, when ethical issues arise. As discussed previously, ethical decision making is a process. Keeping in mind the guides for decision making and the dimensions for clinical judgment, we note that all professions that include working with families have their own codes of ethics. For illustrative purposes, the codes of ethics for the National Association of Social Workers and the American Association for Marriage and Family Therapy are discussed.

NASW Code of Ethics (1996).   The broad ethical principles in the code of ethics of the National Association of Social Workers are based on social work's core values of service, social justice, dignity and worth of the person, importance of human relationships, integrity, and competence. The updated code became effective on January 1, 1997, and serves the following six purposes: It identifies core values of social work; summarizes broad ethical principles reflecting these values and sets standards; identifies relevant considerations and conflicts; provides ethical standards for which the profession is accountable; socializes new practitioners to social work's mission, values, ethical principles, and ethical standards; and articulates standards used to assess unethical conduct.

The code sets forth standards to which all social workers should aspire and which are relevant to the professional activities of all social workers. The standards include the categories of social workers' ethical responsibilities to clients, to colleagues, in practice settings, as professionals, to the social work profession, and to the broader society.

The longest and most in-depth standard is the first one, the responsibility to clients, which is five pages in length. It covers the following: the commitment to clients, which is the primary obligation; self-determination of clients; the provision of valid informed consent to clients; competence in providing services; the understanding of cultural competence, oppression, and social diversity; conflicts of interest, including dual relationships; privacy and confidentiality; access to records;

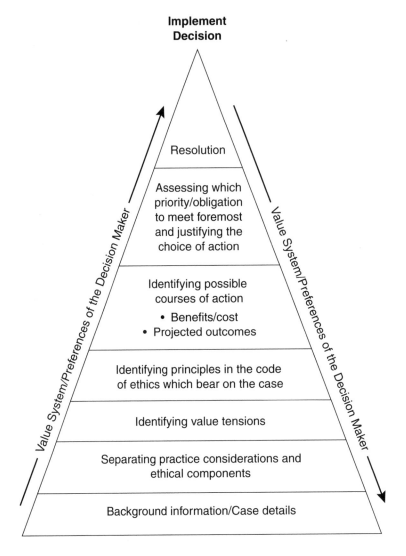

FIGURE 4.2   *Framework to Analyze Ethical Dilemmas*

Source: Mattison, M. (2000). Ethical decision making: The person in the process. *Social Work* 45(3), 206. Copyright 2000, National Association of Social Workers, Inc., Social Work.

sexual relationships with clients, which are strictly forbidden; physical contact; sexual harassment; derogatory language; payment for services; clients who lack decision-making capacity; interruption of services; and termination of services. Special attention must be paid to each of these as practitioners discharge their professional responsibilities to clients in a respectful, caring manner.

Engage in Reflection and Self-Awareness

Be aware of one's ethical preferences
Develop a conscious awareness of one's value patterning

Analyze Current Ethical Dilemma

Begin by isolating the ethical components

Recognize and
appreciate the
value components

Continue the Process of Reflection and Self-Awareness

Acknowledge which factors are influencing the decision

Follow Systematic Steps in the Decision-making Process/Select a Resolution

Use an analytic guide to structure the decision-making process

Reflect on the Choice of Action

Measure the current ethical choice against others from the past
Sharpen and modify conscious awareness of one's value patterning

FIGURE 4.3   *Cycle of Reflection*

Source: Mattison, 2000, p. 210. Copyright 2000, National Association of Social Workers, Inc., Social Work.

AAMFT Code of Ethics (2001).   The revised code of ethics of the American Association for Marriage and Family Therapy, effective July 1, 2001, is binding on members in all categories, including students, clinical members, and Approved Supervisors; also included are applicants for both membership and for the Approved Supervisor designation. It is similar in many respects to the NASW code. Eight categories are addressed. These include responsibility to clients; confidentiality; professional competence and integrity; responsibility to students and supervisees; responsibility to research participants; responsibility to the profession; financial arrangements; and advertising.

The code requires that marriage and family therapists report any alleged unethical behavior of colleagues so that the profession can be self-regulating and can maintain the highest standards of ethical practice. Reports should be made to the AAMFT Ethics Committee and/or to state regulatory bodies as appropriate.

Other professions that work with families, such as psychologists, counselors, chaplains, and nurses, have their own codes of ethics. State licensing boards also have their own codes. In some cases, a state board may have an umbrella code that covers several helping professions. All family practitioners are strongly encouraged to become very familiar with the relevant codes that govern their practice. Although a code of ethics cannot guarantee ethical behavior, it provides an important set of guidelines. Ultimately, however, the ethical behavior of practitioners must come from their personal commitment to engage in informed ethical practice. Similarly, to practice in a manner that is spiritually sensitive requires knowledge as well as a commitment to be aware of and to include this dimension in a responsible manner.

Spiritually Sensitive Practice

The 1996 Joint World Congress of the International Federation of Social Workers and the International Association of Schools of Social Work in Hong Kong heard the proclamation that there is a quiet revolution taking place in social work and other professions which is challenging the sole reliance on a traditional scientific-theory basis in favor of a more inclusive view of the human condition. The suggestion was made that social work's biopsychosocial paradigm be expanded to a bio-psychosocial-spiritual-cosmic paradigm as the integral basis for all courses taught (Schwartz & McGehee, 1996).

Because the majority of the world's families adopt some identifiable form of expression for their spirituality (Campbell & Moyers, 1988), it seems logical that practitioners should attend to the spiritual belief systems of clients if they are to understand better the families with whom they work. As the globe shrinks, long delayed encounters with other cultures have contributed to a widespread increase in spiritual pluralism. Fox (1983) describes what he sees happening as an "ecosystemic" revolution, a paradigmatic shift in our views of spirituality.

The Harvard Medical School held the international conference "Spirituality and Healing in Medicine" in 1996. Of the 900 M. D.'s in attendance, 200 acknowledged using spirituality as a healing tool in their practice. The focus of the conference was on the future role of prayer and religious experience in the healing process. The finding of Harvard medical researchers that spirituality is associated with fewer medical symptoms was shared with conferees (Smith, 1996).

Prominent attention is being given to the subject of spirituality in other secular activities. These include bookstores, various professional conferences, *Time* and *Newsweek* magazines, and countless nonchurch-related associations, such as Celestine Prophecy, A Course in Miracles, Readings of Edgar Cayce, Angels, and so on. Spirituality is becoming part of the mental set of our times. The 25-volume *World Spirituality* series has released its 22nd volume, Peter Van Ness's (1996) *Spirituality and the Secular Quest* (outside the church). Secular spirituality has been defined as "perceiving oneself to be connected to a larger whole through some unitive and transcending principle and living one's life accordingly" (Reed, 1997, p. 45).

The mental health professions have also begun to acknowledge and accommodate recent change in attitudes toward spirituality. The Council on Social Work Education (1994) requires that all master's degree programs in social work provide practice content that includes approaches and skills for practice with clients from varying religious and spiritual backgrounds. The *DSM-IV* (American Psychiatric Association, 1994) has also designated a category for problems related to spiritual issues and concerns.

Past Barriers and Future Directions

In the past there have been several barriers to addressing spiritual concerns of families. One is that, in order to become more scientific, we think we must separate ourselves from nonscientific spiritual constructs. The spiritual dimension is seen as esoteric and unobservable (Cornett, 1992), allowing the entrance of bias and subjectivity. Although subjective constructs, such as spiritual power, psychic energy, and divine intervention, are hard to observe and measure (Prest & Keller, 1993) from a social constructionist perspective, we recognize that subjectivity is inevitable. Further, as Cornett (1992) notes, the failure to integrate spirituality into our clinical thinking represents an impoverishment in our practice.

A second barrier concerns fears about the imposition of a particular frame of reference on clients. Effective practice is predicated on a nonimposing, nonjudgmental practitioner stance. Our spiritual commitments are better expressed through caring behavior. However, rather than monitoring our own spiritual expression in clinical work as we monitor other areas, many practitioners have simply discounted the need to explore the spiritual aspect of clients' lives, often with the assumption that these aspects are conflict-free, functional, or comfortable (Cornett, 1992). Other barriers include rigid conceptions of spirituality and biases against formal institutions (Prest & Keller, 1993).

Despite such barriers, the last decade has been characterized by a tremendous increase in attention to the spiritual dimension in people's lives, as well as permission to include religious and spiritual issues in therapeutic conversations (Becvar, 1997a, 1997b; Frame, 2000). However, several areas relevant to ethical issues have accompanied such a shift. These include the fact that a focus on spirituality in therapy is rarely included in professional training programs (Bowman, 1989); that there are many potential pitfalls requiring attention when including such a focus (Benningfield, 1997); that professionals must respect the autonomy of clients, safeguard their welfare, protect them from harm, and treat them in a just and honest manner when dealing with spiritual issues (Haug, 1998); and that therapists must recognize the limits of the knowledge it is possible to have relative to spirituality (Becvar, in press). Thus the mandate for the future relative to the ability to practice in a spiritually sensitive manner is the requirement for attention to each of these dimensions.

Definition of Spirituality

A definition of spirituality needs to encompass the person's understanding of and response to meaning in life (Cornett, 1992). It must include faith and values as spiritual dimensions (Kilpatrick & Holland, 1990), as well as the process of conceptualizing the individual's connection with others, the world, and the Creator (Campbell & Moyers, 1988). Spiritual expression could also be defined as the individual's response to the events in life over which he or she has no control. Canda (1988) gives an encompassing definition as follows:

> The gestalt of the total process of human life and development relates to the person's search for a sense of meaning and totally fulfilling relationships between oneself, other people and the encompassing universe and ontological ground of existence, whether a person understands this in terms that are theistic, atheistic, nontheistic, or any combination of these.

> Assagioli (1990) considers spiritual as referring to all states of awareness, all the human functions and activities that have as their common denominator the possession of higher values—values such as the ethical, the aesthetic, the heroic, the humanitarian, and the altruistic.

Implementation

As we think about acknowledging spirituality in practice, it is important to be aware that conflicts in values and the search for direction, meaning, integration, and faith underlie many of the problems presented by clients. What is more, despite the difficulties in dealing with such elusive and complex issues, few areas have more importance than these. Even in poor communities, according to Aponte (1995) in his book *Bread and Spirit*, the challenge to the family is not only about bread or basic resources, but as much about spirit. We must build a sense of dignity, purpose, and future in families that have given up hope, meaning, and self-worth, and have succumbed to a sense of despair. Here, optimism and hope are the core elements in building the resilience so necessary when working with Level I family needs.

Practitioners might begin to address this realm by including in the initial assessment questions about the clients' belief system. For example, they might ask, "Where are you about religion or spirituality?" or "How important is or what role does religion or spirituality play in your life?" They might also ask about the spiritual resources clients have available to them—both personal, such as prayer or meditation, and professional, such as a member of the clergy or spiritual guide.

At the same time, it is important that practitioners have an understanding and awareness of their own spirituality in order to be helpful to family members in their pilgrimage of life. Indeed, like other personal issues, the spirituality of practitioners can be an obstacle or an asset. Thus each of us must be sensitive to our own biases in order to avoid value imposition or an inappropriate intrusion on the therapy process.

Effective practice also includes recognizing clients' desires and readiness to deal with spiritual concerns, accepting them, and being as comfortable with discussing this dimension as with discussing the physical, emotional, and intellectual dimensions of practice (May, 1982). Further, whatever clients' belief systems may be, a spiritual orientation on the part of the practitioner would focus on helping clients to define meaning in life and achieve ultimate satisfaction and thus may also participate in the facilitation of deeper levels of healing (Becvar, 1997a). Indeed, as Bardill (1997) states, a failure to account for the spiritual reality in practice means that a powerful reality of life has been ignored.

Hodge (2001) presents a multidimensional framework for spiritual assessment. The two components are a narrative spiritual history outline and an interpretive anthropological framework, as shown in Table 4.1. Using the assessment instrument could help "elicit what may be the most untapped strength among consumers, their spirituality" (p. 211).

Having ascertained the degree of importance attributed by their clients to the realm of spirituality, practitioners may then include this aspect of life as a regular part of the therapeutic conversation. They also may wish to consult with or refer clients to others who have greater expertise in this area. In addition, they may make recourse to self-disclosure as appropriate, sharing the ways in which spirituality has helped them in their own journey toward health and healing.

At the same time, practitioners also must be able to accept the fact that for many clients such explicit discussions may be neither desirable nor useful. Even though spirituality is an important part of their life, some clients may not see it as relevant to the problems at hand. Some may feel it is just too personal or simply may feel uncomfortable discussing this topic with a therapist. Other clients may express lack of belief in any kind of spirituality. Some also may have experienced trauma in the context of their faith tradition (Hickson & Phelps, 1997). Nevertheless, a spiritual orientation on the part of the professional, which includes a nonjudgmental attitude as well as a focus on such issues as clients' values and their search for meaning and purpose in life, may participate in the creation of both a more effective therapeutic encounter and a more meaningful reality for clients

TABLE 4.1   Framework for Spiritual Assessment

Initial Narrative Framework

1. Describe the religious/spiritual tradition you grew up in. How did your family express its spiritual beliefs? How important was spirituality to your family? extended family?

2. What sort of personal experiences (practices) stand out to you during your years at home? What made these experiences special? How have they informed your later life?

3. How have you changed or matured from those experiences? How would you describe your current spiritual or religious orientation? Is your spirituality a personal strength? If so, how?

Interpretive Anthropological Framework

1. *Affect.* What aspects of your spiritual life give you pleasure? What role does your spirituality play in handling life's sorrows? enhancing life's joys? coping with life's pain? How does your spirituality give you hope for the future? What do you wish to accomplish in the future?

2. *Behavior.* Are there particular spiritual rituals or practices that help you deal with life's obstacles? What is your level of involvement in faith-based communities? How are they supportive? Are there spiritually encouraging individuals that you maintain contact with?

3. *Cognition.* What are your current religious/spiritual beliefs? What are they based upon? What beliefs do you find particularly meaningful? What does your faith say about personal trials? How does this belief help you overcome obstacles? How do your beliefs affect your health practices?

4. *Communion.* Describe your relationship to the Ultimate. What has been your experience of the Ultimate? How does the Ultimate communicate with you? How have these experiences encouraged you? Have there been times of deep spiritual intimacy? How does your relationship help you face life challenges? How would the Ultimate describe you?

5. *Conscience.* How do you determine right and wrong? What are your key values? How does your spirituality help you deal with guilt (sin)? What role does forgiveness play in your life?

6. *Intuition.* To what extent do you experience intuitive hunches (flashes of creative insight, premonitions, spiritual insights)? Have these insights been a strength in your life? If so, how?

Source: D. R. Hodge, (2001). Spiritual assessment: A review of major qualitative methods and a new framework for assessing spirituality. *Social Work, 46*(3), 208. Reprinted with permission from the National Association of Social Workers. All printed material is copyrighted.

(Becvar, 1997a). In addition, Canda and Furman (1999, p. 291) list the following as specific examples of spiritually oriented helping activities:

> Active imagination
> Art, music, dance, and poetry therapies

Assessing spiritual emergencies
Assessing spiritual propensity
Biofeedback
Caring for the body
Cooperation with clergy, religious communities, and spiritual support groups
Cooperation with traditional healers
Creating a spiritual development timeline and narrative
Developing and using multicultural teams
Developing mutually beneficial human–nature relationships
Developing and participating in rituals and ceremonies
Dialoguing across spiritual perspectives
Differentiating between spiritual emergencies and psychopathology
Dissolving inner chatter and distractions
Distinguishing between religious visions and hallucinations or delusions
Dream interpretation
Exploring family patterns of meaning and ritual
Exploring sacred stories, symbols, and teachings
Family brainstorming
Focused relaxing
Forgiveness
Guided visualization
Intentional breathing
Journaling and diary keeping
Meditation and prayer
Mindful paying attention
Nature retreats
Physical disciplines for spiritual cultivation, such as hatha yoga or t'ai chi
Reading scripture and inspirational materials
Reflecting on beliefs regarding death and afterlife
Reflecting on helpful or harmful impacts of religious participation
Win–win solution making

Regardless of activities chosen, however, the intentional use of spirituality in practice is unique, not because of words or actions, but because of our assumptions about how these words or actions interface with the transcendent dimension. According to Anderson and Worthen (1997), three assumptions are basic to a spiritual perspective. These are (1) an awareness that God or a divine being exists, (2) a recognition that humans have an innate yearning for a connection with this being, and (3) a belief that this being is actively interested in humans and acts on our relationships to promote beneficial change. Working from these assumptions, practitioners share their own spiritual selves, and then the range of available resources and possibilities for change expands for all.

Accordingly, the practitioner is kind and operates from a place of integrity. Compassion for clients is expressed through a nonjudgmental stance, focused attention, and the creation of meaningful relationships. Humility and respect for everyone involved in the process also characterize spiritually sensitive practice. For example, despite the fact that certain client behaviors are socially unacceptable, the practitioner attempts to focus on understanding the context of clients and their behavior rather than on a blaming or demeaning attitude. Questions such as "How did you learn that it was okay to hit/abuse your spouse?" provide important information about areas in which further learning may be helpful and help to move in the direction of potential solutions. And, as clients are able to experience a respectful process, they may find themselves open to growth and change.

Growth and change in other areas may be facilitated through questions aimed directly at understanding the degree of meaning and purpose in the lives of clients. Some of these questions include the following:

- Are you doing the work you want to be doing?
- Are you satisfied with the education you have obtained?
- Is there any way in which you would like to increase your education or training?
- What are the ways in which you express your creativity?
- Do you have any special talents or skills that you haven't fully developed or expressed?
- Assuming that money and other responsibilities were no object, what would you do with your life if you could do what you truly wanted?
- What would you like to have accomplished by the time you reach 70 in order to feel that your life has been meaningful?
- Have you developed your spiritual life to the extent that you desire?
- What are your most important values?
- What gives your life the most meaning?
- Is there anything you deeply value that you have not yet fully experienced or realized in your life?

The transpersonal or spiritual dimension is one of empowerment by the energies and wisdom that flow from a greater wholeness attained as we recognize that life does indeed have meaning and purpose. It is the bedrock of empowerment for the practitioner and families, and for national and international work. Instead of relegating issues of value to the private sphere, spiritually sensitive practice acknowledges that a transcendent dimension permeates all aspects of life, linking each individual with each other and with the community or public sphere. Such linkages typically prompt spiritual people into actions of concern for others (Elkins, 1990), especially the poor and the vulnerable. Although these persons may not have always spoken with one voice on every issue, they have affirmed in numerous ways their shared faith that the spiritual dimension of life leads to a transcendence of individualism and to a life of commitment and service to others (Leiby, 1985; Peck, 1987).

The convenient popular dichotomy between public and private morality works against the integration of our communities as well as our personal and professional lives. Our shared public interests rely in large part on the development of private virtue. Both private and public order depend on the availability of material resources and fair systems for their allocation to all. Therefore, a commitment to values of social justice and to the difficult tasks of implementing such values in our economic and political systems is essential (Siporin, 1986). Our spiritual heritage further emphasizes that individual self-actualization is gained through committed relationships with others, through investing our own resources and our very selves in furthering the good of others (Kilpatrick & Holland, 1990).

Recognition of the spiritual foundations of our lives and our professional practice leads to a number of implications regarding the client, the practitioner, their relationship, and the social context of the profession. Consistent with our social constructionist framework, clients are acknowledged as our peers. We recognize that they are human beings similar to us and that, just as we have professional expertise, they also are the experts on their personal lives and families. Exploration of spiritual issues is undertaken with respect for the individual's, couple's, or family's spiritual framework, and with the understanding that their belief systems represent their view of reality, which is just as valid for them as ours is for us.

The spiritual, social, emotional, and material or physical dimensions of life are all necessary for our growth and well-being. Thus each should be considered in the therapeutic relationship. A biopsychosocial–spiritual model of human functioning makes spiritual issues a legitimate focus for practitioners and provides for a more complete understanding of the strengths, resources, weaknesses, and problems of families. Policies and services that provide for the accessibility to support in all of these areas are essential for human well-being. Increased openness to addressing relevant spiritual beliefs and metaphors could often provide the practitioner with an important avenue to effective interventions having great potential to participate in the facilitation of growth and change.

Summary

Ethics and spirituality are both involved in inventing, shaping, and reformulating the way we are with ourselves and others. They are at the same time very personal matters and also the blueprints that shape how we relate to others. And both are an inevitable part of the therapy context.

This chapter describes how ethical issues influence what we are able to do with families and the ways in which practitioners must be informed in this area. Current ethical issues raised in this chapter include separating interventions from the larger ecosystems; focusing on individual or family welfare; using informed consent; using confidentiality; and avoiding deception and manipulation. Several models for decision making are presented. These include an overview of decision bases, dimensions of clinical judgment, and codes of ethics. These provide guidelines for making ethically informed decisions in practice.

A final context to be considered is that of spiritually sensitive family practice. Although previously a much neglected area, spirituality is now recognized as an important aspect of people's lives as well as of the therapy process. There are barriers to addressing families' spiritual concerns that must be overcome in order to be able to practice in the future in a more spiritually sensitive manner. Definitions of spirituality include faith, values, how a person understands and responds to meaning in life, and each person's connection with others and the world, as well as a recognition of a transcendent dimension. Several suggestions for including spirituality in the therapeutic conversation are provided. Increased openness in dealing with families' relevant spiritual beliefs may enrich and enhance practice. Spirituality is a resource to draw on not only from within the individual or family, but also in utilizing churches within the ecosystem and the values underlying each person's or system's construction of reality.

Discussion Questions _____

1. Describe and discuss ethical issues that may arise in an intervention with a family with a strong patriarchal tradition.

2. Regarding the ethical dilemma of meeting family versus individual needs, how would you balance the therapeutic responsibility toward both?

3. How do you effectively work with clients who present spiritual ideas that are different from, or even conflicting with, your own?

4. How could you be able to assess when a client or family is ready to or needs to discuss spiritual issues?

5. What are some ethical issues of which to be aware when including spirituality in the therapeutic conversation?

Suggested Readings _____

Assagioli, T. (1990). *Psychos synthesis. A manual of principles and techniques.* Wellingborough, UK: Crucible Press.
   The author defines and maps the geography of spiritual transformation through psychosynthesis. Psychological disturbances may serve as precursors to a more ethically and spiritually refined outlook. The process of spiritual development is described in four critical phases.

Becvar, D. S. (1997). *Soul healing A spiritual orientation in counseling and therapy.* New York: Basic Books.
   This groundbreaking book shows how a spiritual orientation (which can encompass the full range of belief systems) can be used to facilitate healing at the deepest level.

Doherty, W. J., & Boss, P. G. (1991). Values and ethics in family therapy. In Alan S. Gurman and David P. Kniskern (Eds.), *Handbook of family therapy* (Vol. II, pp. 606–637). New York: Brunner/Mazel.
   Of special interest in this article is the discussion of personal and cultural values in family therapy, ideological issues, ethical issues, and gender and ethics in family therapy. Future directions are also discussed.

Dykstra, C., & Parks, L. (1986). *Faith development and Fowler.* Birmingham, AL: Religious Education Press.
   Fowler presents an overview of his faith development theory, and then other authors evaluate the theory and discuss how it can be enhanced.

Huber, C. H. (1993). *Ethical, legal and professional issues in the practice of marriage and family therapy.* New York: Merrill.

A new edition of a very popular text used in many marriage and family therapy professional issues courses. Several chapters are devoted to ethical issues, the professional codes of ethics, and their implications for working with families.

Kilpatrick, A. C., & Holland, T. P. (1990). Spiritual dimensions of practice. *The Clinical Supervisor, 8*(2), 12–140.

This article places values and faith in a historical context within the profession of social work, presents developmental stages of faith, and gives some practical ways that students and practitioners can think about the spiritual dimensions of professional practice.

Mattison, M. (2000). Ethical decision making: The person in the process. *Social Work, 45*(3), 201–212.

Reflective self-awareness can alert the decision maker to the ways assumptions and values influence thinking about ethical dilemmas.

May, G. (1982). *Will and spirit: A contemplative psychology.* San Francisco: Harper.

Within Maslow's hierarchy of needs, May found that spirituality can be found at both ends of the continuum. He states:

It emerges at the bottom, when physiological needs for survival cannot be met and physical existence is threatened. It also arises when most other needs have been taken care of and one has the luxury to ask, "What's it all for? " or "Is this all there is?" Thus, it is in relative affluence or in utter desolation that human spiritual longing most obviously becomes prominent. (p. 91)

References

AAMFT Code of Ethics. (2001). Washington, DC: American Association for Marriage and Family Therapy.

American Psychiatric Association. (1994). *Diagnostic criteria from DSM-IV.* Washington, DC: Author.

Anderson, D. A., & Worthen, D. (1997). Exploring a fourth dimension: Spirituality as a resource for the couple therapist. *Journal of Marital and Family Therapy, 23*(1), 12.

Aponte, H. (1995). *Bread and spirit: Therapy with the new poor.* New York: Norton.

Assagioli, T. (1990). *Psychosynthesis. A manual of principles and techniques.* Wellingborough, UK: Crucible Press.

Bardill, D. R. (1997). *The relational model for family therapy; Living in the four realities.* New York: Haworth Press.

Becvar, D. S. (in press). Moral values, spirituality and sexuality. In R. H. Woody & J. D. Woody (Eds.), *Understanding the 2001 ethics code from the American Association for Marriage and Family Therapy.* Washington, DC: AAMFT.

Becvar, D. S. (1997a). *Soul healing: A spiritual orientation in counseling and therapy.* New York: Basic Books.

Becvar, D. S. (Ed.). (1997b). *The family, spirituality and social work.* New York: Haworth Press.

Becvar, D. S., & Becvar, R. J. (2000). *Family therapy: A systemic integration.* Boston: Allyn and Bacon.

Becvar, R. J., Becvar, D. S., & Bender, A. E. (1982). Let us first do no harm. *Journal of Marital and Family Therapy, 8*(4), 385–391.

Benningfield, M. (1997). Addressing spiritual/religious issues in therapy: Potential problems and complication. In D. Becvar (Ed.), *The family, spirituality and social work* (pp. 25–42). New York: Haworth Press.

Bowman, E. S. (1989). Understanding and responding to religious material in the therapy of multiple personality disorder. *Dissociation, II*(4), 231–238.

Bray, J. H., Shepherd, J. N., & Hays, J. R. (1985). Legal and ethical issues in informed consent to psychotherapy. *American Journal of Family Therapy, 13*, 50–60.

Campbell, I., & Moyers, B. (1988). *The power of myth.* New York: Doubleday.

Canda, E. (1988). Spirituality, religious diversity and social work practice. *Social Casework, 69*(4), 238–247.

Canda, E. R., & Furman, L. D. (1999). *Spiritual diversity is social work practice.* New York: Free Press.

Cornett, C. (1992). Toward a more comprehensive personology: Integrating a spiritual perspective into social work practice. *Social Work, 37*(2), 101–102.

Council on Social Work Education. (1994). *Curriculum policy statement for master's degree programs in social work education.* VA: Author.

Doherty, W. J., & Boss, P. G. (1991). Values and ethics in family therapy In A. S. Gurman & D. P. Kniskern (Eds.), *Handbook of family therapy* (Vol. II, pp. 606–637). New York: Brunner/Mazel.

Efran, J. A., Lukens, R., & Lukens, M. D. (1988). Constructivism: What's in it for you? *The Family Therapy Networker, 12*(5), 27–35.

Elkins, D. (1990). On being spiritual without necessarily being religious. *Association for Humanistic Psychology Perspective,* June, pp. 4–5.

Fox, M. (1983). *Original blessing.* Santa Fe, NM: Bear & Co.

Frame, M. W. (2000). Spiritual and religious issues in counseling: Ethical considerations. *Family Journal: Counseling & Therapy for Couples and Families, 81*(1), 72–74.

Freyman, I. C. (1974). *The American health care system: Its genesis and trajectory* New York: Medcom.

Green, S. L., & Hansen, J. C. (1989), Ethical dilemmas faced by family therapists. *Journal of Marital and Family Therapy, 15*(2), 149–158.

Haug, I. (1998). Including a spiritual dimension in family therapy: Ethical considerations. *Contemporary Family Therapy, 20*(2), 181–194.

Hickson, J., & Phelps, A. (1997). Women's spirituality: A proposed practice model. In D. Becvar (Ed.), *The family, spirituality and social work,* (pp. 43–57). New York: Haworth Press.

Hodge, D. R. (2001). Spiritual assessment: A review of major qualitative methods and a new framework for assessing spirituality. *Social Work, 46*(3), 203–214.

Holland, T. P., & Kilpatrick, A. C. (1991). Ethical issues in social work: Toward a grounded theory of professional ethics. *Social Work, 36*(2), 138–144.

Huber, C. H., & Baruth, L. G. (1987). *Ethical, legal and professional issues in the practice of marriage and family therapy.* Columbus, OH: Merrill.

Kilpatrick. A. C., & Holland, T. P. (1990) Spiritual dimensions of practice. *The Clinical Supervisor, 8*(2), 12–140.

Leiby, J. (1985). The moral foundations of social welfare and social work. *Social Work, 30,* 323–330.

Mattison, M. (2000). Ethical decision making: The person in the process. *Social Work, 45*(3), 201–212.

May, G. (1982). *Will and spirit: A contemplative psychology.* San Francisco: Harper.

NASW Code of Ethics. (1996) Washington, DC. National Association of Social Workers.

Peck, M. S. (1987). *The different drum.* New York: Simon & Schuster.

Prest, L. A., & Keller, J. F. (1993). Spirituality and family therapy: Spiritual beliefs, myths, and metaphors. *Journal of Marital and Family Therapy, 19*(2), 137–148.

Reed, H. (1997). Finding the sacred in the profane. *Venture Inward* (magazine of the Association for Research and Enlightenment, Inc./The Edgar Cayce Foundation/Atlantic University), January–February.

Schwartz, M., & McGehee, E. (1996). Bio-psycho-social-spiritual-cosmic paradigm in social work education. In *Proceedings,* Joint World Congress of the International Federation of Social Workers and the International Association of Schools of Social Work, July, Hong Kong.

Siporin, M. (1986) Contribution of religious values to social work and the law. *Social Thought, 13,* 35–50.

Smith, A. R. (1996). A rising tide lifts all boats. *Venture Inward,* November–December.

Van Ness, P. (1996). *Spirituality and the secular quest.* In *World spirituality,* (Vol. 22). New York: Crossroad.

Watzlwick, P., Weakland, J. H., & Fisch, R. (1974). *Change: Principles of problem formation and problem resolution.* New York: Norton.

Woody, J. D. (1990). Resolving ethical concerns in clinical practice: Toward a pragmatic model. *Journal of Marital and Family Therapy, 16*(2), 13–150.

5

Interventions to Meet Basic Needs in High-Risk Families with Children

R. Kevin Grigsby, D.S.W.

Continuity of relationships, surroundings, and environmental influence are essential for a child's healthy development (Goldstein, Freud, & Solnit, 1973, p. 31). As children develop in the context of the relationship with their primary caretakers, supporting this relationship is of primary importance, as disruptions or termination of the caretaker–child relationship may lead to additional problems for the child. In some families, caretakers have been unable to meet the needs of children or have failed in their attempts to do so. Although there are many families who experience problems, most families have either innate resources or access to support resources that enable them to provide adequate care for their children.

A small portion of families appear to be less able to provide for even the basic needs of nurturing and protection. Weltner (1982) describes these families as having an "ineffective executive system" and designates them as "Level I" families (p. 43). Level I families appear to have difficulty with issues related to food, shelter, protection, medical care, and basic nurturing. Other authors have referred to these families as being "multiproblem families" (Geismar & Lasorte, 1964; Kaplan, 1986; Spencer, 1963) whose children are at "high risk" (Adnopoz, Grigsby, & Nagler, 1996). In the parlance of the social workers who are assigned to work with these families, "perpetual crisis" is often used to describe their level of functioning.

Typical Needs of Level I Families

"Impoverished" is a good, generally descriptive term, as these families are almost always lacking in financial resources. In these families, poverty is not limited to the lack of financial resources alone. Rather, the lack of resources may provide impetus for other negative aspects of these families' lives. "Disease, poverty, alcoholism, chemical dependency, mental deficiency, constitutional inadequacy, parental discord, social isolation, and lack of familial and community support" are common features (Adnopoz et al., 1996, p. 1074), as are parental defects such as chronic mental illness (Rutter & Quinton, 1984) or periodic incarceration. Parents' "executive capacity" (Weltner, 1985, p. 43) is often compromised by the multitude and magnitude of problems facing the family and by a "multiproblem delivery system" (Selig, 1976, p. 526) that may blame families for their inability to make use of traditional supports, such as local social and community services. Therefore, it is important to understand that the designation "Level I" (Weltner, 1985) is merely a tool that can be useful to helpers outside of the family, allowing them to decide "what to do, when, and with whom" (Weltner, 1986, p. 51). If the designation of Level I is seen as a diagnosis, it may lead to a deterministic view, that families on this level are doomed to perpetual crisis. Level I should be seen as a description of families' "level of functioning within an overall intervention strategy" (Weltner, 1986, p. 52), as is used in this book, and not as a "level of pathology" (Weltner, 1985, p. 39). "Level of need" is more accurately descriptive of these families and is used throughout this book rather than "level of pathology." Conceptual clarity is needed here in order to make the distinction between these two concepts, as they are quite different in practice and in theory building. Families may operate at a relatively high level of need and may simultaneously exhibit a high degree of pathology. On the other hand, loving, nonpathological families may find themselves in dire straits if they experience a loss of resources such as income, housing, and physical health. Nonetheless, the framework for categorizing families proposed by Weltner can be very useful, especially to novice helpers (Paquin & Bushorn, 1991).

Assessing the Level I Family: The Case of Ms. W.

All Level I families present with an abundance of problems. Novice helpers are sometimes overwhelmed as they list problem after problem, with seemingly few solutions in sight. On the other hand, experience generally leads helpers to the recognition that nearly all families have some strengths. For this reason, the approach to assessment should focus on family strengths rather than on weaknesses, psychopathology, or the lack of resources. Weltner (1985) suggests that the assessment of the family begin with a "survey of potential resources and strengths" (p. 43). A program that has worked successfully with these types of families operates under the assumption that "there are existing strengths in families that, once identified, can be utilized effectively" (Adnopoz et al., 1996, p. 1077). Focusing on the negative experiences of the past may not be relevant to the present situation.

Assisting the family in utilizing their own resources and strengths to move ahead is as great a challenge as focusing on pathology. Some families may not be aware of their own strengths, as they feel overwhelmed by the plethora of problems facing them. In this situation, part of the task is to instill hope within the family.

The case of S.W. is illustrative of the history and dynamics of a typical Level I family. S.W. is a 27-year-old mother of six children. Three of her children, Tammy, Dwayne, and Kendra, are presently in foster care. Another child, Kenneth, and one other child are living with Ms. W.'s maternal aunt. S.W. is currently living with her newborn daughter (Peggy) in a week-to-week room at a hotel. A DFACS caseworker is assigned to the family and deals with all six children's cases. The caseworker is concerned about S.W.'s ability to care for Peggy, as S.W. has a history of drug abuse in the past and has had "nerve problems," according to other family members. Blood testing completed on S.W. at the public hospital was positive for cocaine on the day of Peggy's birth. As such, state law required that S.W. be reported to the Department of Family and Children Services. At the time of the caseworker's meeting S.W., she denied any continued drug or alcohol use. The caseworker is most concerned about S.W. because she says that "she wishes that she were dead, but that (she) would not kill herself because she has to take care of Peggy." The caseworker reports that S.W. is doing a good job of caring for the child and that the child is thriving. When an offer was made to help S.W. by linking her with a clinician at the community mental health outpatient clinic, S.W. did not agree to go, stating, "There is no use is going. No on can help me."

As S.W. has no telephone at the hotel, the first visit was made without prior notification. Although S.W. was initially suspicious when the social worker arrived at her present dwelling, S.W. was cooperative and verbally expressive of her need for help. Her child (Peggy) appeared to be well cared for and developmentally sound. S.W. had an adequate supply of toys and child-related items but complained of being almost out of groceries. She indicated that Peggy received well-child care at the public hospital primary care clinic and that John L., M.D., was Peggy's pediatrician. The Visiting Nurse Association has been involved with S.W. and her daughter following Peggy's birth.

Written reports supplied by the caseworker documented that three of S.W.'s children who were in foster care (Tammy, Dwayne, and Kezia) were evaluated at the University Child Study Center. The report recommends that Ms. W's parental rights be terminated in order to meet the terms of the permanency plan for the children's care, which is adoption. S.W. is aware of this, but appears to be in a state of denial, as she has continued to request that the Housing Authority supply her with a three-bedroom apartment in order to have enough space so that the children can reside with her. The DFACS case worker and University personnel are working with S.W. to help her to accept that her children probably will not be returned.

S.W. is well nourished, well groomed, and has been to see her physician at the Public Hospital Clinic in the past week to ask for "sleep medicine," as she reported she always wakes up early in the morning (around 5:00 a.m.) and cannot get back to sleep. She reported that her most pressing need is for housing and that she has little hope of finding permanent, affordable housing in the near future.

When asked directly about her other children, S.W. immediately began to sob, and said that she had "lost them" because she is not a good mother. She reported that although the DFACS caseworkers believed that her children were placed into foster care because of substance-abuse related problems, in actuality she did not begin to use cocaine until after they had been placed. When asked why they were placed into care, S.W. explained that she had "spells" when she would just stay in bed all day and would stop eating. She reported that she would "forget" to feed her children and that neighbors had reported her for neglecting them. She reported that the "spells" lasted for weeks at a time, but that she would slowly "get better," especially if her mother would "help her with the kids."

S.W. was well-oriented to time, place, person, and situation. Her immediate, recent, and remote memory were within normal limits, but she reported that when she had "spells" she had a hard time remembering to do simple things like getting up in the morning. There is no evidence that Ms. W. is using cocaine at present. She reports that she used the drug when she felt "really down." When asked if those times were like the times when she had "spells," she replied, "Yeah, How did you know?" She has not been receptive to suggestions (by the DFACS worker and supervisor) that she begin drug abuse treatment and reports, "I don't have a drug problem. You grow up in my neighborhood and you *know* what that is. I just tried it when I felt so bad. When I was pregnant, I felt terrible towards the end— so I smoked some rock when I went into labor. I guess that's why the baby tested positive." She and Peggy appear to have a very strong attachment, and she seems to be doing a good job of caring for Peggy.

S.W. reported that she sometimes hears her mother calling her name, especially when she tries to go to sleep. When questioned further, she reported that her mother died about two weeks prior to Peggy's birth. At this point she began to cry again, saying "Everyone leaves me. The kids' father left me. My mother left me. Even my sister won't talk to me anymore. I guess I'm just no good." When asked about the children's father, S.W. said she had no desire to discuss him.

S.W. has no history of mental health treatment and reports no family history of mental illness or alcoholism. She said that some family members told her that her father's death in an auto accident was actually a suicide. She reported that she was "just a little girl at the time" and did not understand what was meant by suicide.

Ms. W. was referred to the Family Support Service, a program designed specifically to intervene with multiproblem families with children at high risk for being removed from their home. The source of the referral was the hospital social worker at the women's clinic, who was aware of the ongoing DFACS involvement. The social worker feared that Peggy would have to enter foster care placement, as Ms. W. was at imminent risk of becoming homeless and had no other resources available to her that could provide adequate care for Peggy.

There were strengths in this family, if one looked for them. First of all, Ms. W. had a strong relationship with her child Peggy. She had a record of consistent health care and had been consistent in obtaining prenatal care throughout this pregnancy. She also had established a trusting relationship with the women's clinic social worker. As it was revealed that she had waited almost three years between pregnancies, this was also seen as a strength, as it represented her attempt to have some stability in her life and to provide quality care for her child. She had also been successful in maintaining WIC and food stamps and, until the present time, had not experienced any periods of homelessness in an area with a chronic shortage of affordable housing. Finally, strength was found in Ms. W.'s ability to ask for and accept help.

Treatment Goals

The immediate goals in this family were to protect the child; to prevent unnecessary out-of-home placement of Peggy; and to promote, preserve, and support the family as the foundation for Peggy's healthy growth and development. The overarching goal was for Ms. W. to have happy, healthy children who had continuity of relationships, surroundings, and environmental influence (Goldstein et al., 1973, p. 31), thus promoting continued healthy development. Several time-limited objectives were developed with the help and input of Ms. W., which were objectives leading to these treatment goals. These objectives included

- Locating and securing permanent housing.
- Obtaining utilities at new residence.
- Continued health care at the women's clinic.
- Investigating resources that may be available to Ms. W. through her extended family and through traditional community social services.
- Developing and implementing a plan to assist Ms. W. in receiving evaluation and treatment for depression.
- Preparation for ongoing care of Peggy if Ms. W. becomes employed.
- Supporting a continuing relationship with the women's clinic social worker in order to facilitate a contraception plan.
- Arranging for an aftercare plan so that services, supports, and relationships would continue after the Family Support Service social worker was no longer involved in the case.
- Teaching the client assertiveness skills, in order to prevent exploitation and to assist her in securing resources.
- Initiating a caring, positive relationship with the client in order to help the client recognize her own strengths, abilities, and resources.
- Linking with a homeless women's program in order to facilitate shelter care or support if needed.
- If necessary, arranging for shelter care if S.W. becomes acutely homeless.
- Advocating for keeping parent and child together rather than placing the child in temporary foster care if acute homelessness occurs.
- In conjunction with the objective above, providing the client with emergency cash, food, clothing, or other necessities in order to prevent the out-of-home placement of Peggy.

- If out-of-home placement of Peggy is unavoidable, supporting the parent–child attachment relationship by advocating for a local placement and by facilitating parent–child visitation.
- Advocating for the client with the placing agency in order to keep the placement to the most limited duration possible.

The final objective, in any case of this type, is to renegotiate the goals and objectives according to the expressed desires of the family as new issues and opportunities arise.

Treatment Approach

Many services offered to families may be home based or may espouse a "family-centered" philosophy. Level I families may need much more than most families in terms of the intensity and scope of intervention necessary to prevent unnecessary out-of-home placement of children. Over the past several years, home-based, intensive family preservation services (IFPS) have been developed in many areas of the United States. The growth of these programs has been rapid. Several program models have been described and evaluated with mixed findings about their efficacy (Grigsby, 1993; Nelson, K.E., Landesman, & Deutelbaum, 1990; Schuerman, Rzepnicki, & Littell, 1994; Wells & Biegel, 1991; Whittaker, Kinney, Tracy, & Booth, 1990; Yuan & Rivest, 1990). The 1993 Family Preservation and Support Services Act provides federal funding of "almost $1 billion over five years for states to improve the well-being of vulnerable children and their families" (Nelson, H., 1996, p. 18). This level of federal support has led to continued growth of these programs.

Theoretical Base and Basic Tenets

Richard Barth (1990) posits that there are four major theories on which intensive family preservation services draw in order to articulate "ideal service delivery systems and treatments" (p. 89). Crisis intervention theory, family systems theory, social learning theory, and ecological theory appear to be integral to intensive family preservation service delivery. However, they do not appear to completely describe the theoretical framework on which intensive family preservation services are constructed (p. 106). Grigsby (1993) argues that social attachment theory (Ainsworth, 1985; Bowlby, 1969) and functional theory (Dore, 1990; Smalley, 1967) also contribute to the common theory base of intensive family preservation services. All of these theories offer information that is useful in guiding the approach to treating Level I families. No single theory appears to offer a complete explanation of the families' problems, nor can any single theory provide a blueprint for intervention. Just as there is usually no single cause or condition that leads to the problems experienced by the Level I family, no single theory offers a complete guide to intervention. Therefore, it is important that the helper assigned to work with the Level I family have an excellent understanding of a range of theories. Strict adherence or commitment to a single theoretical perspective may lead to a struggle to fit the family to a theory, rather than making use of theory as a guide to intervention.

Application to Level I Families

A common element of the theories described here is that all of them allow for a "strength" rather than a "deficit" perspective. Dennis Saleeby (1996, p. 297) argues "the strengths perspective demands a different way of looking at individuals, families, and communities." That is, the focus of intervention is on the strengths that are inherent in families rather than on the problems that exist within the families. Generally, the strategy for intervention is to identify strengths in the family and then to build on those strengths. In order to do so, the helper assigned to the case must play a number of roles, including those of teacher, role model, advocate, and friend. Helpers working with the Level I family need to be flexible and willing to give up the notion of "therapeutic distance" and objectivity. Rather, the subjective involvement of the helper and the family is often the key to success. In many ways, the relationship between the helper and the family appears to be the "vehicle" of intervention.

Family preservation service models have several common characteristics, including

- Immediate response to families in crisis.
- Service to children at imminent risk of out-of-home placement.
- Assessment and treatment focus on the family as a unit in relation to the community.
- Limited goals and objectives of treatment.
- Service provision in the home or community.
- Offer of concrete and psychological services.
- Making therapists available outside of traditional hours.
- Offer of intensive (5 to 20 hours per week) services, usually short term (6 to 12 weeks) in duration.
- Limiting helpers to small caseloads to facilitate intensity of services necessary to prevent out-of-home placement (Cole & Duva, 1990; Kinney, Haapala, Booth, & Leavitt, 1990).

Intensive family preservation services also share several core values and beliefs, including the following:

- Children should remain with their families whenever possible.
- Families are active agents in the change process.
- Families are doing the best that they can given their circumstances, but they may need help in order to provide better care for their children (Kinney et al., 1990).
- Intervention should be based on family strengths, rather than on diagnosis.

- Therapists should be nonjudgmental and should accept families "as they are," rather than emphasizing deficits.
- Intervention takes place through engagement with a "helper," who assists the family in identifying and building on inherent strengths (Center for the Study of Social Policy, 1988).

Interventions and Techniques

In addition to common characteristics, common core values and beliefs, and a common theoretical foundation, intensive family preservation programs appear to utilize several common interventions and techniques. These interventions and techniques are not limited to IFPS programs alone. Rather, these interventions and techniques appear fundamental to any program that seeks to intervene successfully with the Level I family.

Engagement.   Families are usually first encountered in a state of crisis. The out-of-home placement of one or more of the children is usually under consideration. There is reason to speculate that the "executive capacity" (Weltner, 1985) of the family is inadequate or diminished for one or more reasons. The lack of family organization and neglect of the children may invite the novice helper to place blame on the parents, but there are usually many issues at hand that must be considered. Often, these families are suspicious of anyone who is offering help. However, they are often in such a state of crisis that they will respond favorably to the person who is able to approach them on terms that are comfortable to the family. In general, engaging the family in a helping relationship is sometimes the most difficult part of the intervention process. Several techniques appear to be helpful.

First of all, the social work tenet of "starting where the client is" offers the helper and the family the opportunity to begin. The intervention may begin by asking the family what is most important to them. Many of these families expect that someone is going to tell them, or even demand, that they "do something," as this is the typical intervention to which they are accustomed. In order to successfully intervene with Level I families, families are seen as equals in a partnership that is aimed at building on the families' strengths in order to improve overall functioning.

Some service delivery models team professionally trained (usually M.S.W.-level) clinicians with indigenous community workers. These community workers are often integral in engaging families, because the families view them as peers who truly understand the situation. Sometimes the indigenous community worker may need to make the initial contact with the family, so that the professional helper can then be introduced as the expert on "the system." At all times, it is important, and potentially empowering, to view the clients as the "experts" on their own family. Quite often, family members have been incredibly creative and adaptive in dealing with family and community issues. Much of the help they need may be in the area of intervention with the social system that exists outside of the family. For these reasons, it is vital that the family be engaged and committed to working with the helper or team of helpers from the outset. If the family is not engaged, it is often an indication that they have been approached incorrectly or inappropriately.

Support and Strengths Inventory. In the initial phase of intervention, many families expect that the helpers will want to involve them in in-depth discussions of family problems or, in the jargon of many helpers, "family psychopathology." This approach does not appear to be useful when working with the Level I family. Rather, a listing of potential resources, such as extended family, and a listing of family strengths may lead to a more productive intervention, as these resources and strengths are the foundation on which improved family functioning is based. At times, families may not appear to have strengths. Further investigation may reveal that there were once many strengths, but they are no longer apparent. Sometimes a strength may be simply that things are not worse than they are at present. Another small strength may be that the family is willing to work with the helpers. In any case, it is useful to literally sit down and discuss potential resources and strengths. The use of genograms or social network maps may be useful to professional clinicians. However, some families are intimidated by the use of a written format that they do not immediately understand. Therefore, it may be important—at least during the initial phase of intervention—that clients feel comfortable with the methods of assessment. The use of "ethnographic interviewing" in the natural setting of the family's home or community allows the family members to use their own words to inform the helpers, rather than trying to fit into a prescribed format that may be culturally or ethnically biased, or that may be intimidating to clients who are uncomfortable with certain aspects of self-disclosure. For example, a question such as "How long have you been married?" may seem innocuous to many. To an unmarried mother of four, it may be perceived as somewhat threatening and judgmental. By allowing the client to describe the nature of the family relationships, the helper can quickly get insight into the "life" of the individual family. It is important that the helper or team joins with the clients in valuing the family, rather than imposing a set of "family values" on the clients which may be foreign to them and at times even offensive.

Helpers may envision valuing the family as an integral part of the intervention process. This may not be as easy as it sounds. Some families may place great value on the role of the godparent and expect that the godparent will care for the children if the birth parent is unable to do so. State child welfare agencies may not recognize the godparent as having any ties to the child, because there is no biological relationship. This disparity may place the family and child welfare agency at odds. Often, the helper is expected to resolve this issue within the context of child welfare policy. To truly value the family may require adopting a position that runs contrary to state child welfare policy. Helpers must be prepared to be active participants in the day-to-day world of the clients, or clients will see them as insincere bureaucrats who are not really interested in helping them.

Nurturing the Family. The use of the client-helper relationship is perceived as the vehicle of change, but it is only one of many behaviorally oriented interventions that are utilized in helping families. Experienced clinicians are quick to point out that all behavioral interventions appear to be more successful if they are implemented in the context of a solid, positive relationship between the family members and clinician or team. In effect, many parents in Level I families need a supportive, caring relationship with a person who is genuinely interested in listening to them (Pharis & Levin, 1991). With the parent, indigenous community workers and professionally trained clinicians may take on the helping role of "nurturer." This often takes the form of support provided by actively participating in the day-to-day activities of the parent, such as meal preparation and cleanup or housekeeping. At the same time, these helpers may be the only other adults with whom the parent has frequent contact. The nurturing is often "passed on" to the children in the family as the adults begin to feel more confident in their own capabilities. This is a frequent by-product of the nurturing relationship between the helpers and the parent.

Role Modeling. The relationship between the helper and clients often allows for a great deal of role modeling. If a trusting relationship has been established, many clients will actually ask for help with parenting skills. Very often, the executive capacity of the family may be improved as the parents watch the helpers demonstrating *in vivo* new ways of dealing with old problems. Although this information is available in books about child rearing, these families are unlikely to have access to these materials or may not be able to make use of them without the help of someone who can answer questions or help with reading skills. In many cases, parents have been referred to parenting classes but have not attended because they are unable to arrange for child care or because they are embarrassed that they have been singled out and sent to these classes. *In vivo* intervention takes away the stigma of the parenting class and allows for child care to continue while the learning takes place. It is ironic that clients are often seen as resistant when they do not attend parenting classes, when the reason for not attending is related to the need for child care.

Conflict Resolution. Many Level I families are unable to resolve minor conflict easily within their family or community only because they have never learned methods or techniques of conflict resolution. At times, the simple idea of convening a family meeting where individual members are able to present their own feelings and solutions is a novelty to these families. Through role playing and teaching, families can see firsthand that there are alternatives available to them.

Advocacy. Many Level I families have been repeatedly victimized by unscrupulous landlords, salespersons, and even human services providers. Many families are shocked and surprised that others are willing to help them and that others have enough knowledge of the system that they can get help for families. For example, it has become common for persons who are receiving Medicaid to be denied that benefit unless they appear at a hearing to demonstrate that they still need those benefits. Although many families have no problem appearing for these hearings, a single mother of four preschool children may have a difficult time getting there because of child care issues. As a result, benefits may be terminated. As helpers advocate for the needs of the family, benefits are often reinstated in a timely fashion. In turn, the families are able to learn how to advocate for themselves. In many ways, families begin to see that they have an active role in their own lives, rather than life's "happening to them."

In summary, the interventions and techniques that are used with Level I families vary widely and are used according to the wishes of the families and the issues at hand. Because all families have their own unique strengths and supports, there is no "cookbook" approach. Rather, the helping process is developed in the context of a caring relationship with trained helpers which builds on the particular strengths of the family in question.

Evaluation of Effectiveness

Several questions must be answered when evaluating the effectiveness of an intervention with the Level I family, especially when questions related to the well-being of children in the family have been raised. Most importantly, the issue of child safety must be addressed. Are the children at continued risk for maltreatment? Are the children at risk for out-of-home placement, or has unnecessary out-of-home placement of children been prevented? Careful and thorough risk assessment should be used to determine whether the family can adequately protect the children. Most state protective services agencies have adopted risk assessment procedures that allow workers to make determinations of child safety. Theodore Stein and Tina Rzepnicki (1983) also offer a helpful guide to practitioners in *Decision Making at Child Welfare Intake. The Family Risk Scales* (Magura, Moses, & Jones, 1987) and the *Child Well Being Scales* (Magura & Moses, 1986) have also been developed and utilized as outcome measures for working with families, although one author has been outspoken in his criticism of the validity of the *Child Well Being Scales* (Seaberg, 1988, 1990).

On the other hand, the idiographic or single-case design has been underutilized in work with Level I families. By examining outcome on a case-by-case basis, rather than on a program basis alone, the particular issues within each family can be dealt with in a manner that is useful to the family. Helping each family to examine their own progress toward the goals that they have set can be very useful, because it provides many families with a "success experience." By joining with the helper in the attempt to complete an objective, the family members are able to experience the sense of accomplishment (and success) that many of them have not recently—or, in some cases, ever—experienced. Client outcome should correspond to the agenda set by the family, as well as to the agenda that may have been set for them by "outsiders." Bruce Thyer (1993) argues that evaluators should avoid theory-based research studies and concentrate on systematic efforts to evaluate their own efforts by asking whether the intervention actually helped the family to improve. The use of single-systems designs, rather than large, theory-based social science research studies, appears to be more fruitful when helpers ask themselves the question, "Did I help this family?" Therefore, the evaluation of effectiveness should be considered on a family-by-family basis where the family is involved, from the outset, in determining whether they have met their own goals and objectives in ways that are acceptable to them and to the helpers. To assist with evaluating the intervention, Craig–Van Grack (1997) describes an instrument for process measurement of family preservation service designed to enhance the evaluation of intervention with individual families.

Application to Families on Levels II, III, and IV

There are several aspects of intervention with the Level I family that are particularly applicable to families on Levels II, III, and IV (Weltner, 1985). In general, Level II families may be approached in a manner that is similar to the approach used with the Level I family. The issues of authority and limits that are omnipresent in the Level I family are the prominent issues in the Level II family as well. There is a lack of control in the family system that is due to a dysfunctional executive system. The use of a "strengths perspective" that begins with a support and strengths inventory is often a first step in engaging the family. Flexibility in the provision of home- and community-based services allows the helper to intervene, usually within the context of a family crisis, and to build on the strengths inherent in the family to promote, preserve, and sustain the family while its executive capacity is strengthened. Although a good deal of nurturing and advocacy may be necessary in the Level I family, concentration on role modeling and the development of conflict resolution skills may be more appropriate and fruitful when working with the Level II family.

The salient difference between the Level I and the Level II family may be described as follows: The Level I family is often referred because there have been allegations of abuse and/or neglect, and the child or children are at imminent risk of out-of-home placement. On the other hand, the Level II family is often referred because a parent has *requested* that the child or children go into out-of-home placement, because the child is "out of control." Clinicians also comment that the Level I family is often a family with young children, whereas the Level II family is a family with older, adolescent children. In either case, the approach to the family should be tailored to their needs and should include their active participation in planning, intervention, and evaluation.

Whereas the Level I and II families appear to have many similarities, families on Levels III and IV appear to be quite different from their lower-level counterparts. In general, the Level I and II families are cognizant that things are not working well. In the parlance of family therapists, issues appear to be largely of a "structural" nature. Harry Aponte (1976) has described families like this as "underorganized." Level III and IV families are markedly different in that they have developed patterns of behavior to deal with problems that arise within the family. Although some of these behaviors are adaptive and quite functional, others are maladaptive and resistant to change. In the Level IV family, the task of the helper may be focused on the development of an "inner 'richness'—insight, more sensitive awareness of the relational world, and understanding of the legacies and heritage" (Weltner, 1986, p. 54), rather than on the more basic functions of food, shelter, safety, and authority. The application of the principles and techniques described earlier for working with the Level I family have limited utility and relevance to working with the families on Levels III and IV.

Summary

Level I families present a tremendous challenge to society, because they are the families that are often described as being the most "in need." These families usually come to the attention of the social service system when family members, especially children, are experiencing crisis of some sort. Because children represent our future, it is important that we invest in meeting their needs if we expect them to become productive citizens. Although there are larger issues of social policy that must be addressed if we are truly interested in valuing families, we must also be prepared to intervene at the level of the individual family. The recognition that, in most cases, the family is the solution rather than the problem will lead us to provide services to families that will support, preserve, and sustain healthy families. There is no unitary cause of the problems experienced by the Level I family. Likewise, there is no unitary solution. At this point in our history, it will require significant social investment to solve the problems experienced by Level I families. It may require even greater social investment if we do not act quickly to assist these families and to help them escape the downward spiral of poverty, neglect, and misfortune.

Discussion Questions

1. How does the delivery of family preservation services differ from other models of helping?

2. Name five strengths that are present in a family with whom you are now working. How can a practitioner use the family strengths perspective to work with Level I families?

3. Why is it especially important to use a "strengths" approach when working with Level I families? What might be the result if a problem-focused approach were used?

4. Reexamine the interventions sections. Give your own example for each of the techniques listed.

5. In the family preservation service model, a lack of family engagement is often seen as an indicator that the family has not been approached appropriately or correctly. Are there other reasons that could explain lack of engagement?

Suggested Readings

Adnopoz, D. J., Grigsby, R. K., & Nagler, S. F. (1996). Multiproblem families and high-risk children and adolescents: Causes and management. In M. Lewis (Ed.), *Child and adolescent psychiatry: A comprehensive textbook* (2nd ed., pp. 1074–1080). Baltimore: Williams & Wilkins.

This brief chapter presents one model of family preservation which utilizes a trained clinician teamed with an indigenous community worker as opposed to service delivery models that utilize a single clinician. It is argued that the use of the indigenous worker provides a culturally responsive intervention that maximizes the therapeutic relationship between the caregiver and family preservation team.

Cole, E., & Duva, J. (1990). *Family preservation: An orientation for administrators and practitioners.* Washington, DC: Child Welfare League of America.

Elizabeth Cole and Joy Duva offer a concise orientation to the concept and operationalization of family presevation which does not appear to favor any particular model of service delivery. The authors offer a clear description of the common elements of family preservation practice.

Geismar, L. L., & Lasorte, M. A. (1964). *Understanding the multiproblem family.* New York: Association Press.

This book was written more than three decades ago, but the content is relevant to contemporary social work practice with families that appear to be overwhelmed with the day-to-day difficulty of their lives. It is also interesting from a historical perspective.

Kaplan, L. (1986). *Working with the multiproblem family.* Lexington, MA: Lexington Books.

A solid, practical approach to intervention with multiproblem families. Any person who is working with Level I families would benefit from the material presented in this thoughtful book.

National Commission on Child Welfare and Family Preservation. (1991). *A commitment to change.* Washington, DC: American Public Welfare Foundation.

A recently proposed new framework for child and family services that includes a commitment to family support and community investment based on a family strengths service perspective.

Nelson, H. (1996). *What is appropriate care for the children of troubled families?* New York: Milbank Memorial Fund.

A comprehensive report describing the current crisis in child welfare and suggestions for moving toward an improved system.

Nelson, K. E., Landsman, M. J., & Deutelbaum, W. (1990). Three models of family-centered placement prevention services. *Child Welfare, 69*(1), 3–20.

An excellent, concise description of three of the more common placement prevention program models.

Schorr, L. B. (1994). Making the most of what we already know. *Public Welfare, 52*(2), 22–26.

A succinct description of the common elements in successful programs for children and families.

Selig, A. L. (1976). The myth of the multiproblem family. *American Journal of Orthopsychiatry, 46,* 526–532.

An excellent discussion of the problems faced by families who encounter the "multiproblem service delivery system" as they try to overcome problems in their own lives.

Wells, K., & Biegel, D. E. (Eds.). (1991). *Family preservation services: Research and evaluation.* Newbury Park, CA: Sage.

A collection of chapters related to documenting the effectiveness of family preservation programs.

References

Adnopoz, D. J., Grigsby, R. K., & Nagler, S. F. (1996). Multiproblem families and high-risk children and adolescents: Causes and management. In M. Lewis (Ed.), *Child and adolescent psychiatry: A comprehensive textbook* (2nd ed.), (pp. 1074–1080). Baltimore: Williams & Wilkins.

Ainsworth, M. D. S. (19805). Attachments across the lifespan. *Bulletin of the New York Academy of Medicine, 61,* 792–812.

Aponte, H. (1976). Underorganization in the poor family. In P. Guerin (Ed.), *Family therapy: Theory and practice.* New York: Gardner Press.

Barth, R. P. (1990). Theories guiding home-based, intensive family preservation services. In J. K. Whittaker, J. Kinney, E. M. Tracy, & C. Booth (Eds.), *Reaching high-risk families: Intensive family preservation in human services.* New York: Aldine de Gruyter.

Bowlby, J. (1969). *Attachment* (2nd ed.). New York: Basic Books.

Center for the Study of Social Policy. (1988). State family preservation programs: A description of six states' progress in developing services to keep families together. Washington, DC: Author.

Cole, E., & Duva, J. (1990). *Family preservation: An orientation for administrators and practitioners.* Washington, DC: Child Welfare League of America.

Craig–Van Grack, (1997). A taxonomy and recording instrument for process measurement of family preservation services. *Child Welfare, 76*(2), 349–371.

Dore, M. M. (1990). Functional theory: Its history and influence on contemporary social work practice. *Social Service Review, 64*(3), 358–374.

Geismar, L. L., & Lasorte, M. A. (1964). *Understanding the multiproblem family.* New York: Association Press.

Goldstein, J., Freud, A., & Solnit, A. J. (1973). *Beyond the best interest of the child.* New York: Free Press.

Grigsby, R. K. (1993). Theories that guide intensive family preservation services: A second look. In E. S. Morton and R. K. Grigsby (Eds.), *Advancing family preservation practice.* Newbury Park, CA: Sage.

Kaplan, L. (1986). *Working with the multiproblem family.* Lexington, MA: Lexington Books.

Kinney, J., Haapala, D., Booth, C., & Leavitt, S. (1990). The HOMEBUILDERS model. In J. K. Whittaker, J. Kinney, E. M. Tracy, and C. Booth (Eds.), *Reaching high-risk families: Intensive family preservation in human services.* New York: Aldine de Gruyter.

Magura, S., & Moses, B. S. (1986). *Outcome measures for child welfare services.* Washington, DC: Child Welfare League of America.

Magura, S., Moses, B. S., & Jones, M. A. (1987). *Assessing risk and measuring change in families.* Washington, DC: Child Welfare League of America.

Nelson, H. (1996). *What is appropriate care for the children of troubled families?* New York: Milbank Memorial Fund.

Nelson, K. E., Landsman, M. J., & Deutelbaum, W. (1990). Three models of family-centered placement prevention services. *Child Welfare, 69*(1), 3–20.

Paquin, G. W., & Bushorn, R. J. (1991). Family treatment assessment for novices. *Families in Society, 72*(6), 353–359.

Pharis, M. E., & Levin, V. S. (1991). "A person to talk to who really cared": High-risk mothers' evaluations of services in an intensive intervention research program. *Child Welfare, 70*(3), 307–320.

Rutter, M., & Quinton, D. (1984). Parental psychiatric disorder: Effects on children. *Psychological Medicine, 14,* 853–880.

Saleeby, D. (1996). The strengths perspective in social work practice: Extensions and cautions. *Social Work, 41*(3), 296–305.

Schuerman, J. R., Rzepnicki, T. L., & Littell, J. H. (1994). *Putting families first: An experiment in family preservation.* New York: Aldine de Gruyter.

Seaberg, J. R. (1988). Child well-being scales: A critique. *Social Work Research and Abstracts, 24*(3), 9–15.

Seaberg, J. R. (1990). Child well-being: A feasible concept? *Social Work, 35*(3), 267–272.

Selig, A. L. (1976). The myth of the multiproblem family. *American Journal of Orthopsychiatry, 46,* 526–532.

Smalley, R. E. (1967). *Theory for social work practice.* New York: Columbia University Press.

Spencer, J. (1963). The multiproblem family. In B. Schlesinger (Ed.), *The multiproblem family: A review and annotated bibliography* (3rd ed., pp. 1–12). Toronto: University of Toronto Press.

Stein, T. J., & Rzepnicki, T. L. (1983). *Decision making at child welfare intake.* New York: Child Welfare League of America.

Thyer, B. A. (1993). Promoting evaluation research in the field of family preservation. In E. S. Morton & R. K. Grigsby (Eds.), *Advancing family preservation practice.* Newbury Park, CA: Sage.

Wells, K., & Biegel, D. E. (Eds.). (1991). *Family preservation services: Research and evaluation.* Newbury Park, CA: Sage.

Weltner, J. S. (1982). A structural approach to the single parent family. *Family Process, 21,* 203–210.

Weltner, J. S. (1985). Matchmaking: Choosing the appropriate therapy for families at various levels of pathology. In M. P. Mirken & S. L. Koman (Eds.), *Handbook of adolescents and family therapy* (pp. 39–50). New York: Gardner Press.

Weltner, J. S. (1986). A matchmaker's guide to family therapy. *Family Therapy Networker, 10*(2), 51–55.

Whittaker, J. K., Kinney, J., Tracy, E. M., & Booth, C. (Eds.). (1990). *Reaching high-risk families: Intensive family preservation in human services.* New York: Aldine de Gruyter.

Yuan, Y. T., & Rivest, M. (Eds.). (1990). *Preserving families: Evaluation resources for practitioners and policymakers.* Newbury Park, CA: Sage.

6

A Family Case Management Approach for Level I Needs

Roberta R. Greene, Ph.D., and Nancy P. Kropf, Ph.D.

Case management is a process for assisting families who have multiple service needs. In reality, it may be appropriate for families who have Level I through IV needs whenever they experience multiple complex difficulties that require a range of services from numerous providers. The goals of family case management are to mobilize a family's strengths, to marshal resources, and to maximize family functional capacity. This chapter discusses family-centered case management and focuses on the Level I family.

Family Needs

Throughout the life of the family, members must negotiate changes, shifts, and alterations in their relationships with one another. This movement through the life cycle, known as "family development," requires that families establish, maintain, and adapt to new roles. In making these life transitions, the family builds on strengths and must meet stressful challenges.

Case management can help families cope with and adjust to the stress related to unexpected, or nonnormative, situations. An example of a Level I situation that requires reorganization in the family system is a severe illness of a member. For example, Kaplan (1992) has suggested that case management for families with children with HIV infection demands attention to the special developmental needs of the child over a period of years. Case management has also been found to be effective in promoting apnea monitor usage in families where newborns are at risk for sudden infant death syndrome (Baker & Thyer, 1999). Other Level 1 needs experienced by families include homelessness, chronic mental illness, or a developmental disability of a family member. In addition, inner-city residents, isolated and debilitated by crack cocaine or HIV, require assertive outreach services (Greene, 2000a).

Case management services can also help families with adapting to normative transition phases across the lifespan. Structural changes that occur at family transition points, such as births, reaching adulthood, or retirement, also can disturb the family's balance. For example, a case manager can play an important role in helping a young single mother with family and household responsibilities. (East, 1999; Sun, 2000). A case manager can be instrumental in identifying and linking a new mother with emotional, financial, and medical support for her new role as a caregiver to a young infant.

Case managers need to understand that the family is a social unit that faces a series of developmental tasks. These tasks vary along the parameters of cultural differences but at the same time have universal roots (Minuchin, 1974). The stages of the life cycle have been defined for "intact nuclear families in contemporary Western societies" (Tseng & Hsu, 1991, p. 8) as the unattached young adult, the formation of the dyadic relationship, the family with young children, the family with adolescents, the family launching children, the family with older members, and the family in later years (Becvar & Becvar, 1996; Goldenberg & Goldenberg, 1980; Rhodes, 1980).

However, the structure and development of the family may vary with diverse needs and interests. Groze and Rosenthal (1991) have described the adaptability of families who have adopted special-needs children; Weston (1991), the relationship of gay men and lesbian women in their chosen families; and Kuhn (1990), the normative family crises of confronting dementia in an older family member. McGoldrick (1989) has pointed out that, although women play a central role in families, only recently has there been the idea that they may have a "life cycle apart from their roles as wife and mothers" (p. 200).

Family developmental patterns may be affected by the geographical origin and birthplace of the members, and where they are in the cycle of acculturation to mainstream U.S. society. Ho (1987) has proposed that practitioners should be aware that behaviors differ depending on whether a family and its members are foreign or native born and on the degree to which they are bicultural. Falicov and Karrer (1980) have concluded that studies of the family life cycle should take into consideration the effects of cultural variables such as social class, ethnicity, and religion. For example, in Hispanic-American families, individual needs are viewed as secondary compared with those of the family system (Jordan, Lewellan, & Bandiver, 1994). When making application to family assessment, it would therefore be more appropriate for the case manager to think of several "typical" family life cycles.

Family Case Assessment

An important principle in family case management is that a biopsychosocial change in any one member affects the balance of the whole family group. Greene (2000b) has pointed out that most elderly clients come to the attention of an agency at a time of crisis. At that time, the question—Who is the client?—must be asked. The answer is that the crisis involves the entire family. Consequently, the case manager's assessment and treatment interventions must consider both the elderly person's biopsychosocial needs and the family's role allocations, adapting, and coping capacity.

The following case example involves a family with a member who has a chronic mental illness (Kelly & Kropf, 1995). The son, who is now in middle adulthood, is being cared for by his aging parents. This case clearly illustrates the need to address the issues and needs from an entire family perspective.

Philip Jordan is a 40-year-old, single male with a diagnosis of schizophrenia. He lives at home with his 75-year-old parents in a small southern town where his father is a retired pastor from the local Baptist church. Philip, who has a 22-year history of mental illness, has experienced many psychiatric hospitalizations but has remained out of the hospital for the past two years. Currently he has a flat affect, depressed mood, and mild paranoid ideation concerning his parents. He reports bizarre hallucinations involving religious themes and sexual thoughts.

At the time of his first psychotic break, Philip's parents were in their late fifties. His parents blamed themselves for Philip's illness and prayed for him to be "cured and return to being normal." Instead of regaining his emotional health, Philip's condition has worsened over time. His father retired prematurely, believing that, if he devoted all his time to caring for his son, Philip would improve. However, the retirement has caused the parents to be estranged from their supports and has placed a financial burden on the family.

The family came to the local mental health center to discuss their situation. Their family physician had suggested that they contact the mental health program, because Philip's mother's health had been deteriorating. The parents had begun to realize that their advancing age was creating difficulties in providing care for their son. They were also concerned about Philip's lack of social contacts and the family's worsening financial circumstances due to additional medical expenses.

The mental health center intake worker gathered extensive information about family functioning. Philip's physical, emotional, and social functioning, and medication management were discussed. Beyond Philip's functioning, information was acquired about the other family members. This included the parents' own health status, their knowledge of mental illness, their social support system, and their feelings of competence in managing Philip's caregiving needs in this life stage. Spiritual issues were also explored with the family and were especially significant because religious participation was such an important aspect of family life in early phases. Based on a model developed for older adults (Hays, Meador, Branch, & George, 2001), information about the family's spiritual history was gathered, including their practices, social participation, and social support.

As a part of this family-focused assessment, the parents discussed the stress of this caregiving role and effects on their physical and emotional health. Of particular concern was the evaluation of functional areas in which competence may be furthered or fostered (Bandura, 1997). His father spoke about his disappointment over his early retirement, subsequent financial worries, and loss of status in the community. He also reported that he struggled with the idea that Philip was God's way of testing his faith. In particular, he seemed to miss the fellowship that came from being with other members of the congregation. Mrs. Jordan discussed her worries about Philip's future care and her worsening hypertension and digestive problems. Through her discussion with Philip, the case manager also became aware of his anxiety over the health of his parents and fears about his own future. The interviews with the total family unit allowed the case manager to form a holistic impression about past functioning of the family, their present situation, and future needs.

Treatment Goals

Building on the assessment data, the case manager and family discussed service goals that were formalized into a service contract. The plan included goals that addressed the individual members, the parents as a couple, and the family as a household unit. Additionally, the plan overtly specified the relationship between the mental health service personnel and the family.

The contract addressed the issues of independence, family functioning, and spirituality, that had been discussed by the family during the assessment. For Philip, goals were constructed to assist with vocational training and placement. This plan was intended to decrease Philip's isolation, provide him with structured time during the day, and allow him to contribute to the household finances. To provide the parents with a temporary break, the family decided to have Philip begin taking respite care weekends at a group home. This plan also allowed Philip to experience a residential situation before a family crisis could force him to do so.

Other goals were constructed that related to the parents' issues. They were interested in becoming involved in a psychoeducational group sponsored by the mental health center to learn more about schizophrenia and behavior management. They were also interested in attending an upcoming session on estate planning led by a local attorney. In addition, the case manager discussed spiritual needs within the family, such as reconnecting to their family of faith.

The role of the case manager with the parents was to provide information about resources that they might use to assist in their relationship to Philip. They were also assured that their service plan would be periodically reviewed and that the family would have a voice in formulating future goals.

The case manager and family discussed future plans for Philip. The short-term goals were to have the family begin the process of exploring and considering options for Philip's future care. As an initial step in this process, they prepared a plan that helped the family specify and clarify values and preferences as a part of the process of determining what type of future care arrangements were best suited for a person with a disability (Mount & Zwernik, 1988). Intermediate goals for the family were to visit the group homes in their county, discuss Philip's care with other relevant family members (one other son who lived out of state), begin to use respite care to familiarize Philip with residential living experiences, and work with an attorney to explicate financial issues in case of parental death. These steps were all part of a long-range goal of helping the family make arrangements for the time when the parents could no longer continue as care providers.

Treatment Approach: A Generalist Model of Case Management

A variety of case management models exist, and the choice of using a particular approach depends on numerous factors, including the target client group, staff capabilities, financial resources of the agency, and organizational structure. Rothman (1992) describes four models, each having a different structure or focus. In the *generalist model,* one case manager performs a variety of roles to facilitate a client's movement through the service delivery system (Robinson, 2000). The generalist case management model most closely resembles traditional social casework (Levine & Fleming, 1984).

A second approach is the *case management team,* where a multidisciplinary group functions as the case management system for a client. Each team member is responsible for performing a specialized function (social work, physical therapy, speech therapy, psychology).

A third model, the *therapist case manager,* is used extensively in the mental health system. This approach infuses a therapeutic relationship into the case manager role.

The final model, one of *supportive care,* is based on the natural environment of the client (neighborhood, cultural group). In this model, case management is provided to the client through the natural helping network.

In order to be effective practitioners, generalist case managers must have a broad perspective on human services, one that moves beyond the boundaries of the social welfare agencies in which they work. The use of a social system model can assist the case manager in practice with actual clients. Kuhn (1974) identified three elements of a social system. Dattalo (1992) has taken each and operationalized it in the case management process (see Figure 6.1). The first is the *detector function,* which is an information-gathering phase. The case manager gathers information about both the client problem and resources and service options. The second element is the *selector function,* in which information is screened for use in the treatment process. The case manager uses theoretical frameworks and practice principles to organize information in understanding client preferences, values, and behaviors. The final function, the *effector function,* is the "doing function." After gathering information about the problem and possible solutions, the case manager constructs a plan of action about treatment goals.

Key Features of Case Management

Another way of examining the process is to outline the key features of case management. This practice approach is aimed at ensuring that clients with complex,

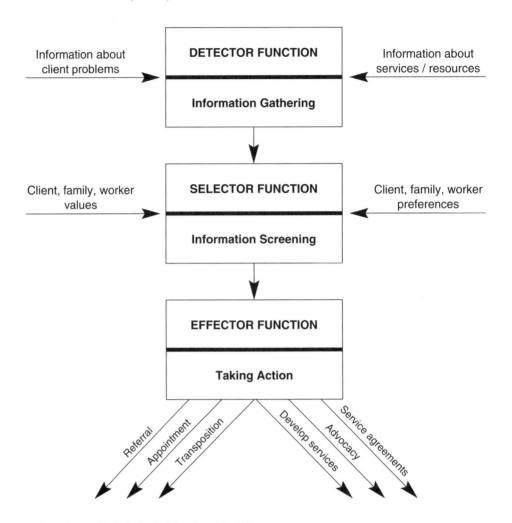

FIGURE 6.1   *Kuhn's Social System Model*

Source: R. L. Schnieder and Nancy P. Kropf, eds., *Gerontological Social Work* (Chicago: Nelson-Hall, 1992), p. 141.

multiple problems and service needs receive all services in a timely and appropriate way. This process has traditionally required that the case manager conduct a skillful assessment of the client's functional capacity and support network and plan, advocate for, and obtain a range of suitable community-based services encompassing economic, health and medical, social, and personal care needs (see Table 6.1).

Community-based case-managed services have been used in all fields of practice, including child welfare, aging, and mental health. Although the presenting problem of the person at risk may vary, the purpose of a case management sys-

TABLE 6.1 Key Features of Social Work Case Management Practice

Social work case management practice

- is a process based on a trusting and enabling client–social worker relationship.
- utilizes the social work dual focus of understanding the person in environment working with populations at risk.
- aims to ensure a continuum of care to clients with complex, multiple problems and disabilities.
- attempts to intervene clinically to ameliorate the emotional problems accompanying illness or loss of function.
- utilizes the social work skills of brokering and advocacy as a boundary-spanning approach to service delivery.
- targets clients who require a range of community-based or long-term care services, encompassing economic, health/medical, social, and personal care needs.
- aims to provide services in the least restrictive environment.
- requires the use of assessment of the client's functional capacity and support network in determining the level of care.
- affirms the traditional social work values of self-determination and the worth and dignity of the individual and the concept of mutual responsibility in decision making.

Source: Reprinted with permission from B. S. Vourlekis & R. R. Greene, (Eds.), *Social work case management* (New York: Aldine de Gruyter 1992). Copyright © 1992 Walter de Gruyter, Inc., New York.

tem is to provide the client with service options along a continuum of care. The concept of a continuum of care suggests that clients may need any one of a comprehensive range of services, depending on each person's ability to function relatively independently. Clients who have greater impairments and lower levels of functioning require more structured environments and higher levels of care.

Case managers increasingly use a strengths perspective practice model (Kisthardt, 1992; Kisthardt & Rapp, 1992; Myers, Kropf, & Robinson, in press; Saleebey, 1992; Sun, 2000; Whitley, White, Kelley, & Yorker, 1999). The strengths perspective documents a client family's present daily living situation and determines what they want to change, achieve, or maintain. The strengths perspective also rests on an empowerment theme that seeks ways for clients to set their own agendas and further engage with others in their environment (Rose, 1992). For example, Kisthardt (1992) has suggested that people who have persistent mental illness not be labeled as being "resistant to treatment" or "lacking in social skills." Rather, clients should be understood as unique, complex individuals, coping with social pressures as well as their "talents, desires, and hopes" (p. 61).

Case management reflects the historic struggle to effect change in the person, the environment, or both (Greene, 1992). In this approach, the case manager assesses the client within the context of his or her environment and provides both direct and indirect service. Direct service is based on a mutually trusting, therapeutic client–social worker relationship in which the case manager evaluates the client's circumstances and intervenes to ameliorate emotional problems accompanying illness or loss of functioning. The emotional problems and the stress associated with loss of functional capacity require that the case manager combine intrapsychic and interpersonal strategies with environmental interventions. Such indirect service involves community-based strategies for resource allocation and advocacy on behalf of the client at risk.

Far too often, clients with many service needs can become "disconnected" from narrowly defined programs, such as those that provide only housing, cash, or nutritional supports (Rubin, 1987). Key features of the case manager's role are responsibility for the development of a mutually agreeable care plan that offers continuity in services and assistance to the client in mediating systems problems that create disruption in service delivery (Roberts-DeGennaro, 1987). Because the case manager needs to understand how systems work and how to access them, and often must coordinate the work of multiple service providers by intervening across service systems' boundaries, case management has been called a *boundary-spanning approach* (Hearn, 1969; Rubin, 1987). Key aspects of a boundary-spanning approach are developing resource systems, linking clients to resource systems, and making systems more accessible and responsible. Central to carrying out this social work approach are advocacy, or negotiating for the equitable distribution of resources, and brokerage, locating and obtaining needed resources.

Interventions: Family Case Management

Family services and case management have long been important components of social work practice. Family-focused social work, with its mission to resolve family social and emotional difficulties, can be traced to the Charity Organization Societies of the 1880s. During those early years, pioneer social workers were noted for meeting with families in their homes to discuss their difficulties and to assess the need for financial relief and other tangible assistance (Hartman & Laird, 1987; Richmond, 1917). Because the Charity Organization Society social workers also were concerned with the lack of coordination among services and fund-raising activities, case management shares similar roots as one of the profession's earliest means of linking clients to service delivery systems (Rubin, 1987; Weil et al., 1985). These common beginnings reflect a strong interest in the family as the focus of intervention and an emphasis on a systematic approach to information collection and assessment, in the value of equity in resource allocation, and in case coordination. Although case management and family-centered practice share a surprising amount of common ground, little has been written about the relationship of these core practice functions.

Although most people in need of case management assistance are receiving the bulk of their care from families and other primary groups, the role of the family in the case management process is ill defined. Although practitioners increasingly have come to appreciate the value of natural helpers, or what Pincus and Minahan (1973) termed "informal resource systems" (p. 15), case management systems are designed largely for the individual client (Caragonne, 1980; Moore, 1990).

Nonetheless, when discussing case management services, some theorists have considered the individual client's resources and natural supports. For example, the National Association of Social Workers (NASW) (1999) *Standards and Guidelines for the Functionally Impaired* has defined the family as critical to the assessment process. Bertsche and Horejsi (1980) have suggested that the family be involved in the initial interview, the formulation of the psychosocial assessment, the decision-making process related to the care plan, followup of service delivery problems, and counseling and emotional support. They go on to describe the case manager's role vis-à-vis the family as a "liaison . . . to help the client make his or her preferences known and secure the services needed" (p. 97).

In addition, Moore (1990) has suggested that a key case manager role is to integrate formal and informal services provided by the family and other primary groups. He noted that health and social services, families, and formal organizations have complementary goals, and that the coordination of shared resources is necessary. According to Nelson (1982), the goal of coordination is to achieve a fit between formal services and primary-group caregiving, not to substitute for family care. Moore (1990) has maintained that it is often the practitioner who acts as a facilitator among the client, the family, and formal caregivers. In addition, Cantor, Rehr, and Trotz (1981) have suggested that, wherever possible, members of the family should be the case managers and that professionals should offer training to support this family responsibility. In this way, the service package is designed to support the family and to maximize its caregiving potential.

Principles for Family-Focused Case Management

Although the family case management literature is limited, the literature on family-centered practice is rich and often consistent with a systems perspective. This perspective generally views the family as promoting positive interdependence and problem resolution, and uses intervention strategies aimed at developing the family as a system of mutual aid. By moving the family to "center stage," the family social work literature recognizes the family as the "primary social service institution" and network for planning and problem solving (Hartman, 1981, p. 7). From a family systems perspective, interventions and case management care plans are designed to preserve and enhance functioning, and to modify dysfunctional family patterns (Greene, 1999) (see Table 6.2).

As no two families are alike, once the case manager has reached out to the family as a unit, it is necessary to assess the family as a group that comprises a causal network. Systems theory suggests that to understand a family, each member should not be viewed in isolation. Rather, it is necessary to examine the relationships among family members, and any one individual's behavior is considered as the consequences of the total situation (Shafer, 1969).

In case management with families, for the social worker to be able to achieve the most effective and culturally sound plan of care, it is important to recognize differences in family forms. For example, persons with AIDS (PWAs) who also are gay or lesbian may want to receive care in conjunction with their family of origin

TABLE 6.2   Key Features of Family-Focused Social Work Case Management

Family-focused social work requires that the case manager

- identify the family as the unit of attention.
- assess the frail or impaired person's biopsychosocial functioning and needs within a culturally sound family context.
- write a mutually agreed-upon family care plan.
- refer client systems to services and entitlements not available within the natural support system.
- implement and coordinate the work that is done with the family.
- determine what services need to be coordinated on behalf of the family.
- intervene clinically to ameliorate family emotional problems and stress accompanying illness or loss of functioning.
- determine how the impaired person and family will interact with formal care providers.
- integrate formal and informal services provided by the family and other primary groups.
- offer or advocate for particular services that the informal support network is not able to offer.
- contact client networks and service providers to determine the quality of service provision.
- mediate conflicts between the family and service providers to empower the family when they are not successful.
- collect information and data to augment the advocacy and evaluation efforts to ensure quality of care.

or their family of choice. Therefore, it is critical for the case manager to establish a helping relationship unique to that particular family.

Application to Families on This Level of Need

Families in need of case management services have a range of needs for flexibility, adaptability, and goal achievement. Although some families may be relatively high functioning, other families experience high levels of tension, use outside resources poorly, and tend to have insufficient organization to meet their goals. These are examples of Level I and II needs where attention to basic resources is indicated (financial, medical), and structural and organizational changes are required within the family. These families may appear disordered and often require many services and clinical interventions.

Because most programs have limited resources, case finding is critical in providing case management services. This process involves delineating a target population and determining who is especially suited to receive a service because their informal support network is unable to provide a particular resource. Some families may require case management briefly during a transition in development, such as discharge from a hospital after an acute illness. Other families may need ongoing services, with the goal of maintaining functioning or preventing regression to the greatest possible extent.

Interventions

The purpose of case management is to provide the client system—in this case, the family—with service options that promote group and individual functioning. To accomplish this task, Dattalo (1992) has identified three sets of roles that a case manager performs:

1. Counselor roles that are client focused, such as being an educator and enabler.
2. Coordinator roles, matching clients with services; as such, serving as a service broker and developing information about the resource network.
3. Advocacy roles that focus on the service system, such as being a mediator and community organizer.

Using these role clusters, the case manager can establish interventions with the family to help them engage in the service system, provide support once services have been initiated, and address shortcomings in the way services are organized. Specific interventions used by case managers in working with families include building positive relationships with the family system, completing a comprehensive assessment, structuring a case plan, linking the family to needed services, monitoring service delivery, and serving as an advocate.

Building Relationships

In all practice situations, building positive relationships with clients is an important initial component. In family case management, the practitioner has the task of promoting alliances to engage all members of the family system in the service contract. Relationship building with a family may include a number of tasks for the case manager, including education about the expectations and responsibilities of both the client role and practitioner roles, assurance about the nature and use of information shared between the family and practitioner, and listening and discussing the perceptions of the family toward using services.

Due to the stigma that is a result of a psychiatric diagnosis, building a positive relationship with families who care for a member with chronic mental illness, such as the Jordan family, is critical. Even mental health professionals may blame the family for their family member's pathology (Fadden, Bebbington, & Kuipers, 1987; Lefley, 1989). This situation has caused antagonistic relationships between families and the mental health system. Establishing rapport and trust, an important phase of any helping relationship, is especially crucial with these families (Cummings & Kropf, 2000).

Completing a Comprehensive Assessment

Case managers use a format for examining the person who is frail or impaired within a family context. The NASW standards (1999) suggest that assessment and practice must be done with cultural competence and respect for social diversity of their clients. Because the family is a unit or interdependent group, it is necessary to assess how a change in one member's functioning affects role expectations throughout the family system (Greene, 1999).

In order to gather this tremendous amount of information, data should be collected from a variety of sources. These include records from other formal service providers in addition to information from the family members themselves. Within a family case management situation, perspectives and experiences of all members of the system must be incorporated. With the Jordan family, for example, the case manager should examine the concerns of the older parents and incorporate their needs into the family service plan. The focus of service provision is broader than just identifying Philip's needs. Frequently, different family members will claim different views about their service needs. In these situations, the case manager will spend time exploring, clarifying, and negotiating with the various family members about these issues.

Structuring a Case Plan

A thorough assessment of a family provides the foundation for a case plan. A service plan is based on a psychosocial study of the client and his or her family. It is a mutually agreed-upon blueprint for deciding what services need to be mobilized on behalf of the impaired person and family (Naleppa & Reid, 1998). It also involves the way in which the family will interact with formal care providers and the cost of that care.

In constructing a case plan, the case manager builds on the informal support network of the family. An ecomap can be used to graphically portray the supports used by the family and the quality of the established relationships. Additional resources, such as available community resources, can be added to the ecomap to demonstrate how the case plan will increase the support of the family.

Linking Clients to Services

Linking involves referring or transferring client systems to services and entitlements that are determined to be necessary and available in the family care plan. This process includes identifying available services and gathering information about service access issues. The case manager can also be involved in helping families to learn about other rzxesources and to transition into another type of service program. Case managers can enable clients to use potential resources by demonstrating how to take appropriate and effective action; for example, how to seek out and join a caregiver support group.

Monitoring Service

The relative success of case management practice is based on seeing whether work among the various services involved in a case is performed in a harmonious fashion (Greene, 1992). The case manager is the coordinator of this effort, making certain that information is exchanged among the numerous service providers who may be involved with a family. Monitoring service delivery to determine if client systems are receiving allocated resources requires that the case manager keep in ongoing contact with the client and his or her network and service providers. Where the family is not successful, it may mean mediating conflicts between the family and service providers. This may also mean that troubleshooting can fill much of the case manager's day (Steinberg & Carter, 1983).

In working with families, monitoring service delivery is intertwined with a dynamic assessment process. Changes that affect the family system precipitate changes in service needs for the family. In the Jordan family, for example, Mrs. Jordan suffered a stroke a few months after the family came to the mental health center. Mrs. Jordan's illness had a dramatic impact on the family's ability to carry out their service goals. The case manager maintained a key role in making certain that services were not disrupted during this family emergency. The case manager was also pivotal in helping the family receive resources, such as homemaker services and transportation, that lapsed as a result of the mother's illness.

Advocacy

Advocacy is a social work intervention strategy that is concerned with poor or inequitable distribution of resources. Data collected from the client system can be used by the family or case manager to augment the advocacy effort to ensure the quality of care.

The Jordan family exemplifies a situation that is becoming an increasing concern in mental health—older parents who provide care to a chronically disabled son or daughter. At this life stage, the older family is concerned with the ability to continue to provide extended care for a person with a chronic mental illness. Case managers who work with older families may need to advocate for services that are specific to issues faced by older families (Cummings & Kropf, 2000). Examples of advocacy efforts include establishing legal/residential workshops specifically oriented to late-life caregivers, structuring an emergency respite care program for instances of health crises of care providers, and exploring the concept of "retirement" for older people who have chronic psychiatric disabilities.

Evaluation

Evaluation of services and service delivery systems is necessary for accountability to the client system, to the funding source, and to policymakers (Greene, 1992).

Measures of quality to the client system help ensure that service conforms to acceptable methods of practice. Case managers engage in effort on two levels: evaluating the progress of the family in the established treatment goals and evaluating the comprehensive quality of available services.

The evaluation of the family's advancement involves measuring progress toward treatment goals. Case plans that are constructed using behavioral objectives and time frames lend themselves to the evaluation phase. Consider the following goal for Mr. and Mrs. Jordan:

Goal
Become involved in a support group for caregivers of people with chronic mental illness.

Objective 1
Contact the support group leader to discuss the content and structure of group. Completed in one week.

Objective 2
Contact neighbors, friends, relatives to identify a companion for Philip so parents can attend meeting. Completed in two weeks.

Objective 3
Parents attend first support group meeting. Completed in one month.

Using these types of behavioral objectives within specified time frames, the case manager can help the family partialize and evaluate progress. Points of inertia, or inactivity in the family, can suggest to the case manager areas where additional support is needed. For example, the inability of the Jordans to accomplish objective 2 suggests that they may lack social support or that they have difficulty asking for support from others. This discovery led to enhancing the treatment plan to address this issue with the family.

Evaluating progress with a family is an empowering experience in itself. Families that cannot partialize problems may feel immobilized and overwhelmed. The case manager can motivate families by presenting them with their own progress.

In addition to evaluation of the client systems, case managers are also involved in evaluating service networks. This level of evaluation can be structured around these basic questions (Dattalo, 1992):

1. What services are available for the families?
2. How accessible are these services?
3. Are there services that are available but not used by families?
4. What needs are unmet by available services?
5. Who are potential providers of needed but unmet services?

By answering these questions, case managers gain a comprehensive understanding about how services are able to meet the needs of the families whom they serve.

Application to Families at Other Levels of Need

Case management may be used with families operating at Levels III and IV. These families appear to have a high level of organization and are well prepared or differentiated in meeting their tasks (Goldenberg & Goldenberg, 1980). Very often, however, the resources secured by the case manager make the critical difference, restoring the functional capacity of the family group in crisis.

In working with clients, regardless of their level of need, the case manager must be acutely aware of the psychosocial effects of the problem situation. For example, families who are dealing with economic survival issues may require help understanding their feelings of fear and anger. Living from day to day can be stressful, and children in particular may experience great anxiety. Such families may benefit from structural family interventions that work to realign hierarchical power positions: Do the parents continue to be seen as providers? Who are the breadwinners (Levels I and II of family functioning)?

The case included in this chapter, which discussed a family with a member who is chronically mentally ill, provides an example of how the case manager will have to fill a number of different roles. He or she needs to build a relationship with and seek resources for the identified client—the member with the mental illness. The practitioner also may not only examine how other family members are adjusting to the member who is mentally ill, but also explore what intimacy, conflict, and self-realization issues may warrant attention (Level IV of family need). In addition, families who are highly functioning may have their equilibrium severely disrupted when important resources are not available.

The key to appropriate choices of intervention rests with assessment of family need. The eclectic choice of an intervention model is carefully selected and is often a blend of approaches depending on a particular constellation of family issues.

Summary

Although family-focused interventions and case coordination have existed simultaneously since the beginnings of social work practice, a family-centered approach to case management has not been widely addressed. This chapter has promoted an inclusive model of working with a family whose needs are primarily on Level I. The model of practice is built on the active premise that one person in the family does not "own a problem"—issues affect all members. The case of the Jordan family provided an example of how a case manager could take a whole-family approach within a mental health context. The service goals did not reduce the family to "identified client and parents" but defined the client system as the family unit.

The role of the case manager in family-focused practice is to meet family needs and promote family harmony. The case manager has the responsibility to empower family members to activate and augment their support network. Formal services are introduced where the support system cannot accomplish tasks and meet the family's needs. The case manager helps the family identify and clarify their service needs and construct a plan of action. The case manager is also responsible for determining that the plan is being implemented and evaluating its success.

Discussion Questions

1. What are the overlapping features of individual- versus family-focused case management? How would the Jordan case study differ if the approach was individual-focused?

2. What are the advantages and disadvantages of having a single case manager, as opposed to team case management?

3. Describe the roles of a case manager using a family approach.

4. How do you maintain a trusting relationship in a case management role in difficult settings (such as public housing) when you feel you have done all you can to obtain trust?

5. How would a case manager address spirituality needs of families as part of treatment goals?

6. B. is a 28-year-old female with a history of substance abuse and incest as a child. She recently made a suicide attempt. Would the family case management approach be useful in working with this situation? What would be the short-term goals? long-term goals?

7. Identify a family from your practice whose primary needs are at Level I and with whom you think the case management approach would be particularly relevant. Briefly identify the family's current supports and needs, and give at least five specific ways in which you could potentially assist this family utilizing relevant family case management methods.

8. Is case management a type of family therapy? Why or why not?

9. Why would the case management approach be utilized with Level I and II families more often than with Level III and IV families?

Suggested Readings

Hartman, A., & Laird, J. (1983). *Family-centered social work practice*. New York: Free Press.
    This book offers a classic rationale for and discussion of family-focused social work practice. It offers a must-not-miss introduction to anyone interested in the field.

Hegar, R. L. (1992). Monitoring child welfare services. In B. S. Vourlekis and R. R. Greene (Eds.), *Social work case management*. New York: Aldine de Gruyter.
    This chapter of an edited text on case management focuses on case management in the child welfare area. It addresses such concepts as permanency planning, protective services, and family preservation.

Naleppa, M., & Reid, W. J. (1998). Task centered case management for the elderly: Developing a practice model. *Research on Social Work Practice, 8*(1), 63–85.
    This study employs a task-centered model of case management and evaluates collaboration between the older client and the case manager in achieving client goals.

O'Connor, G. (1988). Case management: System and practice. *Social Casework, 69,* 97–106.

This journal article discusses the two levels of case management—the systems level, dealing with interagency connections and the continuum of care; and the practice level, focusing on direct service to the client.

Robinson, M. (2000). Case management for gerontological social workers. In R. L. Schneider, N. P. Kropf, & A. Kisor (Eds.), *Gerontological social work: Knowledge, service settings & special populations* (2nd ed., pp. 136–166). Belmont, CA: Wadsworth.

Vourlekis, B. S., & Greene, R. R. (Eds.). (1992). *Social work case management.* New York: Aldine de Gruyter.

This book discusses the eight basic functions of case management through an examination of different fields of practice. There are chapters on private case management with the elderly, programs in child welfare, adult protective services, school social work, and pediatric AIDS.

Weil, M., & J. M. Karls & Associates. (1985). *Case management in human service practice.* San Francisco: Jossey-Bass.

The authors conceptualize eight basic case management functions. Chapters illustrate practice issues in several settings and fields of practice.

References

Baker, L. R., & Thyer, B. A. (1999). Family social work intervention to increase parental compliance with infant apnea monitor use in the home. *Journal of Family Social Work, 3*(3), 21–27.

Bandura, A. (1997). *Self efficacy: The exercise of control.* New York: W. H. Freeman.

Becvar, D., & Becvar, R. (1996). *Family therapy: A systematic integration* (3rd ed). Boston: Allyn and Bacon.

Bertsche, V. A., & Horejsi, C. R. (1980). Coordination of client services. *Social Work, 25*(2), 94–98.

Cantor, M., Rehr, H., & Trotz, V. (1981). Workshop II case management and family involvement. *The Mount Sinai Journal of Medicine, 48*(6), 566–568.

Caragonne, P. (1980). *An analysis of the function of the case manager in our mental health social service settings.* Austin: University of Texas School of Social Work.

Cummings, S., & Kropf, N. P. (2000). An infusion model for including content on elders with chronic mental illness in the curriculum. *Advances in Social Work, 1*(1), 93–103.

Dattalo, P. (1992). Case management for gerontological social workers. In R. L. Schneider & N. P. Kropf (Eds.), *Gerontological social work: Knowledge, service settings, and special populations* (pp. 138–170). Chicago: Nelson-Hall.

East, J. F. (1999). Hidden barriers to success for women in welfare reform. *Families in Society, 80,* 295–304.

Fadden, G., Bebbington, P., & Kuipers, L. (1987). The burden of care: The impact of functional psychiatric illness on the patient's family. *British Journal of Psychiatry, 150,* 285–292.

Falicov, C. J., & Karrer, B. M. (1980). Cultural variations in the family life cycle: The Mexican American family. In E. A. Carter and M. McGoldrick (Eds.), *The family cycle* (pp. 383–426). New York: Gardner Press.

Goldenberg, I., & Goldenberg, H. (1980). *Family therapy: An overview.* Monterey, CA: Brooks/Cole Publishing.

Greene, R. R. (1992). Case management: An arena for social work practice. In B. S. Vourlekis and R. R. Greene (Eds.), *Social work case management* (pp. 11–25). New York: Aldine de Gruyter.

Greene, R. R., (1999). *Human behavior theory and social work practice* (2nd ed.). New York: Aldine de Gruyter.

Greene, R. R. (2000a). Case management with older adults: Developing a new paradigm. Paper presented at the Indiana Social Services Administration, Division of Addiction and Mental Health Services, Building Case Management in the New Millennium.

Greene, R. R. (2000b). *Social work with the aged and their families* (2nd ed.) New York: Aldine de Gruyter.

Groze, V., & Rosenthal, J. A. (1991). A structural analyses of families adopting special needs children. *Families in Society, 72*(2), 469–482.

Hartman, A. (1981). The family: A central focus for practice. *Social Work*, 7–13.

Hartman, A., & Laird, J. (1987). Family practice. In A. Minahan et al. (Eds.), *Encyclopedia of social work* (18th ed., pp. 575–589). Silver Spring, MD: National Association of Social Workers.

Hayes, J. C., Meador, R. G., Branch, P. S. & George, L. K. (2001) The Spiritual History Scale in four dimensions (SHS-4): Validity and reliability. *The Gerontologist, 41*, 239–249.

Hearn, G. (1969). Progress toward an holistic conception of social work. In G. Hearn (Ed.), *The general systems approach: Contributions toward an holistic conception of social work* (pp. 63–70). New York: Council on Social Work Education.

Ho, K. H. (1987). *Family therapy with ethnic minorities.* Newbury Park, CA: Sage.

Jordan, C., Lewellan, A., & Vandiver, V. (1994). A social work perspective of psychosocial rehabilitation: Psychoeducational models for minority families. *International Journal of Mental Health, 23*(4), 27–43.

Kaplan, M. (1992). Case planning for children with HIV/AIDS: A family perspective. In B. Vourlekis and R. Greene (Eds.), *Social work case management* (pp. 76–88). New York: Aldine de Gruyter.

Kelly, T., & Kropf, N. P. (1995). Stigmatized and perpetual parents: Older parents caring for adult children with life-long disabilities. *Journal of Gerontological Social Work, 24*(1/2), 3–16.

Kisthardt, W. E. (1992). A strengths model of case management: The principles and functions of a helping partnership with persons with persistent mental illness. In D. Saleebey (Ed.), *The strengths perspective in social work* (pp. 59–83). New York: Longman.

Kisthardt, W. E., & Rapp, C. (1992). Bridging the gap between policy and practice: Implementing a strengths perspective in case management. In S. M. Rose (Ed.), *Case management and social work practice* (pp. 112–125). New York: Longman.

Kuhn, A. (1974). *The logic of social systems: A unified deductive, system-based approach to social science.* San Francisco: Jossey-Bass.

Kuhn, D. R. (1990). The normative crises of families confronting dementia. *Families in Society, 71*(8), 451–460.

Lefley, H. P. (1989). Family burden and family stigma in major mental illness. *American Psychologist, 44*, 556–560.

Levine, I. S., & Fleming, M. (1984). *Human resource development: Issues in case management.* Baltimore: Center for Rehabilitation and Manpower Services, University of Maryland.

McGoldrick, M. J. (1989). Women through the life cycle. In M. McGoldrick and F. Walsh (Eds.), *Women in families: A framework for family therapy* (pp. 200–226). New York: Norton.

Minuchin, S. (1974). *Families and family therapy.* Cambridge, MA: Harvard University Press.

Moore, S. T. (1990). A social work practice model of case management: The case management grid. *Social Work, 35*(5), 444–448.

Mount, B., & Zwernik, K. (1988). *It's never too early, it's never too late: A booklet about personal futures planning* (Publication #421–88–109). St. Paul, MN: Metropolitan Council.

Myers, L., Kropf, N. P., & Robinson, M. (in press). Grandparents raising grandchildren: Case management in a rural setting. *Journal of Human Behavior in the Social Environment.*

Naleppa, M., & Reid, W. (1998). Task centered case management for the elderly: Developing a practice model. *Research on Social Work Practice, 8*(1), 63–85.

National Association of Social Workers (NASW). (1999). *NASW Code of Ethics,* http://www.naswdc.org/code.htm

Nelson, G. M. (1982). Support for the aged: Public and private responsibility. *Social Work, 27*(7), 137–143.

Pincus, A., & Minahan, A. (1973). *Social work practice: Model and method.* Itasca, IL: Peacock.

Rhodes, S. L. (1980). A developmental approach to the life cycle of the family. In M. Bloom (Ed.), *Life span development* (pp. 30–40). New York: Macmillan.

Richmond, M. (1917). *Social diagnoses.* New York: Russell Sage Foundation.

Roberts-DeGenarro, M. (1987). Developing case management as a practice model. *Social Casework, 68*(8), 466–470.

Robinson, M. (2000). Case management for social workers: A gerontological approach. In R. L. Schneider, N. P. Kropf, & A. J. Kisor (Eds.). *Gerontological social work: Knowledge, service settings, and special populations* (2nd ed., pp. 136–166). Belmont, CA: Wadsworth.

Rose, S. (1992). Case management: An advocacy/empowerment design. In S. M. Rose (Ed.), *Case management and social work practice* (pp. 271–298). New York: Longman.

Rubin, A. (1987). Case management. In A. Minahan et al. (Eds.), *Encyclopedia of social work* (pp. 212–222). Silver Spring, MD: National Association of Social Workers.

Saleebey, D. (1992). *The strengths perspective in social work.* New York: Longman.

Shafer, C. M. (1969). Teaching social work practice in an integrated course: A general systems approach. In G. Hearn (Ed.), *The general systems approach: Contributions toward a holistic conception of social work* (pp. 26–36). New York: Council on Social Work Education.

Steinberg, R. M., & Carter, G. W. (1983). *Case management and the elderly.* Lexington, MA: D. C. Heath.

Sun, A. P. (2000). Helping substance-abusing mothers in the child welfare system: Turning crisis into opportunity. *Families in Society, 81*(2), 142–151.

Tseng, W. S., & Hsu, J. (1991). *Culture and family problems and therapy.* New York: Haworth Press.

Vourlekis, B. S., & Greene, R. R. (Eds.). (1992). *Social work case management.* New York: Aldine de Gruyter.

Weil, M., & J. M. Karls & Associates. (1985). *Case management in human service practice.* San Francisco: Jossey-Bass.

Weston, K. (1991). *Families we choose: Lesbians, gays, kinship.* New York: Columbia University Press.

Whitley, D. M., White, K. R., Kelley, S. J., & Yorker, B. (1999). Strengths based case management: The application to grandparents raising grandchildren. *Families in Society: The Journal of Contemporary Human Services, 80,* 110–119.

7

Structural Family Interventions

Harry J. Aponte, M.S.W.

Structural family therapy (SFT) is a systems-based model that places a special focus on the internal organization of relationships within families vis-à-vis their functioning. It aims to solve problems of dysfunction by making changes in the underlying structure of personal relationships.

Levels of Family Need

Structural family therapy was born to meet the needs of troubled inner-city youth and their families. The model was first presented in a book whose title spoke to the original target population, *Families of the Slums* (Minuchin, Montalvo, Guerney, Rosman, & Schumer, 1967). What most directly influenced the emerging character of this new model was the underorganization (Aponte,, 1994a, pp. 13–31) of these families with Level II needs. The structure of the family relationships lacked "the *constancy, differentiation,* and *flexibility* they need[ed] to meet the demands of life" (Aponte, 1994a, p. 17). The children that Minuchin and his colleagues found at the Wiltwyck School for Boys were most often from families led by a single mother, overwhelmed by life's circumstances. Fathers may or may not have played a consistent role in the children's lives. The youngsters themselves did not have a clear sense of family rules, hierarchy of authority, or whom to depend on within the family for help with life. The model sought to bring effective organization to the family so that its members could better find solutions to their problems.

Given that the original families were "products of slums" (Minuchin, et al., 1967. p. 6), it is no wonder that the model also lent itself from the very beginning to work with families with Level I needs. Families needed to be able to organize themselves with effective authority and hierarchy, clear personal boundaries, and stable relationship alliances, along with the communication skills to negotiate these structural components, in order to meet their most basic needs in the midst of socioeconomic deprivation. Because of the social conditions within which these disadvantaged families faced their problems, the model looked not only at the internal relationship context of the family, but also at the structure of the social environment within which these families struggled with life (Aponte, 1994a, pp. 13–31).

It was not long, however, before the original proponents of the model began to discover the relevance of relationship structure in families to other problems, such as anorexia nervosa (Minuchin, Rosman, & Baker, 1978). Obviously, families in which youngsters were starving themselves in order to manage their emotional distress and family conflicts did not tend to come from the lowest socioeconomic strata. For the most part they were middle-class families with Level III needs. The factor these families had in common with the lower-income families was the direct impact that a dysfunctional family structure had on the functioning of its members. It was evident that family structure directly affected the eating disorder of the child in the family. Insights about structure also contributed to the work with marital relationships (Aponte & DiCesare, 2000). In addition, the model has addressed the dynamics of love and intimacy within personal relationships (Aponte, 1998b), as well as the personal dimensions in the proper and effective relationships between practitioners and clients (Aponte, 1998a).

Given a growing awareness of the crisis in values that the society was undergoing, it became apparent to some that it was not enough to speak only of structure and function in relation to problems. A society that had lost its consensus of values was creating difficulties for families which called for them to consider the values by which they would organize themselves in order to carry out their familial functions. This awareness brought about an integration into the structural model of notions of values and spirituality (Aponte, 1994a; 1994b; 1996). The Level IV spiritual needs of life, relating to moral standards, philosophical perspective, and the social base of spirituality, are all relevant to families in our current age, regardless of socioeconomic status (Aponte, 1999).

Assessment

The core focus of an assessment in SFT is how families are organized in relation to the problems they experience in the present. Structural family therapy views the past as "manifest in the present and . . . available to change by interventions that change the present" (Minuchin, 1974, p. 14). The assessment demands a clear identification of the focal issue, preferably in the operational terms in which it is currently manifested (Aponte & VanDeusen, 1981, p. 316). In SFT the basic context in which family assessments take place is the *enactment* (Aponte, 1994a, p. 21; Minuchin, 1974, p. 141). Structural therapists look to have families relive in the therapy the struggles they have at home around their problems. Witnessing and engaging with an actual interaction with its underlying relationship structure is a more reliable source of data than what people report about their lives.

The underlying structure that draws a structural therapist's attention is composed of *boundary, alignment,* and *power.* These three basic structural dimensions (Aponte & VanDeusen, 1981, pp. 312–313) are

1. *Boundaries.* What defines who is in or out of a family relationship vis-à-vis the focal issue, as well as what their roles are in this interaction.
2. *Alignment.* Who is with or against the other in the transactions generating the problem.
3. *Power.* What is the relative influence of the participants in the interactions that create the problem.

Therapists formulate a level of *structural hypotheses* that describe the current boundary, alignment, and power organization of the family in relation to its problems (Aponte & VanDeusen, 1981, pp. 314–315; Minuchin, 1974, p. 130). They also formulate a second level of *functional hypotheses* that "speak to the *meaning* and *significance* of the current structure" (Aponte, 1994a, p. 36). The present structure of family relationships has a history and a purpose. Functional hypotheses describe the historical background of the family that brought it to the immediate difficulty and the current motivations that drive family members to relate to one another as they do now around this issue. Because structural therapists work through the interactions they witness in the present, their every action with families is based on hypotheses about what they are observing. In fact, SFT considers change-inducing interventions "as occurring through the process of the therapist's affiliation with the family" (Minuchin, 1974, p. 91). In other words, the intentional actions of therapists in their relationships with families have change-promoting impacts. Consequently, every action of therapists should flow from their diagnostic hypotheses, and these hypotheses should be confirmed or altered according to the therapeutic impact of therapists' actions (Aponte, 1994a, p. 38).

In an interview with the Gonzagas, a Mexican-American family, a consultant was presented with a set of parents and five children, ages 4 to 16 (Aponte, 1994a, pp. 32–57). The identified patient was an 11-year-old boy. He was having school problems. In the initial presentation of the case, the mother was outspoken and articulate about the problem. The father, a packer, had been described by the therapists to a consultant as peripheral to the family and not active in the therapy, although he was attending all sessions. The consultant hypothesized that, in terms of boundaries, the father was peripheral to the mother's handling of the 11-year-old's school problems. She exercised the power of the executive parent in relation to this boy's school problems, being the one who communicated with the school and supervised the boy about his school work. However, in terms of alignment, the boy was resisting her guidance. The boy was likely triangulated between parents who had a conflictual marriage. The consultant had little family history to formulate his functional hypotheses, but did speculate that this Latin-cultured father with relatively limited education was not comfortable in the American world of professional agencies, which was mostly populated by well-educated women.

Seeing how little control the mother had over the boy, the consultant further hypothesized to himself that at the heart of her powerlessness with him was lack of the male support of the father. To probe the father's willingness and ability to help his son, the consultant invited him to engage his son in a discussion about his difficulties, hoping for an enactment of the father–son relationship. What became evident was that the boy was frightened of his father, who was too slow to dialogue and too quick to hit. When the other two boys in the family joined the discussion at the invitation of the consultant, the father was confronted by the 16-year-old's painful plea to have his father quit calling him a "liar" and stop hitting him. He felt humiliated. The father came to realize how important he was to his sons and how they needed him to treat them with affection and respect. The father, with some feeling, concluded that he was the problem in this situation and touchingly said that he understood the boys' reactions because he, too, had a father. The consultant worked to bring the father into the parenting in a way that would convince him how needed he was and his wife how able he was to contribute positively to the supervision of the boys. It was left for the therapists to follow up with the couple about their marital difficulties to ease their ability to work cooperatively as parents.

Goals

Structural family therapy aims more to address directly how clients experience life than to talk about and analyze their struggles. It seeks to engage family members around concrete issues, located in the present. The approach looks to achieve quick, palpable results through family members' exercising new attitudes and behaviors with one another around the focal issue. This new experience is meant to form the basis for better patterns of relating.

With the Gonzaga family, the consultant worked to get the father and the boy with the identified problem to interact in a way that encouraged spontaneous, open expression by the boy and an affectionate, supportive, and respectful attitude in the father. The goal was to have that experience take place in the session with the participation of the other boys. The mother's witnessing the father's successful transactions with the boys would, it was hoped, dispose her to appreciate and trust what he could bring to parenting. The father's feeling of competence and the mother's acceptance of his active parental involvement could dispose both to look at doing something about their marital relationship so that they could work together as parents. Structural therapists target achieving new experiences that touch mental attitudes, emotional dispositions, and the power of action-in-practice, to lay the groundwork for new and more effective patterns of family relationships.

Intervention Approach

There are basically seven principles of intervention that form the foundation of structural family therapy.

1. Focus on Concrete Issues

SFT focuses on the urgent issue that holds the family's attention and intensity of concern (Aponte, 1998b). With the Gonzaga family, it was the 11-year-old's school problems. The issue that forces their concern is the issue that will mobilize their efforts toward a solution. For therapy, the problem must be experienced as compelling, because it affects their lives in real and practical ways. What hurts in their everyday lives also becomes an impulse for mobilization. In addition, what draws clients' investment in an issue is its importance to them because of their personal values, that is, what matters to them.

When clients confront their roles in the solution of a problem, they face challenges to change what is difficult for them to modify about their lives. They face hard decisions that must be driven by strong motivation. These choices carry with them reasons to change that draw from philosophical and moral convictions, as well as family and community opinion. Clients' spirituality adds depth and meaning to their motivations. Structural therapists look for concrete issues rooted in current life experience which carry the deepest investment and motivation to change in client families.

2. Locate in the Present

Structural family therapy considers the past "manifest in the present and . . . available to change by interventions that change the present" (Minuchin, 1974, p. 14). The current issue must contain the focal point of today's concern, the dynamics immediately generating the distress, and traces of the family's past experience that contain the whys and motivation driving the issue today. When working through the present, the practitioner not only relates to the immediate pain urging relief, but also to the deeper structural and dynamic forces that are driving the problem. A structural therapist's interventions in the present experience of a problem must reach into the emotions, history, and spirituality that give that experience its meaning and importance. The therapeutic process itself is considered by the practitioner as another context in which the issue is currently alive and compelling attention. The therapeutic context becomes a vital arena in which to address the problem in the present.

3. Mediate Interventions through the Client's Experience in the Session

The principal field of intervention for SFT is the family's enactment of their issue in the session (Aponte & VanDeusen, 1981, p. 329; Minuchin & Fishman, 1981, pp. 78–97). The structural therapist looks to seize the moment when family members spontaneously enact their struggle in the session or to create a situation that draws the family into a characteristic interaction around the issue. Talking about an issue draws from the intellect and memory. The drama of reenacting the struggle in session embodies all the affect and energy that drives the difficulty. With the Gonzaga family, the consultant directly requested the father to talk with his son about how they relate around the boy's school problems. When this boy told of his fear of his father, and the older boy spontaneously spoke of how hurt he was by the father's disrespect of him, the consultant held still and let the father respond with his own intensity to his sons. The situation was an opportunity to see how they interacted, but also suggested a new way for the father to engage with his boys. That enactment is both material for assessment and chance to intervene.

4. Change through Reorganizing the Structure of Relationships

The structural family therapist pays special attention to the structure of family relationships in relation to the focal issue. This transactional structure is the skeleton that undergirds the dynamics that generate the family's problem. In one instance, the pathological structure is the underlying framework of a family conflict. In another circumstance, the faulty structure lacks the stability, flexibility, or richness of development needed to meet the challenges of personal functioning within the family. Structural therapists intervene to resolve conflict, repair brokenness, and build new strength in the underlying structure of issues that clients present.

As noted earlier, at least one perspective on the structural model has evolved to incorporate the spiritual dimension of life into a tricornered vision of human functioning that includes structure, values, and function. People organize themselves internally and in relationships to carry out life's functions, but always in relation to their morals, ideals, and philosophy of life. This spiritual dimension can take a secular form without reference to a transcendent spiritual world or can be embodied in a formal religious belief system and faith community. In either case, people's spiritual framework is a vital link in the process chain that leads to their choices about how to meet and contend with life's challenges. In practice, the structural therapist with a spiritually sensitive perspective brings to the therapeutic effort a recognition of moral choice, personal philosophy, and faith community in the dynamics that influence how people approach the solution of their problems (Aponte, 1996; 1998b; in press).

5. Build on Client Strengths

SFT centers the therapeutic process on the resources and power of the client to grow and change, whether within themselves or in their family relationships (Aponte, 1999). The model works through a "search for strength" (Minuchin & Colapinto, 1980). Structural therapists actively engage with families to block old, pathological transactional patterns (Aponte & VanDeusen, 1981, p. 335–336) while also working to build on families' strengths to create new, effective patterns of interaction. Therapists look for whatever personal resources are potentially present for clients' efforts to contend with their problems. These resources may reside within clients' character, their family relationships, or their communities (Aponte, 1994a, pp. 58–82; Aponte, 1996).

The spiritual dimension of therapy recognizes the ultimate resource of positive, personal power for clients—free will, the seat of our moral choices. The personal power in freedom of the will that Frankl (1963) experienced in the camps, the poor and disenfranchised can also discover within themselves: "For the powerless and invisible, acting on the freedom to choose is to claim their potential and importance in the face of daunting circumstances." (Aponte, 1999, p. 82)

SFT that recognizes the spiritual dimension of therapy pivots its therapy on the free, moral choices clients face. Moreover, spirituality offers clients the resources of their belief system to give meaning and purpose to their struggles. Spirituality can also potentially find a source of strength in clients' faith communities and their God. Every intervention of a structural therapist carries within it a recognition of client strength and builds on that strength for positive change. Speaking to client strength starts with relating to the personal value and dignity of the client, and hinges ultimately on the acknowledgment of clients' personal power and responsibility to freely choose the actions that will determine their destiny. Moreover, because clients are viewed as ensconced in their family and community systems, these systems are also assumed to have the potential to contribute to support clients' efforts to solve their problems.

6. *Aim at Palpable Outcomes*

Although SFT looks into the underlying structure of people's actions and relationships, the model is practiced in palpable experience. The initial formulation of the problem takes the form of behavior, operationalizing the concern of the family (Aponte & VanDeusen, 1981, p. 316). The structural therapist then enters the family's struggle through the *enactment*, an actual reliving of the family drama in session. The therapist follows up with interventions aimed at creating new experiences in session that are transformative, as when the consultant had Mr. Gonzaga talking with his boys in session in ways that elicited mutuality rather than stifling the boys. Structural therapists also assign tasks as *homework* (Minuchin, 1974, p. 151) which takes the therapeutic experience home where the family drama normally takes place. Finally, when structural therapists formulate outcomes, they think in terms of a palpable experience that embodies the structural and dynamic changes within and between the members of a family as a result of the therapy (Aponte, 1992a).

The palpable experience of life carries within it all the motivation, dynamics, and emotions that power life. It is in this arena of living intensity that structural therapists prefer to work. They have immediate access to what moves problems in families and to the potential for change that resides in people. When people experience a change in a new, palpable experience, it reaches deep, taking root more profoundly in the heart of the psyche and the relationship.

7. Intervene through the Active Involvement of Practitioner with Family

Structural therapists actively engage with families to create experiences among family members and between practitioner and family that generate change.

- Initially, therapists look to *join* (Minuchin, 1974, pp. 133–137) families "in a carefully planned way" (Minuchin, 1974, p. 91). This is not only an effort to gain the trust of family members, but also a strategic therapeutic opportunity to relate in new ways that draw out new interactions within families.

- In more stubborn and chronic situations, practitioners may themselves engage with families with greater intensity (Minuchin, 1981, pp. 116–141) or may intensify a family's conflictual interaction (Aponte & VanDeusen, 1981, p. 335) through an enactment to induce emotional reactions that bring clients out from behind their defensive walls.

- Therapists may attempt to block (Aponte & VanDeusen, 1981, p. 335) or unbalance (Minuchin, 1981, pp. 161–190) a pathological pattern of interaction within a family to challenge family members to adopt a more effective mode of operating.

- On the other hand, in more receptive circumstances, practitioners may suggest, reward, and otherwise facilitate new patterns of interaction among family members (Aponte & VanDeusen, 1981, p. 336) through what they teach, what they emotionally abet, or how they personally relate to a client.

- Therapists may intentionally use themselves in personal interactions with clients within their professional roles, to induce different therapeutic experiences for clients (Aponte, 1992b). This use of self requires a knowledge of themselves, an ability to connect to their inner personal experience in session, and the expertise to utilize their past experiences, personality, and spiritual outlook to influence families (Aponte, 1994b; Aponte & Winter, 2000). In SFT this active use of self is employed with specific strategic goals within current transactions in session.

Evaluation

As noted earlier, the structural model grew out of research on the treatment of poor, underorganized families. The results of the research, as published in *Families of the Slums* (Minuchin, et al., 1967), demonstrated the effectiveness of interventions on the family structure underlying specific troubling issues that challenged the old and created new experiences in session. The initial research on underorganized families was followed by research targeting specific symptoms that were not necessarily associated with low socioeconomic conditions. Extensive investigations were conducted about families with members suffering from psychosomatic symptoms (Minuchin, et al., 1978) and drug addiction (Stanton, Todd, & Associates, 1982).

It is evident that the concept of family structure has served as a useful construct for further studies of psychosomatic illness (Kog, Vertommen & Vandereycken, 1987; Northey, Griffin, & Krainz, 1998; Onnis, Tortolani, & Cancrini, March, 1986; Wood, Watkins, Boyle, Noguera, Zimand, & Carroll, December, 1989). SFT has contributed to research on such disparate topics as family therapy with children (Abelshon & Saymin, 1991; Kerig, 1995) and family and culture (Fisek, 1991; Jung, 1984; Santisteban, Coatsworth, Perez-Vidal, Mitrani, Jean-Gilles, & Szapocznik, 1997), as well as applications to the business and industrial world (Deacon 1996). The concept of structure in systems has broad application. There should not be confusion about the abstract concepts and their clinical application, which will reflect the personal social biases of the practitioners. Structure in family systems is a given. What constitutes family is determined by our values and social outlook.

Application to Families on Levels I, III, and IV

The structural model has clearly demonstrated its relevance to Level I, II, and III needs. The theory and intervention techniques are well adapted to address concerns about concrete issues, hierarchical family structure, and personal boundary issues. Although it is not specifically tailored to therapeutic foci about intimacy in relationships and personal self actualization, SFT obviously deals with these issues in the work of relationships in families and couples, and in the personal development and differentiation of children and adults within their family context. The relevance and importance of personal values and spirituality when thinking of human relationships draws attention to Level IV concerns. Although SFT naturally attends to Level I, II, and III needs, it has necessarily had to incorporate into its scope of concern Level IV needs.

Summary

Structural family therapy is not a single, tightly organized model of intervention with a unitary orthodox theory. However, what is common among virtually all the approaches to the model is the emphasis on family structure, the here and now, building on client strengths, aiming at palpable outcomes, and the active style of intervention by practitioners. Some perspectives on the model emphasize technique over therapeutic relationship, whereas others stress the therapist's personal involvement. Structural therapists also differ in their views about normal family structure and in their opinions about the importance of spirituality to the work of therapy. These differences are incidental to the essence of the model, which focuses on actively addressing in the here and now the relationship structures underlying family function. The model has endured and continues to be a dominant approach in the field of family therapy.

Moreover, in today's eclecticism in therapy, it is rare to find practitioners who practice a single, orthodox approach to therapy. Therapists oriented to the structural model use what has been learned from Bowen about the impact of the family of origin on current functioning. From the earliest days, structuralists have employed strategic techniques. What structural therapists today ignore the dynamics of the unconscious? On the other hand, SFT has influenced practitioners from other orientations. The insights of SFT about structure in family systems and how to work with the underlying structure of relationships in the present are no longer the exclusive concerns of the structural model. These ideas have worked their way into the general thinking about family systems and interventions. SFT has made its contributions to the field of family therapy and has learned from the contributions of other family models, as well as individual models of therapy—as it should be.

Discussion Questions

1. What are the essential components of the structural model?

2. How can components of SFT be incorporated into other models of family therapy?

3. How is SFT applicable to Level III and IV needs?

4. What is the special relevance of spirituality to work with socioeconomically disadvantaged families?

5. How does one incorporate spirituality into the structural model, given the diversity of values and spirituality among practitioners and clients?

Suggested Readings

Aponte, H. J. (1992). Training the person of the therapist in structural family therapy. *Journal of Marital and Family Therapy, 18*(3), 269–281.
    This article attempts to apply the notion of the person-of-the-therapist to SFT, the first effort to address more fully the use of self in this model.

Aponte, H. J. (1994). *Bread & spirit: Therapy with the new poor.* New York: Norton.
    This book contains updated revisions of Aponte's basic structural writings, along with some new material. The particular emphasis of the book is on therapy with disadvantaged families and the place of values and spirituality in this work.

Aponte, H. J. (1998). Love, the spiritual wellspring of forgiveness: An example of spirituality in therapy. *Journal of Family Therapy, 20*(1), 37–58.
    This article demonstrates a cornerstone for incorporating spirituality into therapy, with an example of setting the value platform for a therapeutic contract.

Aponte, H. J. (1999). The stresses of poverty and the comfort of spirituality. In F. Walsh (Ed.), *Spiritual resources in family therapy* (pp. 76–89). New York: Guilford.
    This chapter in Froma Walsh's book is a more recent elaboration of the application of a spiritual perspective to therapy with a particular population.

Minuchin, S. (1974). *Families and family therapy.* Cambridge, MA: Harvard University Press.
This book is the most complete representation of Minuchin's concept of structural family therapy.

Minuchin, S., & Fishman, H. C. (1981). *Family therapy techniques.* Cambridge, MA: Harvard University Press.
This book contains Minuchin and Fishman's most comprehensive compendium of SFT's technical interventions.

Suggested Videotapes

Clinical application of forgiveness. (1996). National Conference on Forgiveness, University of Maryland.
This videotape contains the actual session that is discussed in the article "Love, the spiritual wellspring of forgiveness: An example of spirituality in therapy. "

A daughter who needs a mother. (1992). AAMFT Master Series.
Aponte works with an African-American family where the focus is on the relationship between a mother and her emotionally alienated adolescent daughter. The mother struggles with the effects of her own emotionally deprived childhood on her relationship with her daughter.

Family therapy with the experts: Structural therapy with Harry Aponte. (1998). Allyn and Bacon.
This videotape is one of the series Family Therapy with the Experts. It contains not only a full clinical session by Aponte, demonstrating structural family therapy, but also an interview with him about the structural model.

A house divided: Structural family therapy with a black family. (1990). Golden Triad Films.
Aponte works with an African-American family in a complex family situation of a married couple who have children from previous marriages. The father was released from jail for this interview.

Tres madres: Structural family therapy with an Anglo/Hispanic family. (1990). Golden Triad Films.
Aponte works with a three-generation family that has both Anglo and Latino family members. The presenting issue is a very unhappy, sleepwalking little girl. The focus of the therapy is a young mother valiantly struggling to survive a dysfunctional family background, poverty, and cultural difficulties.

Williams family: Strength and vulnerability. (1995). Research and Education Foundation, AAMFT.
This videotape is the interview with the family in Chapter 11 of Aponte's book *Bread and Spirit.* It shows a family that has courageously overcome overwhelming trials and tragedies of racism, sickle-cell anemia, drug addiction, and untimely and violent deaths. Their spirituality has been a key source of their strength.

References

Abelsohn, D., & Saayman, G. (1991). Adolescent adjustment to parental divorce: An investigation from the perspective of basic dimensions of structural family therapy theory. *Family Process, 30*(2), 177–191.

Aponte, H. J. (1992a). The black sheep of the family: A structural approach to brief therapy. In S. H. Budman, M. F. Hoyt, & S. Friedman (Eds.), *The first session in brief therapy* (pp. 324–342). New York: Guilford.

Aponte, H. J. (1992b). Training the person of the therapist in structural family therapy. *Journal of Marital and Family Therapy, 18*(3), 269–281.

Aponte, H. J. (1994a). *Bread and spirit: Therapy with the new poor.* New York: Norton.

Aponte, H. J. (1994b). How personal can training get? *Journal of Marital and Family Therapy, 20*(1), 3–15.

Aponte, H. J. (1996, Fall). Political bias, moral values, and spirituality in the training of psychotherapists. *Bulletin of the Menninger Clinic, 60*(4), 488–502.

Aponte, H. J. (1998a). Intimacy in the therapist-client relationship. In W. J. Matthews, & J. H. Edgette (Eds.), *Current thinking and research in brief therapy: Solutions, strategies, narratives* (Vol. II) (pp. 3–27). Philadelphia: Taylor & Francis.

Aponte, H. J. (1998b). Love, the spiritual wellspring of forgiveness: An example of spirituality in therapy. *Journal of Family Therapy, 20*(1), 37–58.

Aponte, H. J. (1999). The stresses of poverty and the comfort of spirituality. In F. Walsh (Ed.), *Spiritual resources in family therapy* (pp. 76–89). New York: Guilford.

Aponte, H. J. (In press). Spiritually sensitive therapy. In R. F. Massey & S. D. Massey (Eds.), *Comprehensive handbook of psychotherapy, Vol. III: Interpersonal, humanistic, existential approaches to psychotherapy.* New York: Wiley.

Aponte, H. J., & DiCesare, E. J. (2000). Structural theory. In F. M. Dattilio & L. Bevilacqua (Eds.), *Comparative treatment of couples problems* (pp. 45–57). New York: Springer.

Aponte, H. J., & VanDeusen. J. M. (1981). Structural family therapy. In A. S. Gurman & D. P. Kniskern (Eds.), *Handbook of family therapy* (pp. 310–360). New York: Brunner/Mazel.

Aponte, H. J., & Winter, J. E. (2000). The person & practice of the therapist. In M. Baldwin (Ed.), *The use of self in therapy* (2nd ed.). New York: Haworth.

Deacon, S. (1996). Utilizing structural family therapy and systems theory in the business world. *Contemporary Family Therapy, 18*(4), 549–565.

Fisek, G. O. (1991). A cross-cultural examination of proximity and hierarchy: A dimension of family structure. *Family Process, 30,* 121–133.

Frankl, V. E. (1963). *Man's search for meaning.* New York: Washington Square Press.

Jung, M., (1984). Structural family therapy: Its application to Chinese families. *Family Process, 23*(3), 365–374.

Kerig, P. K. (1995). Triangles in the family circle: Effects of family structure on marriage, parenting, and child adjustment. *Journal of Family Psychology, 9*(1), 28–43.

Kog, E., Vertommen, H., & Vandereycken, W. (1987, June). Minuchin's psychosomatic family model revisited: A concept-validation study using a multitrait-multimethod approach. *Family Process, 26*(2), 235–253.

Minuchin, S. (1974). *Families and family therapy.* Cambridge, MA: Harvard University Press.

Minuchin, S., & Colapinto, J. (Eds.). (1980). *Taming monsters* [Videotape]. Philadelphia: Philadelphia Child Guidance Clinic.

Minuchin, S., & Fishman, H. C. (1981). *Family therapy techniques.* Cambridge, MA: Harvard University Press.

Minuchin, S., Montalvo, B., Guerney, Jr., B., Rosman, B., & Schumer, F. (1967). *Families of the slums.* New York: Basic Books.

Minuchin, S., Rosman, B., & Baker, L. (1978). *Psychosomatic families.* Cambridge, MA: Harvard University Press.

Northey, S., Griffin, W. A., & Krainz, S. (1998). A partial test of the psychosomatic family model: Marital interaction patterns in asthma and nonasthma families. *Journal of Family Psychology, 12*(2), 220–233.

Onnis, L., Tortolani, D., & Cancrini, L. (1986) Systemic research on chronicity factors in infantile asthma. *Family Process, 14*(2), 107–121.

Santisteban, D., Coatsworth, J. D., Perez-Vidal, A., Mitrani, V., Jean-Gilles, M., & Szapocznik, J. (1997). Brief, structural/strategic family therapy with African American and Hispanic high-risk youth. *Journal of Community Psychology, 25,* 453–471.

Stanton, M. D., Todd, T. C., & Associates. (1982). *The family therapy of drug abuse and addiction.* New York: Guilford.

Wood, B., Watkins, J. B., Boyle, J. T., Noguiera, J., Zimand, E., & Carroll, L. (1989). The psychosomatic family model: An empirical and theoretical analysis. *Family Process, 28*(4), 399–417.

8

Social Learning Family Interventions

Arthur M. Horne, Ph.D., and Thomas V. Sayger, Ph.D.

Family life has become increasingly stressful during the past century. There has been more isolation of family members due to the urbanization of society and a move toward small nuclear families instead of extended families. The urbanization process has led to a focus on work outside the home for most adults. Increased costs of living have resulted in more parents' working longer hours out of the home, with fewer support systems available to provide parenting and child care. There is a significant level of violence in American society. This, coupled with drug and alcohol abuse, a concomitant increase in sexual experimentation among young people, and more teenage parenting and single-parent households, has resulted in a dramatic growth in the numbers of children and family members living below the poverty level and a corresponding increase in suicidal and homicidal behavior among young people. In many communities, gang membership has supplanted family membership as the primary source of identity.

Family Needs

Within American society there are substantial numbers of families that are functioning above the crisis level, the level at which families need support from the community for their very survival needs. Although the survival needs of these families have been met, they still have very real and serious problems. Examples of families with problems that fall within the second category of need include families with disruptive, acting-out children; families that are experiencing considerable disarray in the form of poor family organization and structure; families with difficulties in communicating and effective problem solving; families that have children in difficulty with school or community agencies; and families experiencing high levels of disruptive affect, as in violent anger or disabling depression.

Many of the families that have needs on Level II are there because of internal and external (environmental) factors that have affected them. These include the following child and family risk factors:

Child
Child perception that parents support fighting as a way of solving conflict
Expects success and no negative consequences for aggression
Lacks problem-solving skills
Attributes aggression where there is none
Holds beliefs that support violence
Depression
Drug and alcohol use
Low academic achievement
Weapon carrying
Negative parental relationships

Family
Lack of supervision
Lack of attachment
Lack of discipline or consequences
Negative relationships
Psychopathology of one or both parents
Antisocial behavior of family members
Susceptibility to stressors
Unemployment
Marital conflict
Divorce

School
Lack of supervision
Lack of attachment
Lack of discipline or consequences
Negative relationships

Families that have sought help have included ones like the following:

The McCallisters called, requesting to be seen at the center because of a referral from the school psychologist. Their son Kevin had experienced high rates of behavioral conduct problems in school for a number of years. Now that he had reached sixth grade, he had become a serious enough problem to be perceived as a danger to other children. The father was a carpenter who worked long hours when employed and who had little time for the family. The mother, a waitress, worked afternoons and was seldom home when the children came home after school. Kevin, the oldest, had been a behavioral problem throughout his school career and had been referred for testing several times.

Each time he was evaluated, Kevin was identified as marginal in terms of special needs; consequently, he had not received any special placement. The two younger children, also boys, had behavioral problems but had not demonstrated the extent of physical aggression that Kevin had shown. The initial interview with the family indicated that the father was quite removed and distant from parenting, seeing the role of parenting as the mother's responsibility. He was angry that he had been called into the situation. The mother, who scored in the clinical range on a depression inventory, indicated that she loved the children but that they had been a disappointment, causing her more pain than pleasure. Kevin was antagonistic to being involved in treatment, whereas the two younger boys were curious and rambunctious.

The Washington family was referred because Randolph Washington, a 15-year-old, had been caught shoplifting. He had a history of aggressive behavior, including attempting to extort money from children at school, threatening to hurt other children if they didn't pay him for "protection," and stealing items from school. Randolph had been arrested at a convenience store and held overnight at a juvenile detention center. He had attended juvenile court, and the judge had ordered that Randolph, his single-parent mother, and the siblings living at home participate in family counseling. Mrs. Washington was angry at the inconvenience, and Randolph was quite rebellious. None of the family members indicated that he or she saw counseling as a positive experience. They indicated that they would participate in counseling only by showing up for the minimum number of times the judge had ordered.

The Prikosovics contacted the center and requested marriage counseling. They indicated that Mr. Prikosovic came from an Eastern European background, and Mrs. Prikosovic was of Irish heritage. They had been married for six years. Although the marriage had started out amicably, the last two years had been marked by conflict, arguments, and recently by physical aggression between the two of them. They had attempted religious counseling by their priest, but he had encouraged them to follow traditional roles of husband and wife, with the wife deferring to Mr. Prikosovic as the head of the household. Mrs. Prikosovic indicated that she had been willing to accept that role when they were first married, but that it was no longer tolerable for her. They both reported significant conflict in the area of sexuality within the marriage. There were no children.

Robert Verde, a recent university graduate, came for his first session at the center and reported that his lover had just left him for another man. Robert was very distraught and reported the possibility of inflicting personal harm on himself. He stated that he had experienced a number of lovers during his university education but that his recent partner had been with him for more than a year. They were very close and trusting with each other. Robert was devastated that his lover left him after such a close and involved relationship. Robert indicated that his family had not been told about the partnership because Robert did not want his fundamentally religious farming family to know he was gay.

Assessment and Treatment Goals

Each family described presented very real pain and need for assistance in addressing the pressing problems that they were experiencing in their lives. There are general goals that are established for all families receiving treatment.

1. Develop a sense of optimism and hope about their particular situation.
2. Appreciate the universality or general nature of their situation.
3. Become aware of the alternative ways of addressing the problems they are experiencing, so that they see more options available to them.
4. Learn more effective basic living skills: communication, problem solving, decision making, environmental interaction.
5. Develop independence in living skills.

The goals of treatment become focused as each family member presents his or her unique and individual issues.

The McCallisters. The McCallisters require a careful negotiation to determine the level of change and restructuring that would be acceptable and agreeable. Mr. McCallister has reported little interest in participating in treatment, seeing the problem as one primarily for the mother. Here, the therapist must make a decision about family responsibility and power: Should the therapist support the traditional roles that have been assigned and accepted by family members, or should there be a focus on realigning the roles and responsibilities of the parents? The goals for the McCallister family might include

- Empowering the mother to take greater control over how family members spend their time (father absent, chaotic family schedule).
- Teaching both parents more effective parenting skills.
- Helping the boys learn anger self-control skills.
- Identifying problem-solving skills and, especially important, couples communication skills.

The Washingtons

The Washington family does not want to participate in treatment. A goal for this family would be to identify ways in which their family is functioning well and to help them see that they are not "bad" or "sick," but doing the best they can, given their economic and social circumstances. However, they need assistance in learning more effective ways of dealing with their environmental circumstances. Specific goals for the Washington family might include

- Empowering the mother to be able to take greater responsibility for the behavior of the children.
- Teaching the family effective disciplinary techniques.

- Helping the boys learn self-control strategies that will help them stay out of trouble.
- Establishing better communication skills within the family.
- Addressing environmental issues (employment, leisure time).
- Working with school issues such that greater success is experienced in the school environment.

The Prikosovics

The Prikosovics have demonstrated difficulties in maintaining and enhancing intimacy. They need to learn more effective communication and basic problem-solving skills. They are experiencing an evolving and developing relationship but have become "stuck" at a level of development that is not acceptable and is, in fact, detrimental to their growing closer together. Goals might include

- Developing more effective problem-solving skills.
- Learning better communication skills.
- Addressing the beliefs or narratives they have about their relationship.
- Discussing the power and role relationships that have become troublesome.

Mr. Verde

Robert Verde is having difficulty managing his needs for intimacy and relationships in light of his homosexuality and negative social pressures. He needs assistance in learning to manage issues of intimacy (being discarded) and sexual orientation, developing personal strength to manage his loneliness, and learning communication skills, both to facilitate meeting other persons and to learn ways of talking with his family members. Goals might be

- Learning to develop the strength to manage developmental passages, such as the loss of a loved one.
- Developing effective coping skills to manage his loss and fear.
- Practicing communication skills that will allow greater means of meeting people and sharing with his current family and friends.
- Developing self-control skills to manage his life more effectively.

Consistent with other families at Level II, the four families in the case examples are experiencing difficulties with inefficient and ineffective family structures. In turn, these faulty structures inhibit the effective solving of current problems, confusion with family rules, roles, and responsibilities, exacerbating the low level of functioning. As a result, these kinds of confusion limit the families' capacity to overcome their life challenges and their feelings of insecurity, dissatisfaction, and discomfort with the level of intimacy within the family.

Social Learning Family Interventions

Several principles aid in our understanding of family needs and the contingencies on which current family interactions are based. The social learning family treatment approach, (Fleischman, Horne, & Arthur, 1983; Horne & Sayger, 1990, 2000; Tolan & Guerra, 1994) has been successfully employed with a variety of families and with many levels of family needs. This model enables the practitioner to utilize a well-structured series of intervention strategies, yet allows for the necessary flexibility when working with diverse, chaotic, and unique family systems. Because social learning family interventions allow for unique family structures and flexibility in implementing change according to the expressed needs of each family, this approach can be effective across racial and ethnic categories, and with varying gender roles and responsibilities. The effectiveness of social learning family interventions has been researched in a variety of clinical settings. It has been shown to be useful in the remediation of difficult child behavior problems, marital conflict, ineffective power structures and coalitions, and poor community–school–home relations (Horne, Glaser, & Calhoun, 1998; Sayger, Horne, & Glaser, 1993; Sayger, Horne, Walker, & Passmore, 1988; Szykula, Sayger, Morris, & Sudweeks, 1987).

Theoretical Base and Basic Tenets

Many theoretical approaches to family intervention have been utilized with Level II families, with varying degrees of success. All of these models attempt to approach clinical work with families from a positive viewpoint, and focus on the families' strengths and current abilities to cope with chaotic and challenging living environments. Clearly, no one theoretical approach provides the answer for all families experiencing difficulties; thus family practitioners must be clear about the needs of each family they plan to assist and how they will develop their intervention to meet those needs. An underlying knowledge of how one believes individuals and families develop and learn their behavioral patterns is the cornerstone for effectively implementing a family intervention.

For those clinicians who practice social learning family interventions, the following beliefs and assumptions about human/family development are the bases for intervention:

1. People learn within a social context through watching how other people in their environment behave, reacting to these behaviors and interacting with those individuals in their social system (spouse, child, parent, extended family members, teachers, coworkers).
2. The problem behaviors demonstrated by the individual or family are logical from a learning perspective, given the contingencies within that family's or person's environment and their personal beliefs.
3. People behave the way they do either because they have learned that behavior, or because they have not learned alternative, and often more positive, ways to behave.

4. People's beliefs and cognitive processes influence their affective and behavioral responses.
5. People attempt to maximize the rewards of their behavior while minimizing the costs. People are more likely to perform in ways that result in what they perceive to be the best outcome for them.
6. In order to change how someone else behaves, a person has to change the way he or she typically responds to that behavior.
7. The more consistent the consequence and the more immediately it occurs after the behavior, the faster the person will learn. Inconsistent consequences make learning harder, because people do not know what to expect.
8. Because people rarely learn from only one act of behaving and receiving a consequence, repeated trying or testing is a necessary part of learning.
9. The family is the expert on what is happening in their life, and each family is unique.

This framework is appropriate for families at the second level of functioning. The intervention focuses on the development of effective communication skills, establishes appropriate limits and levels of authority, encourages strong parental alliances, and aids families in the development and use of self-control and problem-solving skills. It also addresses the cognitive thought processes to replace dysfunctional thoughts with more facilitative thinking. In essence, social learning family interventions help family members learn not only how to survive family life, but also how to make their family life healthier from a psychological perspective and more enjoyable in general.

Applications and Intervention Strategies

Social cognitive learning intervention strategies focus on families at Level II and fall into three general categories. First, cognitive restructuring addresses any disruptive or maladaptive thoughts that might result in painful or disturbing feelings and, consequently, maladaptive behaviors. Second, coping skills training, such as relaxation training, self-control strategies, behavior rehearsal, and modeling, addresses inappropriate learning experiences. Third, problem-solving skills training (behavioral contracts, negotiation, brainstorming) assists families in developing alternative strategies for resolving current and future conflicts or concerns. Perhaps the most important objective of intervention with Level II families is to focus on creating a structured learning environment in which family members can learn and practice new behaviors that alter their currently ineffective family structure.

Therapeutic Relationship. The development of a positive therapeutic relationship is central to effective family intervention. The relationship between professional and client develops in much the same way as all social systems are formed, that is, through modeling appropriate social behavior, coaching the family members in effective social communication, and setting up positive consequences for establishing the therapeutic alliance. To accomplish these goals, the family practitioner must first help the family establish positive expectations for change. Level II families are characterized by a negative view of their chances for remediation. They feel that they have tried everything they know how to do, and nothing has worked. Thus it is important for the practitioner to communicate to each family that she or he believes that the family can successfully deal with its current problems. The process of preparing the family for success can be initiated by

1. *Defining all members in the family as being hurt by their circumstance.* Most families attempt to find someone or something to blame for their problems. Objects of blame may be the child, parent, judge, social service system, neighborhood, teacher, school, social caseworker, extended family members, or therapist. In defining all members in the family as being in pain, everyone acknowledges that each family member is affected by hurtful ways and that blaming will not solve the problem.

2. *Normalizing the family problems.* Families may communicate hopelessness or feelings of "Why me?" when they are first referred for treatment. It is important to inform the family in treatment that all families have problems, and although the family's current problems may seem to be overwhelming and uncontrollable, families in similar situations have been successful in overcoming their conflicts.

3. *Emphasizing the family's strengths and positive motivation.* Although many families may initially proclaim their reluctance to participate in treatment, the fact that they have attended a session shows that they still have some concern for their family and hold some hope for change.

4. *Communicating empathy.* The family must believe that the practitioner understands what it is like for the family to be experiencing these problems. Assuming the position that family members are the experts on their own family can assist the professional in communicating positively to the family that he or she is there to listen, understand, and help the family successfully overcome their concerns.

5. *Communicating hope.* Although the problems facing the family may be enormous and difficult, a positive attitude and an ability to see the hope and irony in the situation are necessary. Most families at Level II have forgotten how to laugh and enjoy themselves; thus the practitioner must attempt to make the treatment intervention enjoyable and even fun, without diminishing the seriousness of the problems being addressed.

Other relationship-building skills that the professional would utilize include

- Breaking complex problems into manageable units.
- Dealing with one issue or task at a time.
- Giving everyone a chance to participate.
- Teaching new skills in specific, nontechnical language.
- Modeling new skills.
- Personalizing in-session rehearsals.

- Predicting feelings and behavior changes.
- Soliciting and anticipating concerns.
- Encouraging client initiative and giving credit for positive changes.
- Determining reasons for client resistance.
- Checking for comprehension and understanding when teaching new skills.
- Sharing the treatment or session agenda.
- Gathering information about what family members do.
- Gathering information about cognitive and emotional reactions.
- Gathering information about behavioral sequences and patterns.

Structuring for Success.   Structuring for success begins with the initial contact between the family and the practitioner. Not only does the professional want to be successful in assisting the family to function in a more effective manner, but the family must also establish a belief in their own ability to succeed. To establish this positive expectation for change and success, interventions begin with clearly and objectively defining the problem, establishing specific behavioral goals, emphasizing consistency and persistence in developing family routines, interacting with respect and dignity, emphasizing family strengths, and enhancing the couple's and/or the parent–child relationship. Families are encouraged to begin tracking the instances of problem behaviors in their family to determine patterns, sequences, frequency, intensity, and duration of the problems. Usually, families will discover that the incidence of problem behavior is less frequent than they had perceived, yet the discomfort, anger, pain, and disruption created by the behavior are no less real. However, in discovering that the behavior occurs less frequently, the family becomes more hopeful that positive change can be achieved, and thus their motivation and commitment to treatment will increase.

Self-Management Skills Training.   Individuals who cannot gain and maintain control of their emotions and behaviors find it very difficult, if not impossible, to interact with family members in a positive and respectful manner. A study conducted by Morris et al. (1988) found that fathers of aggressive boys reported five times more negative thoughts about their families and eight times more negative thoughts about their child than did fathers of well-behaved boys. This finding further supports the belief that the maladaptive thought processes that family members have about their relatives must be altered if they hope to develop a more functional family environment. Self-control strategies that might be utilized to assist family members in gaining and maintaining self-control are

   1. *Relaxation Training.* Learning self control by learning to control bodily reactions through training in deep-breathing exercises, progressive muscle relaxation, or other relaxation strategies is very effective.

   2. *Positive Reframing.* Individuals will typically react to behaviors based on some perception they have regarding the intent of that behavior. For instance, a parent who is constantly being interrupted by a child may assume that the child is being an ill-mannered pest. This belief might lead the parent to respond in a negative manner. However, if the child's reaction were reframed as an attempt to gain the parent's highly valued attention, the parent might respond more positively. Functioning under a more positive frame of reference, the parent can then teach the child more appropriate ways of gaining parental attention. This reframing can also be identified as an attempt to replace upsetting, and possibly irrational, thoughts with calming thoughts which allow the family members to interact in healthier ways.

3. *Child Self-Control Strategies.* The most effective way to implement and train children to use self-control strategies is by aiding the parent in instructing the child. The turtle technique (Schneider & Robin, 1976) assists younger children in gaining control over impulsive, aggressive, and disruptive behaviors, and teaches children to slow down, "pull into their shell," calm down, and think of their behavioral goal. This strategy encourages the child to think before he or she acts.

4. *Disciplinary Strategies.* For families in which parental authority has been undermined, it becomes important to assist them in gaining control through consistent and effective disciplinary methods. Many Level II parents have relied on spanking, lecturing, or grounding to punish children for their misbehavior. These punishments are typically ineffective, particularly if the parents' authority is not secure or respected. Emphasizing modeling, direct instruction, and rehearsal to develop effective discipline, parents can be instructed in the development of strategies that allow the child to fully experience the consequences of his or her misbehavior. The following disciplinary strategies are often recommended:

> *Time-out.* Time-out is useful for general child noncompliance or defiance, or when immediate cessation of the behavior is important. Short-term time-out is most effective with children before the age of 10 and requires the parent to send the child to a nonreinforcing environment for a specified length of time to "cool off" and gain self-control.

> *Premack Principle.* Often referred to as "Grandma's law," the Premack principle requires the child to complete a desired or expected activity before doing something he or she prefers to do. A form of contract, this strategy is often misused and reversed, and therefore rendered ineffective. For example, the child must eat his or her vegetables before he or she has dessert; this is an appropriate contract. However, because the child is whining or yelling, many parents will allow the child to eat the dessert to make him or her quiet. Typically, the child will continue to refuse to eat his or her vegetables. In essence, the child has won the battle.

> *Natural and Logical Consequences.* Particularly useful with irresponsible children, natural and logical consequences allow children to experience the consequences of their behavior; thus a child learns which behaviors have negative costs and which provide positive rewards.

> *Assigning Extra Chores.* Effectively used with older children and adolescents, extra chores are assigned for children who lie, damage property, or steal. The

child should be assigned to do one hour of work for each transgression. It is important that the chore be something that would not disrupt other family functions if not completed (such as cooking dinner). Additionally, the child is restricted from the telephone, friends, food, and fun until the work is completed. In instances of property damage or stealing, the child should also be expected to pay restitution.

Loss of Privileges. To be effective, the loss of a privilege must involve something the child values. For instance, telling the child that he or she cannot use the car on the weekend when he or she does not have a driver's license would not be effective. Also, parents must not go overboard. If the child loses a privilege for too long, he or she will soon find a replacement of equal or greater value, and the suspended privilege will lose its effectiveness. Loss of privileges is often effective when other disciplinary strategies have been unsuccessful.

Communication Skills Training.   Healthy and functional family communication begins with ensuring that the message that is intended to be sent is the message that is being heard. Family members must be specific and brief, and utilize I-messages instead of you-messages if they hope to increase the effectiveness of their communication. Effective communication involves the following:

1. *Speaking your piece.* Individuals in the family must express their desires and opinions instead of relying on others to "read their mind."
2. *Finding out what others are thinking.* Many individuals make the mistake of believing they know what other family members are thinking. To be sure, family members must ask others what they are thinking.
3. *Showing others that they are being heard.* Maintaining good eye contact and otherwise indicating interest, and trying to understand what others are saying will communicate concern and committment to clear communication.
4. *Asking questions when confused.* If family members do not understand what other members are trying to communicate, ask them for clarification.
5. *Stopping and letting others know when communication is breaking down.* During arguments, many things that are said in haste and anger may cause others to feel hurt or angry in return. It is best to stop the interaction before it progresses to this stage and to wait until a more calm and rational discussion can occur.

Other behaviors can derail communication and should be avoided. Such behaviors as put-downs, blaming, denial, defensiveness, mind reading, sidetracking, or giving up only lead to the demise of effective communication.

Problem-Solving Skills Training.   Most families at Level II are relatively unskilled problem solvers in many aspects of their lives. To overcome these deficiencies, interventions will assist family members in problem-solving exercises specifically designed to address the unique problems of each family. Basic to problem-solving skills training is the act of brainstorming alternative solutions for specific problems. An approach that seems particularly useful with such families is to ask these questions:

1. What is your goal? What would you like to see happen?
2. What are you doing to achieve this goal?
3. Is what you are doing helping you to achieve this goal?
4. If not, what are you going to do differently?

At first, most families will require a great deal of assistance to generate positive alternatives to their current behavior. However, through modeling this four-step process, the family will soon be able to generate many alternative solutions. The task for the practitioner then becomes helping the family evaluate the potential consequences for each solution and selecting and implementing the alternative that is deemed to be the most satisfactory in resolving the problem.

Evaluation of Effectiveness

Sayger et al. (1993); Sayger et al. (1988); and Szykula et al. (1987) have measured the effectiveness of social learning family interventions in a variety of settings with children with behavior disorders and their families. The results have been impressive, with significant decreases in negative child behaviors and corresponding increases in positive child behaviors both at home and in school. Sayger et al. (1988) also reported that these behavioral changes were maintained after a 9-to-12-month followup. In a comparison of strategic and behavioral family therapies in an outpatient child psychiatric facility, Szykula et al. (1987) reported that 100 percent of the families participating in social learning family intervention demonstrated gains toward their treatment attainment goals, whereas 67 percent of those in the strategic family therapy group made gains toward treatment goals.

In a study of the impact of social learning family treatment for child conduct problems on the level of marital satisfaction of parents, Sayger et al. (1993) noted that those parents reporting low marital satisfaction prior to treatment reported scores in the maritally satisfied range after treatment.

Sayger, Szykula, and Sudweeks (1992) found that parents participating in social learning family interventions reported significantly more positive than negative side effects of their participation in treatment. These studies suggest that consumer satisfaction ratings show that family treatments are both efficacious and effective in the positive treatment of many aspects of poorly functioning families with problems ranging from marital conflict to child behavior problems.

Application to Families on Levels I, III, and IV

Social learning family treatment offers a structured approach to dealing with a variety of family concerns. As such, it can be effectively employed with families at all levels of functioning. Families functioning at Level I can benefit from the positive focus on structure, organization, and problem solving. Even with families at levels higher than Level I, instances may occur in which their safety and security are challenged through unemployment, death, divorce, or other life events. The need to define and develop a new family structure and organization can become a focus in treatment. Families at Level III can benefit from the focus on establishing clear boundaries and emphases on communication skills building. Level IV families can benefit as they develop self-knowledge and awareness regarding their behavior patterns, goals for the future, and general understanding of family systems and structures.

Summary

Social learning family interventions with Level II families focus on learning more effective social skills. People learn in social settings, with the family being the primary such setting. Through live and vicarious modeling, each member of the family learns to interact consistently with how other family members act, or "You attract more bees with honey than with vinegar" versus "Nastiness begets nastiness." People seek the maximum pleasure and least pain that they can experience in life, and as a result, often use aversive methods of interacting to obtain the greatest payoffs. Frequently, this tendency results in an environment focusing on aversive interactions, the abuse of members of the family, and a lack of family (community) happiness because individual desires at times take precedence over the best interests of the group.

Social learning family interventions present a relearning opportunity, helping family members learn to interact with one another in more pleasant, affirming, and respectful ways. Two primary contributions are teaching family members on how to interact in positive rather than aversive ways, by showing respect and dignity for the members of the family; and a provision of structure and organization that brings order to chaos, predictability to uncertainty, trust rather than fear.

Although this approach is not proposed as the only intervention for all families, it has been demonstrated to be highly effective for assisting families experiencing considerable chaos, with clinicians using aversion to control family members. When families are functioning with inadequate or inappropriate social skills, social learning family interventions facilitate the learning of more adaptive and fulfilling ways of living together.

Discussion Questions

1. Identify the particular population that the social learning family intervention model has been used with the most. Why has this population been targeted? What is there about the social learning family intervention model that particularly lends itself to working with this population?

2. The authors provide evidence substantiating the efficacy of social learning family intervention. Describe why behavioral research methods have been especially applicable to this model of intervention, and discuss whether the information is useful for the clinical practitioner.

3. It often appears that clinicians are guided more by intuition and feel than by research supporting particular models. Family treatment adheres to a research model for evaluating the development and application of principles. Discuss why social learning family treatment makes use of this research model, whereas many other models do not.

4. The authors noted that the social learning family treatment model is not necessarily the only or the best intervention to use. Describe guidelines that could assist you in deciding whether the social learning family treatment model is applicable to a given case.

5. The authors address the "softer" clinical skills necessary to be effective with families. Discuss the importance of relationship skills to a program that is predominantly technique and intervention oriented.

6. Explain from an ethical/professional position how you can justify using or not using a model that is less appealing but more efficacious.

7. Identify the aspects of treatment that seem to be key for families at Level II.

Suggested Readings

Goldstein, A., & Huff, C. (1993). *The gang intervention handbook.* Champaign, IL: Research Press.
  This handbook describes interventions useful for addressing gang problems, including two chapters describing family interventions.

Horne, A., & Sayger, T. V. (2000). Social learning family therapy. In A. Horne (Ed.), *Family counseling and therapy* (3rd ed.). Itasca, IL: Peacock.
  This text presents an overview of models and theories of family therapy intervention. The chapter on social learning family therapy includes a historical foundation for the model and reviews the research supporting the model. The chapter also describes applications to marriage work.

Sayger, T. V., & Heid, K. O. (1991). Counseling the impoverished rural client: Issues for family therapists. *The Psychotherapy Patient, 7,* 161-168.
  Discusses the problems facing family therapists when working with the rural poor and possible strategies for family intervention.

Sayger, T. V., Szykula, S. A., & Laylander, J. A. (1991). Adolescent-focused family counseling: A comparison of behavioral and strategic approaches. *Journal of Family Psychotherapy, 2,* 57-79.
  This article presents a hypothetical case and discusses the application of social learning and strategic family therapy in addressing the family issues.

References

Horne, A., Glaser, B., and Calhoun, G. (1998). Conduct disorders. In R. Ammerman, C. G. Last, & M. Hersen (Eds.), *Handbook of prescriptive treatments for children and adolescents* (2nd ed.). New York: Pergamon Press.

Horne, A. M., & Sayger, T. V. (1990). *Treating conduct and oppositional defiant disorders in children.* Elmsford, NY: Pergamon Press.

Horne, A., & Sayger, T. V. (2000). Social learning family therapy. In A. Horne (Ed.), *Family counseling and therapy* (3rd ed.). Itasca, IL: Peacock.

Morris, P. W., Horne, A. M., Jessell, J. C., Passmore, J. L., Walker, J. M., & Sayger, T. V. (1988). Behavioral and cognitive characteristics of fathers of aggressive and well-behaved boys. *Journal of Cognitive Psychotherapy: An International Quarterly, 2,* 251-265.

Sayger, T. V., Horne, A. M., & Glaser, B. A. (1993). Marital satisfaction and social learning family therapy for child conduct problems: Generalization of treatment effects. *Journal of Marital and Family Therapy, 19,* 393-402.

Sayger, T. V., Horne, A. M., Walker, J. M., & Passmore, J. L. (1988). Social learning family therapy with aggressive children: Treatment outcome and maintenance. *Journal of Family Psychology, 1,* 261-285.

Sayger, T. V., Szykula, S. A., & Sudweeks, C. (1992). Treatment side effects: Positive and negative attributes of child-focused family therapy. *Child and Family Behavior Therapy, 14,* 1-9.

Schneider, M., & Robin, A. (1976). The turtle technique: A method for the self control of impulsive behavior. In J. Krumboltz & C. Thoreson (Eds.), *Counseling methods.* New York: Holt, Rinehart & Winston.

Szykula, S. A., Sayger, T. V., Morris, S. B., & Sudweeks, C. (1987). Child-focused behavior and strategic therapies: Outcome comparisons. *Psychotherapy: Theory, Research, Practice and Training, 24*(3S), 546-551.

Tolan, P. H., & Guerra, N. G. (1994). What works in reducing adolescent violence: An empirical review of the field. Boulder: The Center for the Study and Prevention of Violence, University of Colorado.

9

Solution-Focused Family Interventions

Jeffrey J. Koob, Ph.D.

Solution-focused brief therapy (SFBT) Interventions, as the name implies, focuses on solutions rather than problems. For example, if a child frowns, one could focus on the child's not frowning (problem-focused), or one could focus on the child's smiling (solution-focused). If the child smiles more, then by definition he or she frowns less. To obtain this dynamic interplay, however, certain assumptions must be made (de Shazer, 1985, 1988, 1994, 1997; de Shazer, Berg, Lipchik, Nunnally, Molnar, Gingerich, & Weiner-Davis, 1986; O' Hanlon & Weiner-Davis, 1989).

Assumptions

1. *The Family Is the Expert.* Unlike problem-focused therapies, in which the therapist is viewed as the expert, SFBT therapists believe that families have the knowledge, resources, and strengths to find their own solutions. The therapist is there to help guide them toward those solutions. In addition, because the therapist is not constructing the solution from his or her own cultural perspective, SFBT is sensitive to families' cultural identification, thus allowing cultural differences to help shape the solution.

2. *Problems and Solutions Are Not Connected.* If one can accept this assumption, issues of diagnosis and assessment become moot (although not to managed care). SFBT maintains that at one time a problem emerged due to an antecedent. It is unnecessary, however, to discover that antecedent or to help the client in gaining insight surrounding the antecedent. Rather, one can determine what clients would prefer to be doing instead of continuing the problem, and that exception becomes the solution.

3. *Make Unsolvable Problems Solvable.* Clients present the therapist with what, in their view, are unsolvable problems. The therapist's task, therefore, is to redefine or reframe the problem into solvable terms. Take, for example, a client saying, "I cannot be happy, because I am a depressed person." Now imagine a therapist asking, "Are there times when you are less depressed?" This represents a slight change in the definition, and this definition, unlike the client's, is amenable to change.

4. *Change Is Constant and Inevitable.* This questions the idea of a system struggling to maintain homeostasis. From this view, problems can be seen as not only necessary for change, but also part of the change process. The notion is not to eliminate a problem so that the system can go back to a steady state, but rather to define the problem as part of the change process. This allows the system to become unstuck within the change process (problem) and prompts the system to complete the present change (solution). In other words, "Your child frowns because he or she is sad" (problem) becomes "Your child frowns as a means of communicating with you" (new definition). "How would you like your child to communicate with you?" (client as expert). "I would like my child to smile more" (solution).

5. *Only a Small Change Is Needed.* De Shazer (personal communication, September 15, 1985) uses the analogy of a person walking in the desert. He says that, if the person makes a one-degree angle to the right, it will not seem like much at first, but as time passes the walker will end up miles away from the original destination. This implies that the therapist needs only to effect a small change in the system, rather than solving each problem individually or even attacking the most serious problem, and that small change over time will snowball into dramatic changes.

6. *Keep It Brief.* Due to the focus on solutions rather than problems, the time spent in assessment, clinical diagnosis, and facilitating insight are frequently bypassed. Rather, with an emphasis on how a client would like life to be, the interaction becomes positive, motivating, and future oriented. This shift, however, from "problem talk" to "solution talk," must follow the client's lead, an issue that will be dealt with later in this chapter.

Typical Needs of Level III Families

Level III families tend to have "a structure and a style that is often perceived as working" (Weltner, 1985, p. 46). The analogy for this level is the inner architecture of the house. When one is working with the inner structure, the presence of the outer structure is assumed. In these families it is assumed that "there is sufficient strength and health to allow for resolution" (p. 47). This assumption is congruent with the use of a solution-focused approach to family treatment (Cleveland & Lindsey, 1999).

Assessment

A mother, daughter, and father present at an SFBT clinic. The clinician asks what prompted them to make an appointment. The mother explains rather emphatically that her daughter (who appears to the therapist as being in junior high) "needs to be in school." The mother further asserts that, if it were not for her daughter's boyfriend, her daughter would be in school. She concludes that her daughter "needs to be bad, because her boyfriend is bad." Rhetorically she asks, "Where has my little girl gone, and who is this stranger now living in the house?" The father and daughter sit quietly. The therapist agrees that it is difficult for mothers to lose their "little girls."

The daughter explains, "I know I should be in school." The therapist shows surprise and gives some praise that the daughter knows the importance of education. "Wow, how do you know this? Most children your age don't know this. Mom, did you know your daughter knew this?" The daughter further explains that perhaps if her mother were not so confrontational, she would feel less stressed and then be more comfortable about attending school.

The father diplomatically summarizes the interaction, suggesting that "If our daughter attended school, perhaps my wife would be less confrontational; if my wife were less confrontational, perhaps our daughter would attend school." The mother and daughter sit quietly.

The therapist asks about exceptions to the rule—times when the daughter does manage to get to school; times when the mother and daughter have a non-confrontational conversation. Both mother and daughter agree that their relationship was nonconfrontational prior to the boyfriend. The daughter contends that she is able to get to school when there is a test. The therapist shows surprise, gives praise that she is able to do this, and asks the daughter to elaborate further.

Finally, the therapist asks each of them the *miracle question;* namely, "When you go to sleep tonight, imagine that a miracle happens, but because you were sleeping you were not aware of it. The miracle is that, when you wake up, you will no longer have the problem that brought you to therapy. Upon awaking, what will be the first sign to you that a miracle has happened?" For the mother, it is her daughter going to school and having meaningful conversations with her; for the daughter, it is hearing laughter in the house and everyone talking to one another in a tension-free environment; for the father, it is getting a job (he is currently unemployed and, to the therapist, looks depressed). The therapist then asks them to rate on a scale from 1 to 10, with 10 representing their miracle, how close they are to achieving that miracle.

The therapist takes a consulting break and returns to the family with a list of compliments, normalizations, reframes, and a task. The task is that each of them is to choose a special day in which he or she will pretend that they have achieved their miracle. It will be the task of the other two to guess which day was the special day for each of them.

Theory Base and Basic Tenets

Beyond Milton Erickson

SFBT, similar to strategic (Haley, 1976), structural (Minuchin, 1974), and communication therapies (Satir, 1964), derives its roots from the teachings of Milton Erickson. All of these therapies have in common the use of joining, normalization, reframing, paradox, systems focus, nonpathologizing, focus on small change, and brief number of sessions. SFBT, however, differs from these other therapies in two major aspects. Whereas in these other therapies the therapist is the expert who directs the client toward resolution of a problem, SFBT, on the other hand, views the client as the expert, with the therapist assisting the client in the construction of the solution (de Shazer 1985, 1988; O' Hanlon & Weiner-Davis, 1989; Walter & Pellar, 1992). In other words, clients possess all of the building materials (strengths), the therapist helps them decide what they want to build (solution), and then helps them to build it. De Shazer (personal communication, September 15, 1985) explains that one can follow in the footsteps of Milton Erickson, or one can stand on his shoulders and see what lies beyond. In other words, one can improve on what Erickson started.

This notion of improvement lends a dynamic structure to SFBT. A group of students once asked de Shazer what they should read in order to prepare to learn SFBT. De Shazer said, "Read what I have yet to write" (personal communication, September 15, 1985). The best one can do, however, is to read what he has recently written. As an illustration, if one were to read de Shazer's (1985) earlier works, where he discusses skeleton keys, where one key (solution) can fit many different locks (problems), this would not be as consistent with his later works. De Shazer's (1997) more current idea, that problems and solutions are not related, may make the use of the key obsolete. In other words, SFBT is a continuously evolving treatment method in which some earlier tenets can later become obsolete.

Miracle Question Is the Heart

A tenet not likely to become obsolete is the miracle question. It could be said that the miracle question is the heart of SFBT. In other words, "When you go to sleep tonight, imagine that a miracle happens, but because you were sleeping you were not aware of it. The miracle is that, when you wake up, you will no longer have the problem that brought you to therapy. Upon awaking, what will be the first sign to you that a miracle has happened?"

The miracle question has strong theoretical underpinnings in the works of Polak (1973), Toffler (1974), and Frankl (1963). These researchers conclude that, when people have a positive vision of their future, they will succeed, and without a vision, they will fail.

Polak sought to discover why some nations survive and others perish. He found that this had no relationship to the size, wealth, strategic location, or resources. Nations that had a powerful vision of their future (Constitution, Magna Carta, Declaration of Independence) survived; those without perished.

Toffler's writings inspired teachers to discover which students excelled in life and which students failed. They found that high GPAs, high scores on standardized tests, and upbringing in advantaged families (with wealth, education, and resources) were not keys to success. Rather, they found that those students with positive visions of their future (strong goals of what they wanted to accomplish in their lives) were the students who would be successful.

Finally, Frankl found that prisoners who survived the concentration camp experience were not those who were the youngest and healthiest. Rather, he found it was those prisoners who had something important yet to accomplish in their lives who survived. They had positive visions of their future.

The purpose of the miracle question in SFBT is for the client, with the help of the therapist, to build a positive vision of the client's future. This is a future in which the presenting problems do not exist and in which they would derive additional positive experiences not present in their current lives. This positive vision of the future, therefore, becomes the motivating factor for clients to improve their lives. According to Polak, Toffler, and Frankl, without it, one will fail; with it, one will attain success.

Cup Is Half Full

When clients present with problems, these problems have become the major focuses of their lives. They have for all intents and purposes stopped focusing on any positive experiences in their lives. SFBT therapists believe that a cup that is half empty is a cup that is half full. Clients have been focusing on the empty part; it is the work of the therapist to refocus their attention on the full part. Take for example the coping question: "Given all of these difficulties in your life, how are you able to cope?" This changes the focus from problem talk to solution talk (the positives in their lives). The formula first-session task from the case assessment is also an example of refocusing the client toward the positives (de Shazer & Molnar, 1984).

Language Constructs Reality

SFBT places a great deal of significance on the use of language. Sentences are constructed in such a way as to create an alternative future. For example, "When the problem is solved, what will you be doing differently?" *When* is used instead of *If* in order to suggest a positive future to the client. This use of language is consistent with Erickson's use of hypnotherapy. De Shazer, however, contends that this same suggestive state can be reached through the proper choice of words rather than through formal induction. In fact, de Shazer (1994) more recently wrote a book *Words Were Originally Magic*, describing how the German philosopher, Ludwig Wittgenstein (1974), unraveled Bertrand Russell's (1959) problems of philosophy (we can know nothing for sure), by focusing on words when used in context (creates meaning), and words when used out of context (creates problems), with context being the key. In other words, Russell's asking how we can "know" anything for sure takes the word *know* out of the context in which it is normally used. Wittgenstein argued that Russell makes the question unanswerable. Wittgenstein's asking if we "know" our name uses the word *know* in context and makes the question answerable. Example:

> *Therapist:* "How do things need to change in order to make you happy?"
>
> *Client:* "I can never be happy, because I am a *depressed person*."
>
> *Therapist:* "Then what needs to happen to make you *less depressed*?"

Finally, on the use of language, Berg and DeJong (1996) suggest using "hedging" words. They contend that using words such as *seems, might,* and *perhaps* seeds suggestions in one's mind that later grow to fruitful solutions. For example, "It seems that perhaps you might change too fast."

Treatment Goals

In an ideal SFBT setting, the therapist meets with the family in front of a two-way mirror. The family signs consent forms agreeing to be videotaped and observed by a two-member consulting team on the other side of the mirror. In the room is a telephone that can be used by the team to call the therapist with questions to ask the family. In addition, the family is informed that, after approximately 45 minutes, the therapist will leave the room, consult with the team, and return with some recommendations.

To illustrate a classical SFBT treatment process, a prototype can be illustrated in three sessions.

Session 1

The therapist is initially searching for the "customer." This is the person who is most motivated toward change. Because motivation and other characteristics indicative of the client constitute 40 percent of why clients get better (Garfield, 1994), it is worth the small effort. It is, in fact, this person who will ensure that change in the system occurs. Often this is the person who initiates the phone call for treatment. It may be the person who speaks first in a session. One way to be sure is to ask the family, "Who is most concerned about resolving this problem? Who is second? Who is third?"

Next the therapist listens to the clients, using the basic counseling skills of establishing rapport, empathy, joining, reflection, and summarization, to name a few. As the therapist listens, however, he or she waits for an end to the different problems, repeats the list of all the difficulties, and then asks the client the coping question: "Given all of these problems [list them], how are you able to cope?" The purpose is to move from problem talk to solution talk. If clients change their tone to being more positive, are able to elaborate at least a few, if not several, strengths, and continue on this positive trend, the therapist has set the stage for change. If the client, however, cannot sustain solution talk and keeps going back to the problem, then the therapist goes back to the problem.

If solution talk is enabled, the therapist moves to the miracle question. When the first session is going well, much of the focus will be on the miracle. The therapist will encourage the family to expound on the miracle. For example, "After the miracle happens, what will you notice first? What will you notice next? What will your spouse notice?"

Once the miracle question is elaborated, the therapist asks the scaling question to gauge how close they are to achieving their miracle. If a client says they are at a 5, the therapist expresses praise in that they are halfway there. Next the therapist asks what has to happen for them to move from a 5 to a 6. If the client says that is too far a move, the therapist asks about moving from a 5 to a 5.1.

Finally, the therapist takes a consulting break, whether he or she has a team behind the two-way mirror or not, and comes back with a prescription (recommendation). The therapist starts with compliments, normalizations, and reframes. The formula first-session task is then prescribed: "When people enter therapy, they begin to change. There are things in your life, however, that you do not want to change because they are positive. So, between now and the next time we meet, pay attention to those positive things in your life, and we will discuss them next week."

Session 2

The therapist begins by repeating the first-session task and asking the clients what they found. When the clients mention positive changes, the therapist amplifies (encourages the clients to elaborate) these changes. For example, if the clients say they went to a movie, the therapist asks, "Is this a new behavior? How do you explain it? How were you able to do it? How can you continue to keep it happening?" If the clients say nothing is positive and puzzled prompting does not help ("Nothing!?" "Are you sure!?"), the therapist meticulously unravels every detail of the family's activities that occurred since leaving the therapist's office the week before. Positive changes will surface.

Assuming that this session focused primarily on positive changes, the therapist again asks the scaling question, comparing it to last week's. Invariably, it usually goes up; at the worst, it stays the same. If it were to go down, the therapist would ask, "What did you do to keep it from going further down?"

Finally, the therapist takes a consulting break. When the therapist returns, the family is again given compliments, normalizations, and reframes. The formula second-session task is then prescribed: "Progress is often two steps forward and one step back. If you find yourself taking a step back this week, pay attention to what you do to keep moving forward again."

Session 3

The therapist begins by repeating the second-session task. If there were steps back, the therapist asks, "What did you do to move forward again? How were you able to do this? It must have been difficult, but somehow you were able to do it. How will you continue to do this in the future?" In this fashion, the therapist continues to address all of the steps back, one step at a time. For issues where steps back were not taken, or if no steps back were taken, the therapist asks how they were able not to take a step back. It may be possible to close the case at this time or at least extend the time of the next visit.

Epilogue

As a final note, this is a prototypical treatment process. If clients do not feel bad about what is happening in their lives, it is doubtful that they will be in therapy. If the therapist is not sensitive and empathetic to the client's feelings, the client will not return. Although SFBT therapists do not encourage problem talk ("Tell me more about how the problem is interfering with your life") and elaboration of feelings ("Tell me more about how that made you feel"), it is a serious mistake to move from problem talk to solution talk until the client is ready. If these are feelings they have never expressed or stories they have never told, the SFBT does not move to solution talk until the client is ready. These are probably the most common reasons for a necessary and appropriate increase in sessions.

Application

Using this prototypical treatment process, this process can be customized for the previous family case assessment.

Session 1

In recalling the family case assessment, "How old is the daughter? What grade is she in at school? How many days a week does she miss school? How long have the parents been married? How long has the father been unemployed?" Some might argue that, for a family case assessment, the SFBT therapist missed a lot of critical information. However, if the family is the expert, how does it help the family if the therapist asks questions to which the family already knows the answers? In addition, because problems and solutions are not connected, why ask for information that is not relevant to the solution? These last two questions are consistent with an assessment by an SFBT therapist.

What the therapist does instead is attempt to find the customer. The customer is the person most concerned about the problem. It stands to reason, therefore, that the customer is the most motivated to solve the problem. The therapist helps join with the mother by allowing her to talk first, using her language ("little girl") and normalizing the situation ("difficult for mothers to lose their 'little girls' "). The normalization also begins to help make the unsolvable problem ("Where has my little girl gone?") a solvable problem (she is growing up). As long as the therapist joins with the mother, the mother will keep the family in therapy until it is mutually agreed to terminate.

After the mother has explained the situation, the daughter agrees that she should be in school. Because this is a solution introduced by the mother, the therapist encourages the daughter to discuss this further. In addition, the therapist wants the mother to hear why the daughter thinks she should be in school and the fact that the mother and daughter agree. Already the family has introduced some material that will become compliments during the recommendation or prescription segment. First, both the mother and the daughter agree on something. Second, the daughter is smart enough to realize that school is important. Third, the parents have raised an intelligent daughter.

When the father is asked for his perspective, he is able to briefly summarize the situation between the mother and the daughter. His awareness and diplomacy will also be material for compliments during the prescription segment.

Next the therapist asks about exceptions to the rule—times in the past or in the present when these problems did not exist or were easily solved. This is a source of solutions. It may be discovered that the family had solutions in the past but has forgotten them. Because the family is the expert, the therapist is using the resources of the family. In addition, exceptions to the rule tell the family how the circumstances need to be different in order for the solution to emerge (goes to school when she has a test). The daughter's ability to understand the importance of taking tests can also lead to a compliment during the prescription segment.

Because the family members are able to talk about positives in their lives and to voice positive things about one another, the therapist can introduce the miracle question. If the members reject the question ("Miracles don't happen." "I cannot think of anything."), then it may be that the question was asked too soon. The therapist needs to continue with problem talk. Another explanation is that a client does not entertain the possibility of miracles. In that case, the therapist could ask, "If you were very lucky" or "If you won the lottery," for example. Generally, the client's mood state is perhaps the best indicator of when it is time to ask the miracle question. In this case assessment, the family members are able to elaborate their miracle. If there are similarities in their miracles (the daughter's hearing laughter), this becomes a possible compliment for the prescription section.

To determine how close family members are to achieving their miracle, a scaling question is asked. If a family member says they are at a 5, the therapist expresses praise in that they are halfway there (all the numbers can be defined in a positive way). Even at a 1 (although there are techniques for never getting a 1 as a response), the clients can be told that they are on track toward their miracle or that they are in the game. Next, the therapist asks what has to happen for them to move from a 5 to a 6. If the clients say that is too far a move, the therapist asks about moving from a 5 to a 5.1. In the case assessment, the mother says she is at a 5, so the therapist expresses encouragement that the mother is halfway to her miracle; the daughter is at a 6, so the therapist expresses encouragement that she is over halfway there; the father is at a 5, so he is also encouraged. All of these rankings, of course, provide further material for the prescription section.

Finally, the therapist takes a consulting break, meets with the team to write a prescription, and then returns to the family to administer the prescription. This break is consistent with the suggestible state achieved in Ericksonian hypnotherapy. When the therapist leaves the room, the family is wondering what the therapist and the consulting team will have to say upon their return. De Shazer (1985) believes that this puts the family in a susceptible state, thus making them more receptive to the prescription. Keeping in mind the case assessment, the prescription may sound like the following (except that the client's names would be used):

Prescription

"Mother, the team agrees with you that it is difficult for a parent to see a daughter grow up and wonder where their little girl has gone. A child who was once easy to talk with becomes a daughter who now seems like a stranger. This must be very hard for you. The team is impressed with your hard effort and dedication to deal with this situation."

"Daughter, the team sees your difficulty in juggling school, family responsibilities, and a social life. It seems early for someone your age to try to do this on your own, but given how bright you are and your potential, we can see why you are trying. It seems that you must have inherited your hard effort and dedication from your mother."

"Father, your diplomatic way of looking at the situation between your wife and daughter is impressive. You manage to stay neutral, and by doing so, you may become the diplomat between your wife and daughter."

"Parents, the team congratulates you on raising such an intelligent daughter. She is aware of the importance of school. Few children her age are intelligent enough to understand how important school is to their future."

"All of you have formed miracles that consider not only your own happiness, but also the happiness of the other family members. Mother, your daughter's going to school; daughter, hearing laughter in the house; father, obtaining a job. All of these situations bring happiness to your family. In addition, all of you are already halfway or more to achieving your miracle. Although achieving miracles is not easy, this family possesses the hard work and dedication that is needed to achieve miracles."

"Finally, we want to give each of you a homework assignment. Each of you chooses a special day in which you will pretend that you have moved up your scale one point. For mother and father, that means you have moved from a 5 to a 6; for daughter, that means you have moved from a 6 to a 7. You cannot tell the other two what day you have chosen as your special day. It will be the additional task of the other two to guess which day you chose as your special day."

Session 2

The therapist enters the room, sits down, and notices that the family members are smiling. The mother is dressed more relaxed than in the last session (jeans rather than suit); the daughter and husband are dressed more neatly (new jeans rather than ripped jeans).

The therapist starts by asking about the task. The mother begins by explaining how she got up in the morning, went to the kitchen to make breakfast, and had an enjoyable conversation with her husband and daughter, who in reality were still in bed. When the daughter came home late, she made believe that her daughter and boyfriend were out buying her a gift, and it caused them to be late. When she watched a movie, she told her daughter and husband all about it as if they were interested. The mother said that it was fun. The therapist praised the mother for her creativity. The daughter and father told similar stories, with the father "cracking jokes" and making the mother and daughter laugh (for real, not pretend). Not surprisingly, they were able to identify each family member's special day.

The mother and father went on a date that included dinner and a movie. The daughter smiled, turning to look at both of them, as they told their story. The therapist showed encouragement and asked, "Is that different for the two of you to go on a date? What did you both do to make it happen? How will you continue to keep it happening in the future?" After exhausting all the material regarding the date, the therapist asked, "Are there other positive changes that occurred in the past week?"

The daughter smiles and explains that she has gone to school every day. The therapist gives encouragement and asks, "Wow, how were you able to do that?" The daughter explains that she knows the importance of school.

The father explains that he is willing to take a temporary or part-time job until something better comes along. The therapist gives encouragement and asks, "Is that new for you? Your willingness to look for a part-time job until a full-time job comes along?" He states that, yes, it is new for him.

Finally, the therapist asks them to remember when they rated how close they were to achieving a miracle on a scale from 1 to 10. The therapist then says to the mother, "Last week you were at a 5—more than halfway to achieving your miracle. Where are you now?" The mother says that she is at a 6. The therapist gives encouragement, asks the father and daughter the same question, and finds that each has moved up their scales by one point.

Epilogue

The family was complimented and given the formula second-session task, regarding progress being two steps forward and one step back. At session 3 they continued to show improvement (school attendance, conversations, dates), so a fourth session was scheduled for two weeks later, at which time the therapy ended.

Application to Spirituality

Spirituality, morality, ethics, and religion commonly have different definitions, depending on who is using the word. In SFBT, these concepts become important to therapy only if they are important to the client. Because the therapist is attempting to learn the culture, the language, and the clients' vision of a positive future, the therapist learns the clients' view of these concepts only if the clients believe that they are necessary for a positive solution.

As an example, a client with AIDS said, "I am so angry that I am going to f**k everyone at the bar." The client has introduced an ethical, moral, religious, or spiritual issue, depending on the client's definition. It relates to the "cup half empty" approach. The cup half empty for this client is to use his disease to harm others; the cup half full is to use his disease to help others. The SFBT therapist's response was "And how will this help you?" The client looked puzzled and said, "Well, it won't help me." This nonconfrontational stance tends to puzzle the client, who may have instead expected the therapist to take a confrontational posture. With nothing to fuel the anger, the anger dissipates. Seeing the cup half full and being nonconfrontational, therefore, are ways to deal with spiritual issues.

In a similar case, another client with AIDS who was asked by the therapist, "And how will this help you?" instead replied, "I'll feel better." The therapist then asked, "When will you stop feeling better?" (future orientation). The client looked puzzled and said, "When I feel guilty for what I did." The therapist replied, "So what could you do instead—that, instead of making you feel guilty, it 'might' make you feel proud? And it would keep you feeling better?" The client said, "Help them not to make the same mistake that I did." *Might* is used as a hedging word, in order to suggest the word *proud* to the client, because the client had not used the word. It makes the client more amenable to the word. This future orientation is leading toward the miracle question, in which spiritual issues may play a part in the miracle construction.

Later, both clients spoke of getting involved in social change as a way of helping others affected by the AIDS virus ("How will this help you?" became "How will this help others?"). The therapist complimented the clients on their evolving "social consciousness." One client responded that he had never considered himself "religious" (which he defined as following the teachings of an organized religion) but did consider himself "spiritual" (he defined this as believing that there is something out there greater than humanity). The therapist used this to compliment the client in the delivery of the prescription, stating that "As you find your body becoming less healthy, you will find your mind, on the other hand, becoming more healthy. Or, as you would say, more 'spiritual.' " (Both the therapist and the client were aware of the effect of the virus on the brain; therefore, "healthy mind" was not misconstrued to mean that the virus would leave the brain.)

This movement from expressing the desire to harm others toward a spiritual desire to help others assisted these clients in finding meaning in their lives. This meaning helped them deal with end-of-life issues.

Interventions

Joining

This is basically the therapist's means of establishing rapport with the family. Initially, the SFBT finds the customer and ensures that the therapist joins with the customer. Sometimes small talk is engaged in before the session begins, as a way of breaking down formality and giving an indirect compliment. For example, "People sometimes have difficulty finding us. Did you find our location OK?" "It is often difficult to park around here. Were you able to find a spot OK?" Using the client's language (actual phrases that they use) is critical to joining with the family. When the family hears their words, they know you are listening. An SFBT takes the stance of being nonconfrontational. Clients may say that they are confused or puzzled by some information that seems inconsistent, but an SFBT never confronts. Finally, discarding the notion that clients "resist" (de Shazer, 1984) helps the therapist join with the clients. Berg (1995) states that even clients labeled as "involuntary" do not resist therapy. She contends that if they were "resisting" they would not be sitting in your office.

Normalizing

For clients, problems are issues that are not normal. It stands to reason, therefore, that if the therapist can suggest to the clients that the issue is normal, by definition it will cease to be a problem. For example, "How do you know this is rebellious behavior, and not just being a teenager?" Rebellious behavior is a problem; being a teenager is normal behavior.

Circular Question

People may act based on what they believe others think, rather than on what others are actually thinking. To unravel this mystery, an SFBT therapist might ask, "What do you think your mother thinks about your missing school?" The answer to this question helps the mother see how the daughter believes she views the situation. In our family case assessment, if the daughter were to say that she believes her mother sees her as stupid, this will likely lead to a compliment from the mother regarding the daughter's intelligence. It also helps to clear misunderstandings. A further level of difficulty to this type of questioning would be "What do you think your mother thinks *you* think about your missing school?" In essence, these types of questions help members understand how it is that other family members act in certain ways.

Coping Question

This question helps the family move from problem talk to solution talk. At a point in the session when it seems that the client has described all of his or her problems, this question can be used—basically, "Given all of these problems [list all of them], how are you able to cope?" If the client is able to mention positive aspects and is able to sustain this positive direction, he or she is becoming ready for the miracle question. If, on the other hand, the client has little to say or says some positives but keeps going back to the problems, then the therapist needs to continue to listen to the problems until the client is ready. It may be that positives cannot be discussed until the second session. When the therapist gives the task, it should be directed toward looking for positives (formula first-session task). This sets the stage for asking the miracle question in session 2.

Miracle Question

This question, as stated earlier, provides the client with a positive vision of the future. This vision becomes a motivating factor and a description of when therapy has been successful (when the miracle is reached or the family agrees that they are close enough). In other words "When you go to sleep tonight, imagine that a miracle happens, but because you were sleeping you were not aware of it. The miracle is that, when you wake up, you will no longer have the problem that brought you to therapy. Upon awaking, what will be the first sign to you that a miracle has happened?" One serious caution regarding the miracle question is that it must deal with the possible, never the improbable. For example, you would not say to an AIDS patient that the miracle is that he or she will no longer have AIDS. You would not say to a person in a wheelchair that the miracle is that he or she will be able to walk. Instead, you would say to each of these individuals that the miracle is that he or she will be able to *cope* with AIDS or *cope* with being in a wheelchair.

Scaling Question

This question is used to gauge a baseline and measure progress in a behavior, goal, or construct—essentially, "On a scale from 1 to 10, with 1 being that you are so depressed you can't even leave your house, given that you are at least at a 2 and that 10 would be that you are so happy that you don't need to see me any more, how would you rate your level of happiness?" This example includes a means of not having the client say they are at a 1, and it changes the scale to one of happiness, which may not work for all clients (those who believe that they can never be happy). If a client says he or she is at a 1, you can mention how he or she is on the track to success or in the game toward happiness, for example. At 2, they are almost halfway to being halfway there; at 3 they are halfway to being halfway there;

at 4 they are almost halfway there; at 5 they are halfway there; at 6 they are over halfway there; and so forth. Obviously, other comments can be made to represent the numbers. When a client gives a number on the scale, the therapist then asks what has to happen to move up one number. If a whole number is too large a move for the client, then decimal places can be used (from a 5 to a 5.1). You will get an answer.

Exceptions to the Rule

This is a team search between the therapist and the client to discover solutions to a problem that either the client forgot or never considered using for a different problem. For example, "Was there a time in your life when this problem did not occur? When was the last time the problem did not happen? In the time that the problem has surfaced, has there been a time when you have been able to stop the problem from occurring? Have you had problems in the past that were similar to this problem? How were you able to stop those problems from happening?"

Formula Tasks

These are the tasks that are suggested at the end of an SFBT session as the final part of the prescription. The first session task tends to be "When people enter therapy, they begin to change. There are things in your life, however, that you do not want to change because they are positive. So, between now and the next time we meet, pay attention to those positive things in your life, and we will discuss them next week." Other first-session tasks might include "Do not change anything" or "Do something different." All of these tasks accept the assumption that the client is the expert and therefore can find a solution to the problem. The traditional task encourages the family to make changes. "Do not change anything" is more vague and suggests that they can keep it from getting worse and therefore can at some point make it better. "Do something different" encourages the family to find a solution. Whatever it is that they do differently may in fact resolve the problem.

The second session task tends to be "Progress is often two steps forward and one step back. If you find yourself taking a step back this week, pay attention to what you do to keep moving forward again." Another possibility is "Pay attention to what you do when you overcome the urge to [engage in that behavior]." Both of these tasks are encouraging the client to pay close attention to the solution. The first option provides the additional value of normalizing or reframing relapse. If there is a step back, some families disregard any progress made at that point—"It's right back to the way it used to be." By acknowledging that we do take steps back, this is reframed as part of progress and as an acceptable route toward progress. In addition, sometimes families progress quickly, and members worry or express a fear of relapsing. This task helps them. As a variation on this task, the therapist may suggest that the family take a step back in the next week. This becomes a no-lose situation. If they take a step back, they are following the normal route toward progress; if they do not take a step back, that is certainly positive.

Sometimes when a family is asked to take a step back, they will argue with the therapist, adamantly stating that they refuse to take a step back. That is certainly a positive sign.

Hypnotic Situations

These are situations that make the family more susceptible to what the therapist suggests. Previously it was discussed how the consultation break serves to make the family more susceptible to the prescription—namely, they are wondering what the team has to say. During the compliment segment of the prescription, the therapist attempts to produce a "yes set." If the family nods and agrees to several compliments in a row, they are more likely to agree to the next statement that follows. This may be a statement that the family has struggled to agree on during the session—for example, "Your daughter wants to go to school." Finally, the therapist may word a sentence in such a way that it comes out as a command rather than a suggestion—for example, "You may find that, as you look for exceptions, that you, *Matt, stop overeating*, you will make the right choices for yourself." The italicized words are said as a statement while looking directly at the client. The sentence is clumsy and another sentence follows, so the statement (hypnotic suggestion) is more hidden to the client.

The Team

When one has the luxury of working with a team, they become an invaluable source of intervention material. They may keep track of the client's pet phrases, possible compliments, and suggestions for a task. In addition, they can call you when you are meeting with a family and offer suggestions for change. Finally, they can allow the therapist to join with the family against the team—for example, "I agree with you. You should not take a step back. But the team thinks that you should." In this way the team can also parallel the struggles that the family is experiencing regarding the possibility of relapse.

Evaluation

Stalker, Levene, and Coady (1999) argue that SFBT has been adopted too quickly by human service professionals as a panacea for clients' problems. Addressing what they believe is an acceptance of an approach that has scant empirical research promoting its efficacy, they caution against the indiscriminate adoption of SFBT as the one solution to all problems. Finally, they recommend that students should be introduced to a wide variety of evidence-based treatment methods, to better prepare them to be successful in a multicultural, multiproblem environment.

Gingerich and Eisengart (2000), on the other hand, although not disputing the necessity of adhering to evidence-based therapies, reviewed all of the controlled outcome studies on SFBT (N = 15) up to and including 1999. They focused on studies employing some form of accepted experimental control (use of a comparison group or single-system design). Although all of these 15 studies met criteria for controlled outcomes, 5 studies were determined to be superior to the other 10 in terms of degree of experimental control. Those 5 studies will be reported here.

Sundstrom (1993) randomly assigned 40 female college students suffering from depression to one of two groups: SFBT group (n = 20) and interpersonal psychotherapy for depression group (ITP; N = 20). Using a MANOVA to determine differences in the two groups from pre to post on several standardized measures, Sundstrom found a statistically significant treatment effect for both groups from pre to post. Sunstrom did not, however, find any differences between groups. It was concluded, therefore, that SFBT is as effective as a well-established treatment for depression (ITP), but not superior to that treatment.

Zimmerman, Jacobsen, MacIntyre, and Watson (1996) compared 30 parents in an SFBT parenting group to 12 parents on a waiting list. A t-test was conducted to compare the two groups from pre to post on a number of standardized measures. Results indicated that there were more statistically significant differences in the SFBT group compared to the waiting-list group—namely, the SFBT group improved on parenting skills. It was noted, however, that due to self-selection and small samples, nonspecific effects could have been responsible for the success of the SFBT group.

Cockburn, Thomas, and Cockburn (1997) randomly assigned 48 orthopedic patients to one of four groups: groups 1 and 3 were SFBT plus standard rehabilitation; groups 2 and 4 standard rehabilitation only. ANOVAs were conducted to compare the groups on a number of standardized measures. Results indicated that there were statistically significant differences between the two SFBT groups and the two comparison groups. The SFBT groups improved on their ability to cope with their disability. In addition, and more importantly, the SFBT groups were able to return to work in a shorter period of time. This was a well-controlled study with impressive support of the efficacy of SFBT.

Lindforss and Magnusson (1997) randomly assigned 60 serious criminals with high recidivism rates to one of two groups: an SFBT group (N = 30) and a control group (N = 30). Comparing the two groups on recidivism rates, results indicated that the SFBT group had a lower recidivism rate compared to the control group (statistically significant), in addition to less serious offenses and shorter sentences for the SFBT reoffending prisoners compared to the control reoffending prisoners.

Seagram (1997) matched 40 adolescent offenders on severity of antisocial behaviors to form two groups: an SFBT group (N = 21) and a standard institutional care group (N = 19). Comparing the two groups on a number of standardized measures, Seagram reported several statistically significant findings for the SFBT group compared to the comparison group—namely, the SFBT group improved in prosocial behaviors. Improvements, however, were only modest.

Applications to Families on Levels I, II, and IV

Weltner's (1985) analogy for the issues of those families who might be considered at Level I is the basement of a house. These issues are life-and-death issues, such as housing and health care needs, and sufficient parenting to nurture and protect the family. The goal for intervention is to add resources. The Level II analogy is the foundation and refers to authority and limits within the family unit. At Level IV, the goal is "the development of an inner 'richness'—insight, more sensitive awareness of the relational world, an understanding of legacies and heritage" (p. 47). The utility of this approach in dealing with these issues has not been established. It is probable that this approach is more effectively used with issues at Level III than with those at Levels II and IV (Cleveland & Lindsey, 1999).

Summary

Solution-focused brief therapy (SFBT) stands in contrast to mainstream approaches, with its rejection of insight, problem-focused, detailed assessments, and expert stance. Rather, SFBT learns the language, culture, and expertise of the clients in order to assist them in constructing a positive vision of their future. Once this vision is formed, it becomes the task of the therapist to help lead the clients toward that vision from a stance that is one step behind. SFBT is more than the sum of its techniques. Once you look through SFBT lenses and see that resistance does not exist, that the cup is always half full, and that change is constant, you can never see the world as it used to be. The significance of this change is that you do not use SFBT, you become SFBT. The caution, however, is not to accept SFBT until you are convinced that it is right for you.

Discussion Questions _____

1. How can treatment be successful if the therapist does not know what the problem is that brought the family to therapy?

2. Because we do not have a clinical diagnosis for "normal," how do we know when a family no longer needs therapy?

3. How does language change perception?

4. How does a belief that resistance does not exist help the family?

5. How does SFBT respect cultural differences?

Suggested Readings _____

DeJong, P., & Berg, I. K. (1997). *Interviewing for solutions.* Belmont, CA: Brooks/Cole.
   Excellent resource for teaching solution-focused brief therapy to practitioners. Particularly valuable because the authors use the model with clients who are generally con-

sidered to be multiproblem, difficult, and unmotivated. In addition, the book has a companion student workbook and an instructor's manual (sold separately).

De Shazer, S. (1997). *Putting difference to work.* New York: Norton.

As with any of deShazer's books, these are more for the theoretician than for the clinician. This one is selected only because it is more recent than the others. Again, if you are interested in the theory of solution-focused brief therapy, any of de Shazer's books would be the logical choice.

Miller, G. (1997). *Becoming miracle workers: Language and meaning in brief therapy.* New York: Norton.

Written by an ethnomethodologist who for 12 years sat behind the team, who sat behind the mirror watching the therapist. A clinician will see therapy through different eyes; but, be warned, it is possible that one will never look at therapy the same way again.

Walter, J. L., & Pellar, J. E. (1992). *Becoming solution-focused in brief therapy.* New York: Bruner/Mazel.

If one is looking for an SFBT primer, this is it. The authors use common cases, explain the model clearly, and offer step-by-step instructions on how to do it.

References

Berg, I. K. (1995). *I'd hear laughter* [Film]. (Available from Brief Family Therapy Center, P. O. Box 13736, Milwaukee, WI 53213–0736).

Berg, I. K., & DeJong, P. (1996). Solution-building conversations: Co-constructing a sense of competence with clients. *Families in Society, 77,* 376–391.

Cleveland, P. H., & Lindsey, E. W. (1999). Solution-focused family interventions. In A. C. Kilpatrick & T. P. Holland (Eds.), *Working with families: An integrative model by level of need.* (2nd ed., pp. 139–154). Needham Heights, MA: Allyn and Bacon.

Cockburn, J. T., Thomas, F. N., & Cockburn, O. J. (1997). Solution-focused therapy and psychosocial adjustment to orthopedic rehabilitation in a work hardening program. *Journal of Occupational Rehabilitation, 7*(2), 97–106.

de Shazer, S. (1984). The death of resistance. *Family Process, 23,* 11–17.

de Shazer, S. (1985). *Keys to solution in brief therapy.* New York: Norton.

de Shazer, S. (Sept. 1985). Personal communication

de Shazer, S. (1988). *Clues: Investigating solutions in brief therapy.* New York: Norton.

de Shazer, S. (1994). *Words were originally magic.* New York: Norton.

de Shazer, S. (1997). *Putting difference to work.* New York: Norton.

de Shazer, S., Berg, I. K., Lipchik, E., Nunnally, E., Molnar, A., Gingerich, E., & Weiner-Davis, M. (1986). Brief treatment: Focused solution development. *Family Process, 25,* 207–222.

de Shazer, S., & Molnar, A. (1984). Four useful interventions in brief family treatment. *Journal of Marital and Family Treatment, 10*(3), 297–304.

Frankl, V. E. (1963). *Man's search for meaning.* Boston: Beacon Press.

Garfield, S. L. (1994). Research on client variables in psychotherapy. In A. E. Bergin & S. L. Garfield (Eds.), *Handbook of psychotherapy and behavior change.* (4th ed., pp. 190–228). New York: Wiley.

Gingerich, W. J., & Eisengart, S. (2000). Solution-focused brief therapy: A review of the outcome research. *Family Process, 39*(4), 477–498.

Haley, J. (1976). *Problem solving therapies.* New York: Grune & Stratton.

Lindforss, L., & Magnusson, D. (1997). Solution-focused therapy in prison. *Contemporary Family Therapy, 19,* 89–103.

Minuchin, S. (1974). *Families and family therapy.* Cambridge, MA: Harvard University Press.

O'Hanlon, W. H., & Weiner-Davis, M. (1989). *In search of solutions.* New York: Norton.

Polak, F. (1973). *The image of the future.* San Francisco: Jossey-Bass.

Russell, B. (1959). *The problems of philosophy.* Oxford: Oxford University Press.

Satir, V. (1964). *Conjoint family therapy*. Palo Alto, CA: Science and Behavior.

Seagram, B. C. (1997). The efficacy of solution-focused therapy with young offenders. Unpublished doctoral dissertation. York University, North York, Ontario, Canada.

Stalker, C. A., Levene, J. E., & Coady, N. F. (1999). Solution-focused brief therapy—One model fits all? *Families in Society: The Journal of Contemporary Human Services*, 468–477.

Sundstrom, S. M. (1993). Single-session psychotherapy for depression: Is it better to focus on problems or solutions? Unpublished doctoral dissertation. Iowa State University, Ames, IA.

Toffler, A. (1974). *Learning for tomorrow: The role of the future in education*. New York: Random House.

Walter, J. L., & Pellar, J. E. (1992). *Becoming solution-focused in brief therapy*. New York: Brunner/Mazel.

Weltner, J. (1985). Matchmaking: Choosing the appropriate treatment for families at various levels of pathology. In M. Marikin & S. Koman (Eds.), *Handbook of adolescents and family treatment*. New York: Gardner Press.

Wittgenstein, L. (1974). *Philosophical investigations*. Oxford: Basil Blackwell.

Zimmerman, T. S., Jacobsen, R. B., MacIntyre, M., & Watson, C. (1996). Solution-focused parenting groups: An empirical study. *Journal of Systemic Therapies, 15*(4), 12–25.

10

Family Systems Interventions

Joseph Walsh, Ph.D.

Since its introduction in the 1960s and 1970s, family systems theory has thrived as an influential and widely utilized theory of family assessment and intervention. The theory provides a comprehensive conceptual framework for understanding how *emotional ties* within families of origin (including extended family members) influence the lives of individuals in ways they often fail to appreciate and may tend to minimize. The theory is sometimes called *family emotional systems* theory to underscore this point and to distinguish it from the generic *family systems* term. This theory is unique in its attention to multigenerational family processes and also in its prescriptions for working with individuals in a family context (Bowen, 1978; Kerr & Bowen, 1988).

Murray Bowen, creator of the theory, was trained as a psychoanalyst. This helps to explain why family systems theory has implications for the treatment of individuals as well as families. The nature of healthy human functioning in the theory includes the acquisition of a *balance* of emotion and reason. The concept of *differentiation* is used to characterize one's ability to achieve this balance. The concept also describes one's ability to function effectively both apart from and within the family of origin. Differentiation is made possible by a facilitative family environment in which the person can establish an identity related to, but also separate from, the identity of the nuclear family. This is primarily an "objective" self, a bias that further reflects analytic influences on Bowen's thinking.

Within most cultures of American society, people typically accelerate the processes of physically and emotionally separating from their family of origin during late adolescence. This is a major life transition for those who leave and for those who stay behind. According to family systems theory, people who have achieved differentiation will be successful in this transition, and those who have not (or are *enmeshed*) will have difficulty. One's capacity to develop positive new relationships in adulthood is affected by learned patterns of managing family-of-origin relationships. In every case, positive or negative, the influence of the family is pervasive throughout life.

Needs Presented by Level III Families

As discussed in Chapter 1, families come to the attention of clinical practitioners for a variety of reasons. Their concerns may be related to a lack of material resources, family crisis or disorganization, relationship difficulties, or a desire for greater self-actualization. The concepts from family systems theory may be useful to the practitioner with families at *all* levels of need as a means of assessing the nature of family interactions. Understanding the quality of family relationships, a hallmark of this theory, may be significant in treatment planning regardless of the family's specific needs. The intervention strategies suggested by family systems theory, however, are not appropriate for all problem situations.

Family systems interventions are generally appropriate when the focus will be on the quality of nuclear or extended family interpersonal processes and on the desire for one or more family members to become more differentiated. Level III families often appear to be functioning well to the outside observer. It is their interpersonal lives, including issues of boundaries, enmeshment, and emotional distance, that are the sources of their problems. These processes may be evidenced in a variety of presenting problems that represent too much or too little investment of some members in family activities, relationships, and well-being. The practitioner will require some structural stability in the family to help members become aware of their patterns of behavior that may be contributing to problem situations.

Titelman (1998) has edited a book that includes examples of a range of problems for which family systems interventions may be appropriate. These include family problems related to marital fusion, emotional dysfunction in children, a child with a medical problem, college students with adjustment problems, concerns about elderly members, depression, phobias and obsessive compulsive disorder, alcoholism, incest, divorce, and remarriage.

Assessment

What follows are the major concepts of family systems theory that are central to the process of assessment. These are drawn primarily from Bowen (1978).

The Multigenerational Perspective

One of Bowen's greatest contributions to the field of family theory was his principle that individual personalities and patterns of interaction among family members have their origins in previous generations. Additionally, he demonstrated that extended family relationships might be as important to personal development as nuclear family relationships. In these ways Bowen foreshadowed recent developments in the field of family therapy, of moving beyond the nuclear family unit into a consideration of other influences on family life.

Bowen recommended a three-generation assessment of families, partly because of realistic limits on the availability of information and also because of his early career work with families who included a member with schizophrenia. His schizophrenia research in the late 1950s focused on 14 families whom he studied for time periods of six months to three years (Bowen, 1959; Dysinger & Bowen, 1959; Howells & Guirguis, 1985). Bowen concluded that the type of family anxiety that results in one member's developing schizophrenia required three generations to unfold. In his sample, the first generation's parents were relatively mature, but the child acquired their combined immaturity, manifested as anxiety and fusion. The same process repeated in the next generation produced sufficient emotional fusion for schizophrenia to develop. Bowen is criticized for being one of a group of influential family theorists who produced literature blaming the development of schizophrenia on parents. It is now understood that schizophrenia is largely biological. Still, Bowen's work of that time was helpful to family therapists for understanding the manner in which anxiety can be passed down through generations.

The practitioner does not have to have information about three generations to effectively provide family interventions. Family structures are more diverse and fragmented today than they have ever been in American life. Clinical practitioners experience reconstituted families, dissolving families, single parent families, and gay and lesbian families. Geographic mobility is such that many people have limited awareness of their blood or territorial origins. It is always important to acquire as much information as possible about nuclear, extended, and cross-generation family relationships, but the practitioner can proceed with whatever data are available. In fact, the trend in family systems theory in the past 20 years has been developing strategies to work with families with a focus on only one generation (Titelman, 1998).

Differentiation of Self

Healthy or adaptive individual functioning is characterized by *differentiation of self*. This is a key concept in family systems theory which has two meanings. First, it represents a person's capacity to distinguish between and balance his or her *thinking* and *feeling* selves. Both aspects of experience are important. The thinking process represents one's ability to detach from, or look objectively at, personal reactions or biases. Emotional processes provide important information about the significance of the situation. The "total" human experience involves both emotion and reason.

The term also refers to the ability of an individual to *physically* differentiate from his or her family of origin in a manner that preserves aspects of those emotional ties while not being constrained by them. Differentiation is thus a characteristic not of a person, but of a relationship. The person develops the capacity to maintain a balance in being separate self and maintaining old and new emotional ties.

In some ways it is ironic that family systems theory provides such a rich understanding of the emotional lives of people within their families, because it emphasizes the importance of reason in the formulation of "health." This is consistent with the psychodynamic theory in which Bowen was initially trained. It is the function of the ego to "tame" the drives, or channel them into healthy outlets. Highly charged emotional interactions can cloud one's ability to appropriately separate his or her feelings from those of others and to have an independent existence. Bowen felt that it was important for one's reasoning ability to develop so that it could keep emotional experience from becoming the only basis on which decisions are made.

Triangles

In family systems theory, the interpersonal *triangle* is the primary unit of analysis. All intimate relationships are inherently unstable; they require the availability of a third party to maintain their stability. On first glance this might seem to be a paradoxical notion, but it makes common sense. The price of intimacy in any relationship is the experience of occasional conflict. People cannot exist in harmony all the time. When in conflict, people usually rely on a third person (different third persons, depending on the circumstances) for mediation, ventilation, or problem-solving assistance. This is a natural, healthy process. Serious problems related to one's differentiation may develop, however, when he or she is drawn into certain types of triangles within the family. When a "weaker" (undifferentiated) person is drawn into a triangle in a way that does not facilitate the original two people's resolving their conflict, the person may be deprived of the opportunity to become a unique individual. He or she may assume the ongoing role of helping the other two people avoid their problems with each other. Problematic triangulation in families occurs when conflicted adults draw in weaker family members, often the children, to maintain the stability of their relationship.

Anxiety and the Nuclear Family Emotional System

Anxiety is an unpleasant but normal and functional affect that provides people with warning signs for perceived threats (Marks, 1987). Its symptoms include tension and nervous system hyperactivity. An anxiety-producing situation may be perceived as an opportunity for growth or as a threat to well-being. Anxiety becomes problematic when it interferes with one's capacity for problem solving. The concept of anxiety is central to psychodynamic theory, and Bowen adapted it to family systems theory. Family systems feature levels of anxiety, just as individuals do.

The nuclear family emotional system includes four relationship patterns that may foster problem development (Georgetown Family Center, 2001). With *marital conflict*, each spouse projects his or her anxiety onto the other and attempts to control the other person. With the *problematic emotional functioning* of one spouse, the other spouse makes accommodations to preserve relationship harmony but may develop heightened anxiety as a result. If one or more children exhibit a physical or emotional *functional impairment,* the parents will focus their anxieties on that child, who in turn may become emotionally reactive to them. With *emotional fusion,* family members distance themselves from one another to reduce the intensity of their relationships, and they may become isolated in the process.

A family system that is characterized by psychological tension for any of the above reasons may produce an atmosphere of anxiety that is shared by all of its members. As described earlier, this system anxiety can be passed on and increased through generations. An individual who is not differentiated experiences relatively high levels of tension in family relationships and will tend to be drawn to friends, spouses, and partners with similar levels of anxiety.

Parental Projection

Psychological defenses are processes by which people protect themselves from intolerable anxiety by keeping unacceptable impulses out of their awareness (Goldstein, 1995). Defenses are positive coping mechanisms when they help the person function effectively and do not significantly distort reality. Projection is a common defense mechanism, in which one person attributes to someone else his or her unacceptable thoughts and feelings. The projector is not aware of having the feelings or thoughts but believes instead that the person on whom they are projected is experiencing them. For example, a wife may feel anger toward her husband for spending too little time in the household. If she is threatened by the idea of being angry with her spouse, she may project that feeling onto a child. She may decide that the child is angry with the father and report that "fact" to her husband.

Projection may involve significant distortions of others' feelings, attitudes, and behaviors. Parents often use the defense of projection with their children as "targets," because children are vulnerable family members. Children tend to accept the pronouncements, insights, and beliefs of their parents. Within family systems, children may suffer if the parents project negative feelings and ideas onto them. They may believe that they possess the negative thoughts and feelings attributed to them, and behave as such. In family systems theory, parental projection is a major source of transmitted family anxiety.

Fusion and Emotional Cutoff

Emotional fusion is the opposite of differentiation of self. It is a shared state involving two or more people, the result of a triangulation in which one member sacrifices his or her striving toward differentiation in the service of balancing the relationship of two other people. When one person is emotionally fused with another, his or her emotional reactivity to the other person becomes strong. The person does not "think," but "feels," and does so in response to the emotional state of the other person. The feelings of the mother, for example, become those of the son. When she is happy, he is happy, and when she is sad, he is sad. The son does not have an emotional life apart from that of his mother. Neither person is consciously aware of this state because they lack the capacity to reason about or reflect on the situation. This happens because, for a significant length of time during childhood and adolescence, prior to having an opportunity to differentiate, the fused person began to serve an ongoing function within a triangle that served the needs of two other family members.

People tend not to have insight into the fact that they are fused, but they experience high levels of emotional reactivity to the other person and may attempt to extricate themselves from the relationship. A common strategy is the *emotional cutoff*. This term refers to a person's attempts to emotionally distance him- or herself from certain members of the family or from the entire family. Emotional cutoff is the result of a person's inability to directly resolve issues of fusion, which in turn prevents him or her from forming a unique identity or satisfying relationships with others.

In situations in which the family is living together, emotional cutoff may be characterized by physical avoidance of another person or, more commonly, not discussing emotionally charged topics. For example, a son in conflict with his mother may be pleased to talk about what happened at school, but they may avoid discussing how they feel about each other or the family. This pattern can continue after the family member leaves home. The son and mother may enjoy each other's company to an extent but have superficial interactions. The son may look for substitute families at work, at college, or at church.

Emotional cutoff is often seen in physical distance. Adolescents may be eager to leave home as a solution to their family problems. Again, this may represent a normal family transition. However, when distance alone is seen as a solution to ongoing family tensions, the person may be disappointed. A first-year college student may feel that he can at last become his own person, when in fact his fusion with another family member prevents him from fully experiencing other people. An important aspect of emotional cutoff is that the person experiencing it is usually not aware of the strength of the pull of the primary relationship. The process is denied or minimized.

Other Concepts

Bowen believed that *sibling position* within a nuclear family is a partial predictor of a child's personality development. For example, oldest children tend to be more responsible and conservative, whereas younger children are more sociable and rebellious. These differences are due in part to the constellations of triangles that exist in families of different sizes. Research during the past 10 years, however, has tended to dispel the notion that personality types can be validly predicted on the basis of family position alone (Brody, 1998). There are many other variables to be considered, including gender, number of years between siblings, innate temperaments, and the nature of external environments. Still, being alert to the different triangulation possibilities for each sibling is useful in assessing family systems.

The concept of *societal emotional processes* refers to the manner in which social systems can be conceptualized as similar to the family with regard to the rules that govern interpersonal behavior within and among them. Family systems concepts may be helpful for understanding these other systems. For example, the social service delivery system itself has been described as one-third of a triangle, along with participating individual members and the family, with implications for the differentiation and fusion of participants (Moore, 1990). The church congregation has also been conceptualized as a family (Howe, 1998). Each member's relationship patterns acquired in the family of origin may be replicated with the congregation, and it is this body from which the individual must strive for appropriate differentiation. Although interesting, the concept of societal emotional processes is not yet as well developed as those concepts that are specific to the family unit.

The Genogram

A major tool for assessment is the multigenerational *genogram*. This is a visual representation on one sheet of paper of a family's composition, structure, member characteristics, and relationships (Kerr & Bowen, 1988; McGoldrick, Gerson, & Shellenberger, 1999). It typically covers a span of three generations. Information provided on a genogram includes basic facts about family members (such as dates of birth and death, marriages, moves, and illnesses); the primary characteristics and levels of functioning of each member (education, occupation, health status, talents, successes, and failures); and relationship patterns among members (closeness, conflicts, and cutoffs). Overall family characteristics that may be assessed include structure (roles, rules, and boundaries) and the impact of life events, life transitions, and relationship patterns across generations. The advantage of the genogram as an assessment tool is its presentation of complex family data on one page. It is also an excellent means of eliciting family medical information (Sawin & Harrigan, 1995).

   Some practitioners may be reluctant to construct genograms at the level of detail suggested by family systems theory because it is time-consuming and may be annoying to clients who are eager to move into problem resolution activities (McGoldrick, 1996). Despite these concerns, it is important to understand that, in the first session, it engages all family members in the discussion and usually represents an interesting new way for them to think about the family system.

Assessment Questions

Having reviewed the core concepts of family systems theory and the nature of problems that it suggests, the following list of assessment questions for the clinical practitioner is offered:

- What are the family's current stresses? How are they expressed?
- What physical and emotional symptoms are evident in this family?
- How do the evident symptoms affect family relationships?
- What is the nature of this family's relationship system?
- How does the nuclear family interact with the extended family?

- How stable is the family now? How successfully does it handle anxiety?
- How well differentiated are the family members?
- What triangles exist in the family? Which are primary? Are they functional?
- Are any emotional cutoffs operating?
- How has the family handled stress historically?

Goals of the Intervention

The nature of change in family systems theory involves an *opening up* of the system (Kerr & Bowen, 1988). Presenting problems involve triangles, fusion, and emotional cutoff. Change requires detriangulation and new alliance building among members of the nuclear and extended family. The practitioner attends to the following goals:

- Lowering family system anxiety.
- Increasing the reflective capacity (insight) of all members.
- Promoting differentiation of self by emotionally realigning the family system (which includes the opening of closed relationships).
- Instilling member sensitivity to the influences of multigenerational family patterns.
- Enhancing habits of problem sharing.
- Redressing inequalities within the family by inhibiting dominant members.

Intervention Approaches

Family systems therapists do not work with a set of explicit, concrete intervention *techniques.* The theory offers instead intervention *strategies* with which the practitioner can design techniques in accordance with a family's particular concerns (Bowen, 1978; Kerr & Bowen, 1988). These are summarized below.

The Clinical Relationship

As a prerequisite to change, family members must experience the clinical setting as safe and comfortable, relatively free of the anxiety that tends to characterize their natural environment. The practitioner acts as a *coach.* He or she remains on the sidelines of family interaction, asking questions and making suggestions that the family members discuss and enact with each other. The practitioner strives to be the focus of the family's attention and to set the tone of their exchanges. He or she must be calm, promote an unheated atmosphere, and maintain professional detachment. The purposes of this posture are to avoid emotional reactivity and negative triangulation with family members. The practitioner also serves as a model for rational interaction.

In the early stages of intervention, the practitioner may ask family members to talk directly to him or her about sensitive issues, rather than to one another, to minimize interpersonal tensions. If tensions are so high that productive interactions cannot proceed, the practitioner can use *displacement stories* as a means of taking the family's focus off itself and giving it some distance from its own concerns. This is a technique in which the practitioner provides an example of a hypothetical family with processes and problems similar to those of the actual family. The practitioner asks the actual family to share observations and suggest interventions.

The Genogram

By participating in the construction of the genogram, family members gain insight into their family processes. They learn about interpersonal patterns and how triangles operate within the family. With these insights family members learn to appreciate that their behavior is related to larger systemic processes and the ways in which those processes support or inhibit member functioning. The process normalizes some family problems, particularly those related to transitions. Family members may become able to identify their own strategies to enhance family functioning. The genogram often stimulates a process of life review among older adults. Another way in which the genogram serves as an effective early intervention is that, during the construction, each member is observing a diagram rather than looking at others. This brings a shared focus to the discussion and displaces any negative feelings onto an object rather than onto another person.

Detriangulation

This represents any strategy by which the practitioner disrupts one triangle and opens up the family members to new, more functional alliances or triangles. There are many ways in which the worker can detriangulate the family (Guerin, Fogarty, Fay, & Kautto, 1996). He or she can shift alliances with tasks to be performed within the session or when members are at home. Within the session, the practitioner might encourage role reversals, or situations in which members interact with each other in different ways. A child who is accustomed to complaining to his mother about the annoying behavior of a sibling might be asked to confront the sibling. When a couple is triangled with a child as a means of avoiding issues in their relationship, they might be instructed to spend a certain amount of time together talking about whatever is on their minds that day. If they need the assistance of a third party to bring an issue to resolution, they might be encouraged to talk with a different adult family member. In these ways members are guided into new functional attachments with nuclear or extended family members. Any strategy that contributes to members' opening up the family to new attachments can be pursued. The practitioner should always encourage the development of new attachments that have the possibility of promoting a member's differentiation.

Increase Insight

Family systems theory shares with psychodynamic theory a belief that understanding can lead to change. The practitioner facilitates reflective discussions that promote insight about the effects of relationships on one's personality and behavior. Two techniques that promote insight are person–situation reflection, focused on the present, and developmental reflection, focused on the history of the person, the family, and its patterns (Woods & Hollis, 2000). Children and adolescents may appear to have a lesser capacity for reflection, but insight can be defined for them simply as understanding that one person's behavior always affects another person's feelings and behavior. Two related techniques that the practitioner might use are "externalizing the thinking," or helping each member put into words what is generally kept inside, and encouraging the "I" position. In the latter practice the practitioner asks each person to speak about his or her own thoughts and feelings, label them as such, and accept responsibility for them. This works against the tendencies of many clients to blame others for what they think and feel.

Education

Families often benefit from understanding that their patterns of interaction have sources in the family's history and that improving family life may involve "going backwards" to revisit relationships with various extended family members. This helps family members feel less confused and guilty about their behaviors. In teaching families about family system processes, the practitioner helps each member to observe the self within triangles and to examine behavior in terms of family themes. This also serves as a normalizing strategy for families who worry that they are uniquely dysfunctional or beyond help. The practitioner must decide when to integrate teaching moments with other interventions. The practitioner should always provide this information in terms that the family can understand.

Working with Individuals

This is a book about family intervention, but it must be mentioned that one of the strengths of family systems theory is its utility for working with any subset of a family or even with individual clients (Braveman, 1995). Family systems intervention requires an *awareness,* but not necessarily the presence, of all family members. In individual therapy, the practitioner can construct a genogram with the client and examine the client's behavior in terms of emerging family themes. The practitioner helps the client observe the self in triangles and then detriangulate by developing new or different relationships with family members who are available. The practitioner can also help the client develop insight and use this knowledge of the effects of family relationships to disrupt the repetitions of unsatisfactory relationship patterns with others.

Applications

Two examples of family systems intervention are described below. The first involves a family with marital conflict and substance abuse, and represents a two-generation intervention. The second example involves emotional fusion, the functional impairment of an adolescent member, and issues related to the adult children of elderly family members.

The Reeves Family

Although every family system is unique, some dynamics are common in families characterized by the alcohol abuse of an adult member. There is often an enmeshment, or codependency, of the adults. This pattern has its origins in the adults' families of origin (Bowen, 1991a; Prest, Benson, & Protinsky, 1998). Spouse interactions tend to be characterized by fusion, control and defiance patterns, inadequate conflict resolution habits, and tendencies for the negative triangulation of others (Scaturo, Hayes, Sagula, & Walter, 2000). The nonalcoholic spouse may be overresponsible. This is a form of pursuit that diverts the person away from his or her own self by focusing instead on the behavior of another person. It features boundary crossing and an avoidance of issues central to the relationship. The alcohol may keep the couple's focus away from core relationship issues.

There are common patterns of triangulation in alcoholic families. One child becomes a "hero." Typically the oldest child, the hero stabilizes the family as his or her responsible behavior ensures that no additional problems occur in the system. The hero becomes the pride of each parent and a refuge from their conflicts. Such a child may be detached from his or her feelings. The "scapegoat" is the child whose negative behaviors divert others in the family from the problem of alcoholism. This person acts out and is often in trouble. Substance abuse may be among this child's problems. The parents are often upset with the scapegoat, but they need the negative behaviors to maintain their façade of cohesion. The "lost" child copes with family anxiety by separating him or herself from the family, emotionally and perhaps physically. Although this may seem to be a healthy strategy, the lost child is empty, undifferentiated, and without a stable sense of self on which to build an independent life. Finally, the "mascot" also diverts the couple's attention from each other but is more of an entertainer or clown. This person is well liked in the family but is superficial and seems immature. The parents resist the mascot's efforts to grow up.

Marcia was the identified client of the Reeves family. She was 22, living at home, working part time, and attending community college. She was referred for individual therapy following a short-term hospitalization for depression. Marcia had been anxious, crying frequently, and failing her courses. She admitted to feelings of dread about finishing school but added that it wasn't "right" to feel that way. Her stated goals were to finish school and then get her own apartment and full-time job in the business field. Marcia was likable and had a good sense of humor. She said her family had always been supportive of her. She got along particularly well with her father, the only child to do so.

The practitioner, whose agency encouraged work with individuals, did not meet with the family for several months, but he eventually came to know them all (see Figure 10.1). Mr. Reeves, 53, owned Reeves Roofing Services, a successful local business. The family was financially well off. He was an alcohol abuser with daily heavy drinking and generally kept to himself. He verbally berated his wife of 31 years when angry, often within earshot of the children. Mr. Reeves was a domineering man who intimidated his family. Mrs. Reeves, 51, was attractive and sociable, but passive and prone to anxiety. She voiced no complaints about her family. She was nurturing of the children and bought them gifts frequently. She talked with them about anything but their emotional lives.

There were three other children. Carolyn, 24, was married and had a 2-year-old daughter. She was in contact with the family mostly on formal occasions, such as holidays, but also during family crises. She saw her role in the family as that of a peacemaker. She became frustrated with her siblings and parents whenever conflicts developed. Patrick, 20, worked for his father as a manager and lived with

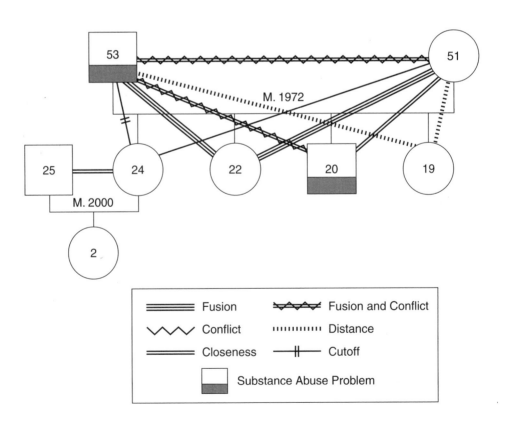

FIGURE 10.1 *The Reeves Family*

friends. He had been the "problem child" in the past, engaging in substance abuse and oppositional behavior. Dad had bailed him out of trouble many times. Patrick was loyal to the family but not close to any of them. He and dad were often in conflict, but since he moved out of the house they experienced less friction. Kathleen, 19, lived with a cousin and attended modeling school. She was attractive and socially sophisticated. She had been away from home for most of the past three years, attending boarding schools. She was popular, independent, and talented. She was a favorite of her mother, who was impressed with her career direction and personal style. Kathleen tended to be parental with her sister Marcia.

Interventions

The practitioner's assessment of Marcia included an exploration of her coping style, dependency issues, and the circumstances of her depression. He suggested that Marcia keep a diary of her emotional experiences to help her become aware of any patterns to her stresses and mood cycles. He helped Marcia, through graduated tasks, to resume her previous level of part-time school, part-time work, and social interaction with friends and family. The psychiatrist prescribed antidepressant medications for Marcia but supported counseling as the primary intervention. The practitioner quickly developed a close relationship with Marcia. Therapy intensified, focusing on developing Marcia's insight about her fears, lack of confidence, interpersonal patterns, and self-image.

When Marcia came to feel safe with the practitioner, she admitted that her goals of self-sufficiency were false and that she wanted to maintain dependence on her parents. She was strongly enmeshed. Marcia viewed her college graduation as the end of an adolescence beyond which she could not function. She was reluctant to share these fears with anyone because, she said, she did not want to be "found out." The pull of the family system was enormous. Adolescent and early adult depression is frequently related to a lack of differentiation and the "sacrificial roles" fulfilled in triangulation with parents (Lastoria, 1990). The practitioner realized that he needed to slow down the pace of his interventions and initiate a family systems focus.

Marcia's parents and siblings reluctantly agreed to participate in family therapy. Her father was particularly ambivalent and seemed to attend primarily to make sure that nothing negative was said about him. For these reasons, only six family meetings were held, and at two of them one or the other of the parents was not present. The family's conversations during the genogram process and other interventions tended to be superficial and noncritical. Still, the practitioner came to understand that, because the other children had left home, Marcia's parents were dependent on her presence to keep themselves in balance with each other. They sabotaged her initiatives toward independence with critical comments. Marcia had previously revealed to the practitioner that they were privately critical of his interventions.

Despite this relatively short-term family intervention the practitioner had an impact on the system. He educated the family about systems influences by discussing in a positive way their mutual roles in helping each other function. He did not directly confront Mr. and Mrs. Reeves about their triangulation of the children, as this would have been destructive to the intervention process. He framed family conflicts in terms of stage-of-life issues (empty nesting, children leaving home) which the parents could relate to and which also kept the focus off Marcia. He encouraged new functional alliances and triangles by enforcing the value of sibling relationships. He encouraged Mrs. Reeves to spend time together with Marcia and her oldest daughter. This might weaken the triangle of Marcia and her parents, and also allow Mrs. Reeves to have time away from her husband. There was no extended family living in the area, so Marcia was encouraged to join social groups as structured means of developing extrafamily relationships. One of these was an Al-Anon group (Marcia had privately admitted to the practitioner her concern about dad's drinking).

None of these task activities included Mr. Reeves, but the practitioner was careful to engage him in discussions, recognize his contributions to the family's financial stability, and suggest new ways for him to interact with his children *outside* the home (to deemphasize his dominance). The practitioner was not sure whether Mr. Reeves did these things, as he continued to seem withdrawn. Nor did the practitioner assume that he had any influence over his drinking. Some of the practitioner's questions in family sessions left the door open for the issue of dad's drinking to be raised by the others, but it never was.

The practitioner continued to see Marcia individually, and she made progress. She slowly made changes in her role within the family in response to the practitioner's interventions including education, suggestions of small changes in her patterns of interaction within the family, and her developing relationships outside the family. The practitioner needed patience to give Marcia the time she needed to work toward differentiation. Marcia never graduated from college, but she did move into an apartment with a friend from work and spent less time in the company of her parents.

The Charles Family

Normal life transitions can create problems in functioning for individuals and families. Among family systems theorists, Carter and McGoldrick (1989) have identified six general stages of a family's life span, including young adulthood (between families), the young couple, families with young children, families with adolescents, families at midlife (including launching children), and families in later life. As families enter each new stage, they may experience difficulty coping with the challenges inherent in that stage. The following case provides an example of family stresses related to two lifespan stages—adolescence and the declining health of older members. Concepts from family systems theory are useful for understanding the heightened anxiety and emotional tumult that creeps into a family with aging or dying members (Bowen, 1991b; Margles, 1995).

Dan Charles was a 16-year-old high school sophomore referred to the mental health center because of poor grades, negative attitudes about school and his peers, and reports by his parents of suicidal thinking. The Charles family had moved from Ohio to Virginia six months earlier when Dan's father, Jeff (age 41), accepted new employment. According to Dan and his parents, Dan was unhappy about living in Virginia. He was irritable, argumentative, and in persistent power struggles with them. Dan usually stayed in the house when he was not in school and had made no friends. He complained about life in Virginia and said he wanted to move back home. Dan complained about his classmates and refused to participate in school activities. Dan's two younger siblings (Adam, 10, and Robyn, 8) resented Dan's anger and how he took it out on them. They enjoyed living in Virginia and had made new friends.

During the practitioner's assessment, however, other family issues emerged as significant to the present situation (see Figure 10.2). She learned that Claudia (age 42), Dan's mother, was concerned about the poor health of her aging parents in Ohio. Claudia's mother was in the middle stages of Alzheimer's disease, and her father was physically limited by congestive heart failure. Within her own

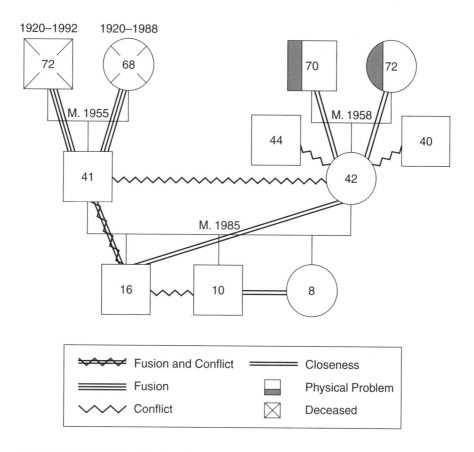

FIGURE 10.2 *The Charles Family*

family of origin, Claudia (who had two brothers) was the "caretaker" child, unofficially delegated responsibility for her parents' welfare. She felt guilty about moving away from Ohio, leaving her parents to the care of her brothers who tended not to be as attentive. Her husband, Jeff, felt that Claudia tended to go overboard in worrying about her parents. He often became angry with her for paying more attention to them than she did to him and the children. They argued about this often. Jeff was the only child in his own family of origin. He was born when his parents, now deceased, were in their forties. They had been quite doting, and Jeff was accustomed to being taken care of. Jeff seemed to want Claudia to attend to him in the ways she did for her parents. Claudia, being a natural peacemaker, tried to see Jeff's side of the issue. Still, she resented his insensitivity to her experiencing a midlife role reversal with her parents.

The practitioner also learned that Dan had tended to be triangled with his parents over the years as a diversion from their conflicts. When they were angry with each other, they found fault with Dan and ventilated their feelings at him. The practitioner wondered if Dan took on the role of troublemaker when his parents experienced prolonged conflict. It was true that the recent move was hard on Dan, more so than the other children, due to his stage of life. But the combined family stresses may have resulted in an increase in Dan's efforts to divert his parents' attention from each other, his mother from the guilt about not fulfilling her nuclear family role, and his father's anger about his unmet needs to be cared for. Although the younger children did not seem to be adversely affected by these processes, the practitioner was concerned that the system anxiety was rising and might begin to affect them as well. Their "staying out" of the situation put them at risk for emotional cutoff.

Intervention

The practitioner met with the family 10 times over a period of four months. She focused with the family on systems issues rather than on the presenting problem of one member's maladjustment. She framed the family's functioning in a context of everyone's need to better adjust to the move, and the family was agreeable to work on this. One motivator for the family was that, because they were not rooted in their new location, they had a strong need to support one another. The practitioner educated the family about life cycle stresses and complimented all of them on the many good decisions they had made in their transition. Dan was pleased to have the focus taken off him. As they reviewed the genogram, the practitioner suggested that they could help one another with their adjustment by interacting in new ways. She included the grandparents in this process. Recognizing the entire family's concern for the aging couple, she integrated strategies to see that all of their needs were addressed.

The practitioner helped the family develop a plan for groups of them to travel to Ohio every three weeks to look after Claudia's parents. Claudia and two of the children might make one trip, enabling them to spend two full days together. Jeff and two of the children might travel to Ohio on another weekend. Jeff and Claudia could travel only with the entire family, so the practitioner encouraged them to spend time together in Virginia away from the children. Their lives had centered on the children for years, and they decided to meet once a week for lunch.

Claudia felt good about this plan, and it lowered her anxiety. The practitioner helped the family appreciate Claudia's need to provide support to members of two generations. Jeff and the children were encouraged to complete minor renovation projects at their new house during the absences of the other members. The practitioner hoped that this would both enhance their sense of mastery and positively change the nature of their relationships. In all of these strategies the practitioner was helping the family form new alliances and differentiate. The children, with the encouragement of the practitioner, spent some of their time in Ohio talking with their grandparents about their mother's and father's lives when they were younger. This helped the children to see their parents in a new light, as "regular people." The activity also strengthened their relationships with their grandparents.

Another effective intervention strategy was the practitioner's encouraging the family to follow through with their vague desire to join a church in Virginia. The family had not been active in their church in Ohio but had more of an interest in doing so now, partly because of their relative social isolation. Claudia had become more conscious of her religious roots since her parents had become ill and were facing existential concerns more directly. The practitioner supported the idea, as it provided the family with a bonding experience. This practice enabled them to consider family functioning within a spiritual context. The family joined several church activity groups which helped them to initiate social ties. In the past, their church affiliations had not provided them with a basis for family-focused activity, but it became more a part of their lives now.

When therapy ended, the family had made a better adjustment to life in Virginia. Relationships improved among the members, and Dan was feeling better about his parents, his siblings, and his school. Jeff had helped Claudia confront her brothers about their need to be more attentive to her parents, and Jeff and Dan continued to spend recreational time together. The family had talked about possibly moving Claudia's parents to Virginia if their health continued to deteriorate. They continued to make monthly trips to Ohio.

Evaluation of Effectiveness

There is no persuasive large-scale empirical evidence that family systems theory is an effective guide to intervention. This is not to say that it is not effective. Rather, it has not been the subject of outcome studies that go beyond case narratives. If this seems discouraging, it must be emphasized that evaluating the effectiveness of family theories is generally difficult, and family systems theory is among the most difficult to operationalize. Bowen did not believe that empirical study was an appropriate way to determine the usefulness of his theory. He believed that such methods overlooked its richness in focusing on limited variables. He believed that what people say they do is not always the same as what they do, so he did not put great faith in standardized clinical self-report measures (Georgetown Family Center, 2001).

Although family systems theory is rich in concepts to guide the conceptualization of family dynamics, its intervention techniques are not highly specific. Family systems practitioners can be creative in their intervention approaches and may operate differently in practice. One practitioner may tend to be didactic, another may be task focused, and a third may use reflective methods. As Frank and Frank (1993) postulate in their cross-cultural study of healing practices, it is the healer's possession of a guiding theoretical framework that is one significant predictor of effectiveness. In this sense, the attractiveness of this theory to clinical practitioners for over 30 years supports its utility.

Family systems theorists emphasize research on process rather than outcome, and on single cases or small samples. Such studies are currently in progress at the Georgetown Family Center (2001) and include the topics of families and cancer, families with substance-abusing adolescents, family processes in immigrant families, relationships and physiology, relationship processes and reproductive functioning, the process of differentiation, and the workplace as an emotional system. Previous center studies have focused on AIDS and the family (Maloney-Schara, 1990), aging and the family (Kerr, 1984), family violence, and managing diabetes. The theory is also used as a model for adolescent group work to promote member growth through differentiation (Nims, 1998).

The literature does include examples of tests of the utility of the theory's *concepts*, and several are presented here. In a study of family-of-origin influences on career decision making, 1,006 college students were surveyed using measures of fusion, triangulation, intimidation, anxiety, and career decision making (Larson & Wilson, 1998). Results indicated that anxiety does serve a mediating role for the management of fusion, but triangulation was not related to career decision problems. Larson, Benson, Wilson, & Medora (1998) studied the effects of the intergenerational transmission of anxiety on 977 late adolescents' attitudes about marriage. The participants' experiences of fusion and triangulation were found to be related to negative opinions about marriage. Timmer & Veroff (2000) studied the relationship of family-of-origin ties to marital happiness after four years of marriage for 199 black and 173 white couples. One predictor of marital happiness for wives, particularly those from disrupted families, was closeness to the husband's family of origin. When husbands' or wives' parents were divorced or separated, closeness to the husband's family reduced the risk of divorce. Avnir and Shor (1998) operationalized the concept of differentiation with a set of indicators so that the concept may be qualitatively assessed during family intervention.

The clinical practitioner can evaluate his or her own effectiveness with family systems theory through the application of *single-systems* (comparing baseline and treatment measures) or *pre-experimental* (comparing pretreatment with posttreatment measures). All that is required is a background in basic research methods. The practitioner can translate a family's goals into observable indicators that can be monitored. Coco and Courtney (1998) provide one example. They initiated and evaluated a family systems intervention for preventing adolescent runaway behavior using pre- and postintervention measures of family satisfaction and cohesion.

Application to Families at Other Levels of Need

Family systems theory interventions require that the client, whether an individual or a family, has the capacity to interact in an atmosphere of relative calm and be able to reflect on relationships with significant others. There must be a stable enough family structure that the practitioner can maintain a detachment from family processes. Because this is a historical approach to intervention, the ability to focus on several generations is desirable. Family systems theory would not be appropriate for *most* Level I and *many* Level II families. The practitioner's focus in Level I is meeting basic material and support needs. There is an urgency to those needs that suggests interventions that do not rely on sustained reflection. Nor is there time for multigenerational assessment in critical situations. Likewise, Level II families are often characterized by chaos that derives from structural instability. The high level of worker activity necessary to adjust the family structure is inconsistent with the family systems perspective.

Family systems theory might be appropriate for some families at other levels of need after their initial problems are resolved. After the Level I family acquires access to basic needs, its members may struggle with issues related to enmeshments or cutoff. A structural breakdown of a Level II family may be related to a triangulation in which an adolescent accedes to an inappropriate position of power. The practitioner's ability to assess those dynamics may be helpful in determining how to help the family organize problem-solving activities, strengthen certain subsystems, or plan for growth after the primary intervention ends.

Summary

Family systems theory is unique in its attention to overt and subtle emotional family processes that develop over several generations. It is an appropriate guide to assessments and interventions that focus on the quality of nuclear and extended family interpersonal processes and the desire for family members to become differentiated. The theory is an effective means of working on issues related to boundaries, enmeshment, and emotional distance. It is versatile in its applicability to individuals and subsets of families. Its potential for use across cultures has also been articulated, although not yet extensively (Hines, Garcia-Preto, McGoldrick, & Weltman, 1992).

Family systems theory has been criticized, however, for two related reasons (Bartle-Haring, 1997; Knudson-Martin, 1994; Levant & Silverstein, 2001). First, it has not adequately attended to variations in how men and women experience differentiation and fusion. The theory has incorporated a male bias in its valuing of reason over emotion and prioritization of separation over connection. Beginning with Gilligan (1982), developmental theories about women have considered their relational and communication styles to be different from those of men. Second, even with its attention to societal emotional processes, the theory has not been sufficiently contextual in its identification of males as the dominant cultural group and their uses of power in family systems. Although these criticisms are valid, they have begun to be addressed by theorists in the 1990s. Family issues of gender difference and power can be productively addressed in therapy (McGoldrick, 1996).

Level III families pose a challenge to clinical practitioners because they are well defended and cope well in many ways. They are also a challenge because of the potential vulnerability of the practitioner to the influence of his or her family issues on the clinical work. The struggles of the presenting family may resonate with the practitioner's family experiences, and he or she may be inclined to take sides or be blind to certain family dynamics. Titelman (1987) has written extensively about the practitioner's need to be sensitive to these forces and to utilize clinical supervision to maintain neutrality in the intervention process.

Discussion Questions

1. Imagine that a professional colleague asks you to describe family systems theory. What three core concepts would you emphasize, and why?

2. Describe a point of fusion you have observed in your work with an individual, a family, or a family subsystem. Describe one way that you might (or did) proceed to modify that relationship.

3. Why is the triangle considered to be the smallest stable relationship system? What does attention to this concept imply about family assessment and intervention strategies?

4. Describe how the genogram can serve as both an assessment tool and an intervention strategy.

5. What is the ideal position of the practitioner in family systems work, so that both engagement and therapeutic distance can be achieved?

6. One intervention strategy in family systems theory involves guiding members into new attachments with nuclear and extended family members. Why should extended family members be included in this process when possible?

7. Consider a case of family dissolution in which the primary issue in the three-member family is the adolescent child's adjustment to the divorce of her parents. Describe one possible intervention strategy if the child will be in joint custody but is disengaged from one parent.

8. You are working with a family in which the mother is dying of ovarian cancer. The two children are grown and live independently in the same city as the parents. The son, like the father, is highly involved in the mother's care. The daughter shows minimal concern with her mother's imminent death. How might you organize an intervention to help the mother communicate more openly with her daughter?

9. Consider a situation in which you are working with an individual adult client whose problem is related to an inability to risk intimacy (however you define it) in relationships with significant others. In the assessment you learn that this person was the hero child in a family where the father was an alcohol abuser. Describe one possible intervention strategy.

10. Consider a situation in which you are working with a single mother who is having trouble "letting go" of her 19-year-old daughter, who is moving toward independence in a normal way. There are two other children, aged 14 and 10. The mother fits the profile of the hero child in her own nuclear family, in which there was an alcoholic parent. Describe one possible intervention strategy for helping the mother "let go."

Suggested Readings

Bowen, M. (1978). *Family therapy in clinical practice.* New York: Jason Aronson.
This is the essential source of founder Murray Bowen's major writings on the topic of family systems theory.

Guerin, P. J., Fogarty, T. F., Fay, L. F., & Kautto, J. G. (1996). *Working with relationship triangles: The one-two-three of psychotherapy.* New York: Guilford.
This is the most recent book by Guerin, a major proponent of family systems theory, and his associates. With its focus on the triangle, the theory's primary unit of analysis, the book has broad clinical application.

Kerr, M. E., & Bowen, M. (1988). *Family evaluation: An approach based on Bowen theory.* New York: Norton.
This book focuses on developments in family systems theory since the publication of Bowen's earlier volume (described above). Its coauthor, Michael Kerr, is widely acknowledged to be the theory's major proponent since Bowen's death.

McGoldrick, M., Gerson, R., & Shellenberger, S. (1999). *Genograms: Assessment and intervention* (2nd ed.). New York: Norton.
This is the most comprehensive source of information about genograms and their application in the professional literature. The book is readable and even entertaining in its selection of examples.

Titelman, P. (Ed.) (1998). *Clinical applications of Bowen family systems theory.* New York: Haworth.
This book includes descriptions of family systems theory interventions for a variety of presenting problems. Each chapter is authored by a different practitioner who helps the reader get a sense of the creative approaches that can be used in family intervention.

References

Avnir, Y., & Shor, R. (1998). A systematic qualitative evaluation of levels of differentiation in families with children at risk. *Families in Society, 79*(5), 504–514.

Bartle-Haring, S. (1997). The relationships among parent–child–adolescent differentiation, sex role orientation and identity development in late adolescence and early adulthood. *Journal of Adolescence, 20*(5), 553–565.

Bowen, M. (1959). The family as the unit and study of treatment: I. Family psychotherapy. *American Journal of Orthopsychiatry, 31*, 40–60.

Bowen, M. (1978). *Family therapy in clinical practice.* New York: Jason Aronson.

Bowen, M. (1991a). Alcoholism as viewed through family systems theory and family psychotherapy. *Family Dynamics of Addiction Quarterly, 1*(1), 94–102.

Bowen, M. (1991b). Family reaction to death. In F. Walsh & M. McGoldrick (Eds.), *Living beyond loss: Death in the family* (pp. 79–92). New York: Norton.

Braveman, S. (1995). The integration of individual and family therapy. *Contemporary Family Therapy, 17*(3).

Brody, G. H. (1998). Sibling relationship quality: Its causes and consequences. *Annual Review of Psychology, 49*, 1–25.

Carter, B., & McGoldrick, M. (Eds.). (1989). *The changing life cycle: A framework for family therapy* (2nd ed.). New York: Gardner.

Coco, E. L., & Courtney, L. J. (1998). A family systems approach for preventing adolescent runaway behavior. *Adolescence, 33*(130), 485–497.

Dysinger, R. H., & Bowen, M. (1959). Problems for medical practice presented by families with a schizophrenic member. *American Journal of Psychiatry, 116*, 514–517.

Frank, J. D., & Frank, J. B. (1993). *Persuasion and healing: A comparative study of psychotherapy* (3rd ed.). Baltimore, MD: Johns Hopkins University Press.

Georgetown Family Center. (2001). http://www. georgetownfamilycenter.org/index.html

Gilligan, C. (1982). *In a different voice.* Cambridge, MA: Harvard University Press.

Goldstein, E. G. (1995). *Ego psychology and social work practice* (2nd ed.). New York: Free Press.

Guerin, P. J., Fogarty, T. F., Fay, L. F., & Kautto, J. G. (1996). *Working with relationship triangles: The one-two-three of psychotherapy.* New York: Guilford.

Hines, P. M., Garcia-Preto, N., McGoldrick, R. A., & Weltman, S. (1992). Intergenerational relationships across cultures. *Families in Society*, 323–327.

Howe, L. T. (1998). Self-differentiation in Christian perspective. *Pastoral Psychology, 46*(5), 347–362.

Howells, J. G., & Guirguis, W. R. (1985). *The family and schizophrenia.* New York: International Universities Press.

Kerr, K. B. (1984). Issues in aging from a family theory perspective. In *The Best of the Family 1978–1983* (pp. 243–247). New Rochelle, NY: Center for Family Learning.

Kerr, M. E., & Bowen, M. (1988). *Family evaluation: An approach based on Bowen theory.* New York: Norton.

Knudson-Martin, C. (1994). The female voice: Applications to Bowen's family system's theory. *Journal of Marital and Family Therapy, 20*(1), 35–46.

Larson, J. H., Benson, M. J., Wilson, S. M., & Medora, N. (1998). Family of origin influences on marital attitudes and readiness for marriage in late adolescents. *Journal of Family Issues, 19*(6), 750–769.

Larson, J. H., & Wilson, S. M. (1998). Family of origin influences on young adult career decision problems: A test of Bowenian theory. *American Journal of Family Therapy, 26*(1), 39–53.

Lastoria, M. D. (1990). A family systems approach to adolescent depression. *Journal of Psychology and Christianity, 9*(4), 44–54.

Levant, R. F., & Silverstein, L. B. (2001). Integrating gender and family systems theories: The "both/and" approach to treating a postmodern couple. In S. H. McDaniel & D. D. Lusterman (Eds.), *Casebook for integrating family therapy: An ecosystem approach* (pp. 245–252). Washington, DC: American Psychological Association.

Maloney-Schara, A. (1990). Biofeedback and family systems psychotherapy in the treatment of HIV infection. *Biofeedback and Self-Regulation, 15*(1), 70–71.

Margles, D. (1995). The application of family systems theory to geriatric hospital social work. *Journal of Gerontological Social Work, 24*, 45–54.

Marks, I. M. (1987). *Fears, phobias, and rituals: Panic, anxiety, and their disorders.* New York: Oxford University Press.

McGoldrick, M. (1996). *The legacy of unresolved loss: A family systems approach.* New York: Newbridge Communications.

McGoldrick, M., Gerson, R., & Shellenberger, S. (1999). *Genograms: Assessment and intervention* (2nd ed.). New York: Norton.

Moore, S. T. (1990). Family systems theory and family care: An examination of the implications of Bowen theory. *Community Alternatives: International Journal of Family Care, 22*(2), 75–86.

Nims, D. R. (1998). Searching for self: A theoretical model for applying family systems to adolescent group work. *Journal for Specialists in Group Work, 23*(2), 133–144.

Prest, L. A., Benson, M. J., & Protinsky, H. O. (1998). Family of origin and current relationship influences on codependency. *Family Process, 37*(4), 513–528.

Sawin, K. J., & Harrigan, M. P. (1995). *Measures of family functioning for research and practice.* New York: Springer.

Scaturo, D. J., Hayes, T., Sagula, D., & Walter, T. (2000). The concept of codependency and its context within family systems theory. *Family Therapy, 27*(2), 63–70.

Timmer, S. G., & Veroff, J. (2000). Family ties and the discontinuity of divorce in Black and White newlywed couples. *Journal of Marriage and the Family, 62*(2), 349–361.

Titleman, P. (Ed.). (1987). *The therapist's own family: Toward the differentiation of self.* Northvale, NJ: Jason Aronson.

Titleman, P. (Ed.). (1998). *Clinical applications of Bowen family systems theory.* New York: Haworth.

Woods, M. E., & Hollis, F. H. (2000) *Casework: A psychosocial therapy* (5th ed.). Boston: McGraw-Hill.

11

Narrative Family Interventions

Nancy R. Williams, Ph.D., and P. David Kurtz, Ph.D.

The creation and sharing of stories as a way to understand and communicate about experience is a common thread that spans cultures and has woven its way through the ages and stages of human development. It is the way we come to make meaning out of our lives and interpret the experiences that shape our belief systems about self and others (Goldenberg & Goldenberg, 2000). Walsh (1998) describes the story-telling process as a way to transmit cultural and family beliefs that guide personal expectations and actions (p. 48). Narrative therapy is an innovative approach to working with individuals, couples, and families which utilizes the stories and narratives people create as the point of intervention in cocreating new versions to bring about change. This postmodern approach incorporates a strong social justice orientation, challenging abuses of power embedded in the cultural narratives that perpetuate oppression and marginalize people who are different from the cultural norm. Emphasis is placed on the process of empowerment, as reflected in the collaborative relationship between client and therapist. This theoretical model, referred to as the "third wave" in family therapy theory (behind psychodynamic and family systems), has been gaining momentum in the family therapy field since the 1980s and continues to broaden its appeal and influence practice in the human service arena (Nichols & Schwartz, 2001).

Proponents of narrative therapy regard this approach as much more than a set of techniques, but rather a revolutionary paradigm shift that challenges the tenets adhered to in family systems theories and traditional clinical approaches to mental health treatment. Narrative theorists hold the view that people seek out therapy when the narratives that dominate their lives become "over-saturated" with problems—their life story no longer works for them (White & Epston, 1990). The restorying process within the narrative approach challenges the status quo viewpoint and creates possibilities for alternative meanings and, correspondingly, alternative ways of acting. An essential aspect of this approach is that the family members are viewed as the experts of their own lives through the validation of the meaning that their problem stories are given. It is through this respectful collaboration with families that clients are enabled and empowered to bring forth their alternative stories. The purpose of this chapter is to present the underlying philosophy, theoretical roots, intervention techniques, and strategies that are identified with the narrative model.

The Role of Culture

The social constructionist philosophy, on which narrative therapy is based, argues that reality is a subjective interpretation of experience based on many factors, not the least of which is the dominant cultural narrative that profoundly shapes people's thoughts and choices. Knowledge of the self is described as being defined largely by the cultural practices that clients and therapists alike engage in (Semmler & Williams, 2000). In fact, Laird (2000) argues that culture is not just a static cluster of enduring characteristics but it is "emergent, contextual, improvisational, performative and political" (p. 346). Freedman and Combs (1996) support this idea by observing

> A central tenet of the postmodern worldview in which we base our approach to therapy is that beliefs, laws, social customs, habits of dress and diet—all the things that make up the psychological fabric of "reality"—arise through social interaction over time. In other words, people together, construct their realities as they know them. (p. 23)

The narrative approach directly addresses social issues of power and oppression, often overlooked in more traditional intrafamilial and intrapsychic models of practice. In this approach, the impact of the cultural experience on the members of those diverse groups who remain outside the dominant cultural narrative of any given culture is considered central (Goddard, Lehr, & Lapadat, 2000; Laird, 2000; O'Dell, 2000; Semmler & Williams, 2000; Waldgrave, 1998; White, 1991). Laird (2000) elaborates on this notion by suggesting that cultural narratives are so impactful that they are, in fact, the pivotal metaphors that clinical practitioners should focus on in work with individuals, couples, and families. She describes cultural narratives as a reflection of a constantly changing landscape of beliefs and attitudes, and adds her voice to White and Epston (1990) and Madigan (1991) in cautioning professionals to be aware that, because the therapeutic situation lies within the domains of power and knowledge, the therapeutic process always includes the possibility of social control and is never value free, apolitical, or context free. Additionally, therapists approach the therapeutic situation with their own narrative which may limit or shape what they think is relevant or important in a client's story (Hart, 1995). As a result, therapists and family members alike are subject to the constraints of race, gender, culture, and theoretical position (Fish,

1993; Laird, 2000; Waldgrave, 1998; White, 1989a). Emphasis is placed on therapists' being aware of their own cultural narrative and the necessity of helping professionals' vigorously attending to a process of "deprivileging" their own stories
to be able to hear the narratives of others.

The narratives or stories that people adopt act as filters that determine which
features of their experience will be chosen to be focused on and what meaning will
be given to the experience (White, 1989). White (1993) claims that the under-
standings that shape actions and behavior are influenced by the meaning people
make of their stories. He suggests that, although narratives offer strategies for
adapting to the inevitable adversities in life, this process can also become the vehicle for cultural oppression. It is through the construction of narratives that the
dominant culture is translated and becomes embedded in our personal frame of
reference as "truths." These adopted truths can serve to shape self-destructive and
constricting thoughts and behaviors even while providing a template for survival.
Thus a narrative approach to family intervention addresses and challenges stories
that disempower and pathologize individuals and families.

Theory of Problems/Needs

Gregory Bateson (1972, 1979) suggests that individuals behave in response to information that they have selected out according to its meaning or significance. If
it has no significance and doesn't fit into the individual's perceived pattern or
dominant story, then it has virtually no existence as fact (White & Epston, 1990).
Problems develop as the inevitable consequences of "vicious cycles" of events that
are inadvertently reinforced. Problems are maintained, even though solutions may
have been attempted, because nothing has happened to break the cycle and allow
new information or "news of a difference" to enter the individual's world of meaning. In fact, nothing has changed because no change has been perceived.

Narrative therapists believe that problems are *not* inherent in individuals or
families but that "problems arise because people are induced by our culture into
subscribing to narrow and self-defeating views of themselves and the world"
(Nichols & Schwartz, 2001, p. 192). Thus these restricted views may prevent people from noticing at-hand information about their own strengths and abilities to
deal with the problem. For instance, a battered woman may escape to a shelter and
then return to her abuser because she believes she cannot survive economically
without him. Or a middle-aged man may remain miserable in a tedious, unfulfill-
ing job, seeing no options because he fears the scorn of family and friends should
he make a career change. In fact, his culture probably does not sanction or support
making a quality-of-life change over his role as a stable and dependable bread-
winner. Societal labels such as "midlife crisis" and "second adolescence" convey
some of the judgment that this man might encounter if he were to challenge his
current story.

In the above examples, individuals held fixed notions about themselves that
were reflected in their dominant stories ("I can't survive without him"; "I'd be

crazy to leave this steady job") and which conflicted with an alternative version (an independent woman, a man with a more challenging career). This is the point at which families and individuals often seek therapy (White & Epston, 1990). The problem and its oppression of individuals can be deliberately "placed" by the therapist outside the individual or family. The cause is not sought, and White argues that the search for a cause is itself a problem, leading to vicious cycles of blame and guilt.

Case Example: Rob

Rob, 36, came to see his new therapist following the breakup of his latest and most long term relationship with a woman named Alice. He was filled with sorrow for the lost relationship and had many self-recriminations as he described himself as "bossy, overbearing, controlling and grasping." He reluctantly acknowledged that he had been physically abusive in the relationship and admitted that he used alcohol as an escape and blamed himself for "pushing her away." Each time he drank to excess, he would experience a great deal of self-loathing and depression, and he had gotten caught in a cycle of loneliness, despair, alcohol abuse, self-hate, and withdrawal. In his previous therapy, some years before, he had recognized that, as the son of an abusive, alcoholic mother, he was following in his mother's footsteps. Though he felt he had made peace with his mother, now deceased, he believed that he was operating under the shadow of nothing less than a biological mandate. His depression had affected his work as a successful musician in a band, and his preoccupation with Alice was keeping him on an emotional roller coaster.

Assessment and Goals

Assessment from the narrative perspective is not concerned with diagnoses or classification into pathologizing categories, but rather as an intervention itself, concerned with the bringing forth of stories from a stance of respectful curiosity. Assessment occurs through enactment of a person's stories, rather than through the uncovering of "facts." When stories and their meanings are revealed, strengths emerge at every step of the therapeutic process. Alternative stories can "deconstruct" and challenge the old story, and are being cultivated throughout the process. Thus assessment and treatment are not considered separate processes but become blurred and intertwined.

The concept of a symptom's function is foreign to the narrative approach (Chang & Phillips, 1993; Nichols & Schwartz, 2001) and serves only to distract from the problem and its effects on the individual or family. In the narrative model, symptom functionality is replaced by the view that problems are inevitable, that restraints have prevented the discovery of effective solutions. As these negative explanations are employed, the pertinent question is not "Why are things this way?" but "What has stopped things from being different"? (Anoretic & Anoretic, 1991).

Labeling Rob an alcoholic, or a child of an alcoholic, or an abusive boyfriend, or controlling, overbearing, and so on, did not solve his problem. In fact, based on prior therapy experiences in which he did receive labels, it seemed to heighten his sense of hopelessness and despair. How does one combat biology? Rob's dominant narrative was about being bossy, controlling, overbearing, and grasping, and that was what he believed he was as a human being. It didn't help that he had been raised in a household where alcohol ruled or that he was of Irish ancestry, where the cultural legacy embraces alcohol as a symbol of identity.

Treatment Goals

Because narrative therapists are not problem solvers, they are more interested in partnering with people to enhance their awareness of the way in which cultural forces have lulled them into accepting problem-saturated ways of living. Therapists are less concerned with formulating therapeutic goals than they are with coauthoring with clients new preferred stories about themselves. The focus is on enabling people to separate themselves from the problem—the problem is the problem and not the person. Once free from the old problem, people have room to rewrite the stories of their lives.

Intervention Approach

Major Tenets

The narrative approach is first and foremost a philosophy, a way of thinking about the world, with its roots deep in ideological precepts and value assumptions primarily in the areas of culture, social justice, and contextual development. As described by Nichols & Schwartz, 2001, "For many of its adherents, then, the narrative approach is more than simply another school of therapy, it's an orientation to life" (p. 393). Michael White, an Australian social worker, is credited with the initial conceptualization of this model. His ideas, however, evolved in collaboration with David Epston, a clinician from New Zealand who introduced him to the concept of the narrative, and Cheryl White, who introduced him to the feminist perspective. The model that evolved from their collaboration is rooted in a postmodern framework that recognizes social and political influences and constraints, and embraces the constructionist contention that "reality" is a social construct.

The narrative tradition claims to stand theoretically distinct and independent from other traditional theories and frameworks of human behavior that view pathology as the root of problems. Depending on the framework, narrative theorists suggest that pathology or blame has been passed between the individual or the family system in traditional practice theories like a hot potato. Epston (1984) argues that these approaches seek to rank individuals according to notions of pathology and "correct" behavior that is predetermined. The implication is that "truth" is possessed by the therapist (messenger of society) and will somehow be forced on the "dysfunctional" and probably "resistant" client. Conversely, the narrative model asserts that a more objective and hence nonjudgmental attitude toward human variation is assumed, which avoids pathologizing and places particular value on personal responsibility and empowerment (Anoretic & Anoretic, 1991).

Although sharing similar theoretical roots, narrative therapy and the solution-focused therapy defined by Steve de Shazer also have distinct differences (Chang & Phillips, 1993). Specifically, these authors note differences in therapeutic intent and the stance toward the problem. Despite important differences, narrative and solution-focused therapies are focused on strengths and solutions, placing these methods at the cutting edge of the social constructionist, postmodern perspective. Some of the major theoretical and philosophical influences that profoundly influenced White and Epston include the writings of Michel Foucault, Gregory Bateson, and Jerome Bruner. Their contributions are reflected in the assumptions that underscore the narrative model: Foucault's theory of power and oppression, Bateson's theory of problems, as previously discussed, and Bruner's theory of change.

Theory of Power and Oppression

Michel Foucault (1965, 1979, 1980) a French philosopher, focused his work on the distribution of power within society that objectified, marginalized, and dehumanized some social groups while upholding the social status of others. He asserted that power is maintained based on standards that are set by the standardbearers of a society (doctors, teachers, politicians, therapists, celebrities), who promote oppression of deviant groups through "expert" judgments that serve to categorize and stereotype these groups. Society adopts the position of its model experts through the internalization of a shared narrative (social construction) that perpetuates oppressive attitudes and beliefs. Thus the culture shapes behavior and trains individuals to conform, and in turn to judge those who refuse or are unable to follow the prescribed norms. Those who conform to the dominant or expert knowledge are accepted, but nonconformists come under the "gaze" of others and are viewed in a pejorative way.

Psychotherapists are trained to identify deviations in behavior and to label individuals with clinical diagnoses like those in the *DSM-IV* (American Psychiatric Association, 1994). Labels like "obsessive-compulsive," "alcoholic," "codependent," and even "borderline" have found their way into everyday language. Family therapists also have their own language for categorizing or labeling families, by calling them, for example, "enmeshed," "blended," "triangulated," or "parentified," which serves to place blame and pathologize the family. The language of the broader society is also filled with words and phrases that convey less-than-acceptable or normal behavior such as "gay/alternative lifestyles" or even "single parents." People who deviate from the norm are often isolated and persecuted, and such reactions can provoke and perpetuate further deviant behavior (Besa, 1994). Drewery, Winslade, and Monk (2000) emphasize the importance of recognizing the power and influence of the use of words in creating frameworks for tangible consequences that inscribe people's lives and become predictors of expectable future behavior

Drawing extensively on Foucault's ideas, Michael White espouses forming a therapeutic coalition with individuals and families to protest oppressive social and cultural forces that become incorporated in problematic beliefs. One of the cornerstones of his approach is the claim that the person/family/system is not the problem, but "the problem is the problem." The creative exchanges he calls "*externalizing* conversations" (Tomm, 1993) are not merely reflective of a technique designed to depersonalize the problem but are a political process of empowering families to objectify the problem and to protest its oppression. For example, Western women have labored under the cultural construct that to be thin is to be beautiful and seek to attain physical perfection (control) through their weight. Many of these women have come to see themselves as under the influence of anorexia (rather than being anorectic) and have begun to take a stand for antianorectic ways for self and others. In fact, antianorexia and antibulimia leagues, the brainchild of David Epston, have sprung up in Australia, New Zealand, and Canada. The purpose of these leagues is to mobilize individuals and families who are being tyrannized by those disorders to unite their energies (Nichols & Schwartz, 2001). Vodde and Gallant (1999) suggest that this sort of political activism demonstrates a unique bridge provided by the practices in narrative therapy between micro and macro practice in the field of social work.

Theory of Change

According to Edward Bruner (1986) and Jerome Bruner (1990), *stories* provide the primary means for individuals to structure or organize their lived experiences. As life stories are told, with their inevitable gaps and inconsistencies, lives are changed through the process of interpreting situations and filling the gaps with both experiences and imagination. As narratives or stories are enacted or performed, they affect lives. In fact, White asserted, life is enactment of text, and the *enactment of text* is a process of reauthoring lives and relationships (White, 1988/1989). Hart (1995) warns therapists to be aware of their own narrative, which may limit or shape what is chosen for reauthoring in a therapeutic situation.

The narrative therapist who is presented with a dominant, problem-filled story challenges it by focusing predominantly on previously disregarded exceptions (or "unique outcomes") to this story. The narrative therapist attempts to cocreate with the family new ideas, new information, and new perceptions around the exceptions that will challenge former presuppositions and create a context for change (Anoretic & Anoretic, 1991). Problem-saturated beliefs are challenged, and possibilities for alternative ways of behaving are enhanced. These alternative ways compose the new story, which can gradually replace the steadily less influential old story. In the case of children, it is often effective to tune into their fantasies and imagination as well as their behaviors. These can be rich sources for identifying exceptions and authoring solution-focused stories.

Rob's therapist believed that it was important to hear and amplify how Rob's new story was different from the old, problem-saturated version in which Rob saw himself as pathological, biologically doomed, and flawed. His first step, though, was to validate the feelings that Rob was feeling in relation to his loss, to hear Rob's story, and to acknowledge its power and influence on him, thus conveying an atmosphere of respect, trust, and safety for Rob.

Social Constructivist View of Resiliency

The focus in the narrative model is on the *meanings* that are attributed to problems, rather than on their causes. Because the underlying assumption is that reality is invented, narrative therapists believe that the concept of the self as a monolithic entity does not exist, because the self is essentially determined by the situation and with whom the self is interacting. Drawing from the work of Markus and Nurius (1986) and Parry and Doan (1994), McQuaide (2000) describes this process as a "confederacy of selves." For example, the "self" we are with our friends is different from the self we are with our family, which in turn is different from the self we are at work. Even within those groups, we are different with different group members and different depending on our mood and circumstance. Who we are is constantly in flux and always in the process of being reinvented. White refers to this notion as "the constituted self" in describing how meanings are cocreated between individuals and others as they communicate. McQuaide (2000) postulates that each of these selves has its own narrative and that "The different ways a person can story his/her life (self-narratives) can be sources of strength and resilience or sources of weakness and vulnerability" (p. 72). Thus we all have parts that are resilient and other parts that are less so, depending on the circumstance, and it is the job of the therapist to enhance and empower the already-existing, if dormant, resilient selves.

The Spiritual Narrative

Spirituality stories have been woven into the historical fabric of mankind and serve as a powerful reservoir for drawing forth strength, teaching endurance, and providing emotional sustenance. The spiritual beliefs that are reflected in personal narratives speak to an individual's metaphoric sense of connectedness to self and others, and an ability to see a larger meaning or purpose in the events of his or her life (Shuler, Gelberg, & Brown, 1994). These beliefs provide protection and ways to cope with the trials of everyday life (Feinstein, 1997). Spirituality as reflected in spiritual narratives can deepen and expand a person's values and perspectives, allowing for the possibility of viewing adversity as an opportunity for personal growth and knowledge. It creates a container for humans to accept their foibles and lays the foundation for self-acceptance and tolerance of others, as it provides a context for understanding the unfathomable. Most important, the development of resiliency is reportedly tied to the ability to have hope and find reassurance in the face of distress. For many people, this support and nurture can be found within an organized spiritual community and for others within a personal relationship with a higher power. Spirituality has recently received acknowledgment as a viable and substantive resource in helping people develop the strength to redirect their lives, as well as a powerful metaphor for strength and unconditional love (Abels, 2000).

Spiritual narratives are embedded in cultural differences (Faiver, Ingersoll, O'Brien, & McNally, 2001), and as such, social constructionists believe they are contextually determined. Spiritual narratives can serve to inspire and provide meaning for surviving adversity and offering hope (Ramsey & Blieszner, 2000), but also can tell stories of disappointment and become the basis for shame-based and self-doubting cognitions (Abels, 2000). They are always richly metaphoric and can serve as "grist" for narrative restorying. In one case study, a woman's personal identity narrative became clearer when viewed through the lens of her personal relationship with God. In reauthoring her spiritual story, it drew on how her relationship with God influenced and reflected her relational identity story with others. In fact, the metaphor that was represented by her spiritual beliefs was used as a basis for the reauthorship of her personal relationships in a new, more satisfying version (Carlson & Erickson, 2000).

The Therapeutic Process

According to White (1991), a central component of this approach is a *deconstruction*, which involves "procedures that subvert taken-for-granted realities and practices" (p. 121). The dominant story of a troubled family is usually fraught with a sense of helplessness and blame-filled descriptions of each member and the relationships among the members. Using a narrative approach to treatment, the therapist facilitates the bringing forth of what is called the "problem-saturated story"—typically the presenting problem. Each selected memory carries meaning or personal significance that allows people to make sense of and find continuity in their experiences. The meanings that humans attach to situations and events influence their behavior around those events. Without planning or intending to, individuals support and maintain problems by cooperating with the problem until it seems to develop its own lifestyle or "career" (White & Epston, 1990). Through the use of empathic listening and carefully constructed questions, the narrative therapist "maps" the influence of the problem (Monk, Winslade, Crocket & Epston, 1997), thus acknowledging its influence on the family. Primarily through the use of curious questions that enable family members to attend to other features of their lived experiences, they are able to recall alternative stories that often draw on previous successes.

Narrative interventions include an eclectic collection of treatment methods, of which any or all may be used. Several of the more commonly used techniques are described in the following paragraphs. The order is intended to reflect a somewhat logical sequence, although some interventive methods can be repeated many times or possibly even eliminated. The process should be seen as rather more like loops and curves than like steps. It becomes the therapist's job, through a process of therapeutic conversations, to assist in drawing out and identifying experiences from the past that are exceptions to the individual's problem-saturated old story. The exceptions or unique outcomes are evidence that, on occasion, the person has successfully challenged the problem, has mustered the strength to overpower it. As the significance and impact of the exceptions are explored and elaborated, the individual's sense of personal efficacy intensifies. Exceptions with their new, reauthored meanings contribute to the new story's past history. The therapist and eventually the client can then decline to accept the validity of the old story (White & Epston, 1990; Hewson, 1991).

Therapeutic Strategies (Application and Interventions)

1. *Normalizing the Problem.* The success of the narrative model is dependent on the collaborative bond that is established between the therapist and the client. One of the impacts of shared stories is the cultivation of empathy in the listener, which has been described as a coconstruction of a relational process considered central in developing strong helping relationships (McLeod, 1999).

Rob's therapist, in seeking to understand Rob and his problem, began by asking many questions and phrased them in a way that helped Rob think about his situation in a slightly different way. This questioning process helped Rob to feel validated and safe with the therapist and allowed him, in the process, to begin to view his story more objectively. After hearing Rob's detailed description of his story of depression and accompanying problem behaviors, his therapist normalized Rob's experience by observing that, although Rob appeared to be under the influence of a great deal of sadness, depression, and loneliness, it was completely understandable, given that he had suffered the loss of his relationship with Alice and was encountering the new skill called "letting go" and all that it represented for him.

The therapist believed that it was his role to hear and amplify how Rob's new story was different from the old, problem-saturated version, in which Rob saw himself as pathological, biologically doomed, and unlovable. He also spent quite a bit of time listening to the language Rob was using to tell his story so that he could hear the metaphors that were meaningful to Rob and within them "news of a difference." As it turned out, Rob was an artist and musician, and this information was used later in therapy as a powerful intervention tool.

2. *Externalization of the Problem: The Problem Is the Problem.* Frequently, individuals and families have had previous experience with therapists who have labored with them to work through or come to terms with particular pathologies or dysfunctions. As a result, clients are often restrained by the belief that blame needs to be assigned to someone who has intentionally maintained or caused a problem, or that the problem reflects a character defect or personality weakness. Externalizing the problem challenges these notions.

Rob's therapist deliberately externalized or separated the oppressing problem of depression and alcohol abuse from Rob. This removed blame from Rob as the identified patient with a long history of problems, including a "doomed" family history and previously failed therapies. One of Rob's previous therapists had suggested that he was genetically at risk for developing alcoholism, based on his family history, and that his bouts of physical violence were likely linked to his alcohol abuse. His current therapist, however, focused on the *problem as the problem* and encouraged Rob to explore the detrimental effects the problem had on him. He encouraged him to organize his strengths and resources in challenging his oppressive story of failure in relationships and alcoholism. He actively facilitated Rob's finding significance and meaning in his occasionally successful encounters with self-control, letting go, and alcohol, which was soon labeled "Al."

The sometimes-humorous technique of naming the problem, as in naming alcohol Al, enables clients to focus their energies toward combating the problem itself. This externalization process allows people to visualize the solution in terms of the collaborative process of forming a team to combat the problem. Externalization is more than a reframing and depersonalizing of the problem. It is a way for families to gain control over the problem. Therapist and family members work together to define the problem situation or pattern as something outside of and distinct from the identified patient. As the problem is shaped through metaphor into an entity that can be named, the individual or family can distance themselves from the problem, challenge it, and defeat it (Neimeyer, 1993a; Winslade & Smith, 1997).

3. Mapping the Problem.

As part of the early assessment/intervention phase, reciprocal patterns emerge that have been supporting the problem. The problem and its impact on the individual's and family's life and relationships are scrutinized at length. The narrative therapist asks each family member to give a detailed, no-holds-barred account of the distressing effects of the problem and the extent to which each individual has been supervised (dominated, pushed around, controlled) by it. Part of the mapping process is exploring the influence (effect) of the person on the problem. White (1986) has referred to these combined questions as mapping the relative influence of the problem in the life of the person and the person in the life of the problem.

Rob's therapist began by assessing the influence that the problem was having on Rob. Together they discovered that the problem was interfering with his maintaining social connections with others. Rob also felt quite down on himself and was extremely self-critical. He reported that he was feeling creatively stifled, and because he was a musician, it was seriously interfering with his ability to write music and perform. On two occasions when he went out in public and saw Alice, he was catapulted into feelings of jealousy and anger that triggered anxiety. He struggled with the feelings that seeing Alice stirred up for him and saw himself powerless to stop the self-destructive drinking behaviors that he relied on to cope with the discomfort.

On one particular occasion, Rob came to the session hung over from a bout with drinking the previous evening. He reported that he had been feeling quite anxious during his performance the previous evening, following a telephone conversation with Alice, and used Al to help him gain control of himself. He conveyed feeling ashamed and physically drained through both his self-report as well as his physical demeanor. When asked how Al had seduced him, he thought about it and commented that Al was very slow and subtle. "He sort of sneaked up on me—took me by surprise." The therapist then asked him whether Al gave him control or took it away from him. Rob quickly and profoundly realized that the latter was the case.

4. News of a Difference. "News of a difference" is news that makes a difference. It provides a twist that allows the individual and the family to see and experience the old story in a new way. The changed meaning provides a new story line for daily living. The individuals are encouraged to acknowledge their progress through amplifying and recognizing the significance of small changes and shifts of behaviors away from the problem. In being helped to recognize the incremental improvements that they are implementing in their life—how they are going against their dominant storyline,—the family members are empowered to change the story that dominates their view of themselves. People tend to cling to the story they are used to, long after it serves them or is even an accurate depiction of their current reality. News of a difference empowers the family to recognize and acknowledge that changes are occurring and that they are responsible for the change. This is accomplished through a collaborative process of cocreating and witnessing the new or alternative stories which emphasizes optimism and empowerment.

Rob did not immediately notice that his depression and anger had slowly diminished—that he, in fact, had begun to do things in a different way. He had not realized that he was not thinking about Alice every waking minute as he had been. He mentioned in his session that he had seen her downtown and had not suffered his usual gut-wrenching anxiety and accompanying urge to follow her. In fact, though it was painful, he had waved to her. He had not realized it was a big deal. After hearing about Rob's successful encounter, most of the rest of the session was spent exploring Rob's extraordinary triumph in conquering the pain that seeing Alice in public had formerly triggered. The therapist also inquired about how his handling of this separation from Alice was different from previous occasions in his life when he had suffered serious loss. In the past, Rob had responded by burying himself in his work and drowned his sorrows in drinking with friends. The therapist helped bring forth the emergence of a different narrative, one in which Rob reported spending quiet time reflecting on himself and his relationship with Alice. Further, he was less caught up in drinking with his buddies. This episode helped Rob frame how he planned on dealing with Al in the future, when he would be frequently tempted by Al, particularly in his profession as an entertainer.

5. Therapeutic Questions. The narrative therapist asks many gentle, curious, respectful questions in the process of interventive interviewing. It is assumed that questions will elicit *experiences of exceptions,* which is the stuff of restorying (Tomm, 1987; White & Epston, 1990). Curious questions, by and large, are the means by which restraining patterns are revealed and challenged, and new opportunities are discovered for positive, affirmative, more flexible action around the problem. As part of this search, any information that represents positive moves toward change is noticed, seized upon, and highlighted. Language and metaphors are used creatively to highlight the relative influence of the problem. The following are illustrations of types of questions that lay the groundwork for the restorying of the person's narrative.

6. Exceptions Questions.   These questions focus on situations of successful, exceptional outcomes that don't square with the dominant, problem-filled story. These are the overlooked times when the problem didn't get the upper hand, but are not recognized yet as victories worth acknowledging by the client.

One of the therapist's questions for Rob was "How much have you been able to stand up to Al and not allow Al to dominate you?" The therapist inquired about occasions when Rob had been able to resist the seductive efforts of Al. The dilemma of whether to cooperate with Al or to protest against it was raised. Rather than taking a moral or professional stand against alcohol, which would invite either shameful feelings on Rob's part or a rebellious reaction, Rob was presented with the options of resisting or acquiescing to the seductive power of alcohol. Refusal to cooperate with the problem began to undermine its effects and life-support system. Rob was encouraged to build on successes so that his story might be reauthored into a new story of a man who has broken the family curse of alcohol.

7. History of Exceptions Questions.   Sometimes called "unique account questions," they discover past clues to accounts of current competence. Michael White (1991) urged therapists to treat these discoveries as significant and as intriguing mysteries "that persons can only unravel as they respond to the therapist's curiosity about them. As persons take up the task of unraveling such mysteries, they immediately engage in storytelling and meaning-making" (p. 30).

Rob was encouraged to remember and describe situations in which he defied Al and refused to fall for Al's attempts to trick him into "getting bombed." Rob came to recognize that he had outsmarted Al during those times and in fact, that it had happened on many occasions.

Some other examples of questions from Rob's sessions:

- How did you achieve this? Have you been advising yourself differently?
- What led up to it?
- What have you witnessed in your life that could have provided a clue that this development was a possibility for you?

8. Significance Questions.   These questions search for and reveal the meanings, significance, and importance of the exceptions. Questions of significance help draw attention to the importance of the exception and the possibility of new meanings. For example, Rob was asked

- What do you think these discoveries reveal to you/me/your family about your motives and what is important to you and your life?
- In more fully appreciating your achievement, what conclusions might you reach about what you stand for?

9. *Spectator Questions.* This type of questioning is sometimes called "experience-of-experience" questions; they invite individuals to imagine how other people that they have known might experience them. For example, Rob was asked

- If I had been able to look in on your earlier life, what might I have seen you doing that would reveal to me how you have been able to take this step?
- Of all who have known you, who would be the least surprised that you have been able to challenge Al, and what would they have seen that would enable them to predict it?

10. *Collapsing Time and Raising Dilemmas.* This technique highlights the relative influence of the problem. It also allows individuals to peer into the past and future, and predict how the problem (Al) might have developed, how it is likely to evolve, and then to make a decision around the resulting dilemma: Is it worth the effort to challenge Al? Some questions that Rob's therapist introduced to Rob are as follows:

- Is Al more of a problem for you now than, say, six months ago?
- How is the influence of Al different in your life now than it was then?
- If you were to continue to allow Al to get the best of you, in what other ways would you invite your friends and future relationships to treat you as fragile and protect you from their opinions?

11. *Enhancing Changes.* Reinforcing changes can be accomplished through the respectful challenge of a client's dominant story. This serves to motivate individuals to reexamine their narratives, leading to an amplification of changes already under way. The goal here is to demolish the problem-saturated version and to begin to reauthor a more adaptive story. Children and adolescents seem particularly open to this method and respond with energy and devotion to proving the problem-saturated story to be wrong. Motivational questions or comments may include the following:

- To a teen: "But wait a minute, you told me that you were always sad, and now you're telling me that you were happy on Saturday! Are you telling me that you were able to keep sad out of your life on Saturday?"
- To a parent: "You said you noticed that Billy kept fear from pushing him around, and you were able to go to the mall. I don't get it! I thought you said fear controlled him all the time! Something is different here. What happened?"

12. *Predicting Setbacks.* This can be done before the dilemma is even settled. Because the problem-saturated story still dominates, setbacks are virtually inevitable, and thus they must be anticipated and their distress expected and planned for. However, this needs to occur in a manner that highlights and encourages self-efficacy. In the following examples, Rob's therapist cautioned Rob, "If you are really determined to make a radical change in your relationship with

Al, do you think you'll be able to handle a setback? Or will you be tricked and seduced by Al into returning to cooperate with Al?"

13. Letters and Audiotapes.   This is a powerful tool for continuing and reinforcing the dialogue between therapist and family members. Therapist-authored letters and tapes can be rich sources for summarizing sessions, writing up case notes and sharing them with the client, highlighting emerging new stories, and rendering lived experience into a narrative or story. The therapist can ask curious questions (such as those discussed earlier) which may give cause for individuals to further reflect on their circumstances and which may unearth new meanings, affirming exceptions, and unique outcomes, and pose new ideas or possibilities. Below is a copy of a letter that Rob's therapist sent him following the session previously described in which Rob faced Al's subtle, yet powerful, control of him:

> Dear Rob,
>
> I have been thinking about our meeting today and thought it would be useful to both of us if I put into writing some of the things we talked about. Please let me know next time we meet if there are things that I missed or need to understand more fully.
>
> Rob, when we first met, you explained that you've had a long relationship with alcohol (Al). Over the years, Al has subtly stolen away more and more of your self to the point where, at times, it has seemed as though you were Al's man rather than your own. Over the years, Al has persuaded you that you were controlling and bossy and needed to hate yourself. Al has stolen away your ability to love others, like Alice, and convinced you that all was hopeless. Also, at times Al has seduced you into behaving in ways that do not fit with your value system and has taken you by surprise on more than one occasion. Al has even stolen your creative energy
>
> Rob, I am very curious how you have managed in the past to resist Al's seductive powers. I understand that this has been far from easy. In fact, I can't help wondering what Al has not managed to steal away from you that helped you at other times to stand up to Al like you have done before. I wonder what you have previously kept secret from Al that has enabled you, first, to decide that Al is playing havoc with your life and that's unacceptable and, second, that you have a right to something different and better in your life.
>
> You also talked about how preoccupation about Alice was leading you by the nose and I couldn't help wondering how you managed to stand up to preoccupation a few weeks back, in spite of the formidable power it has. I was thinking how, even in our meeting, preoccupation attempted to convince both of us that alcohol was the only remedy. From your experience, do you think that it's true that alcohol is a remedy? Do you think that alcohol and preoccupation have teamed up against you to strengthen each other's place in your life, or have they assisted you to develop your full potential?
>
> I have many more questions but am hoping I haven't already overwhelmed you. If any of these thoughts or questions are interesting to you, we can discuss them more fully when we meet or, if you feel inclined to write or draw a response, that would be great.
>
> Yours in allegiance against the tyranny of Al, (adapted from Winslade & Smith, 1997)

14. *Reflecting Team.* This is a method introduced by Tom Andersen (1991) as a way to explore available but unasked questions during family therapy conversations. A team of observers (from one to several) functioning as an audience silently listens to the therapist and family. At a designated time, the therapist invites the team to share its observations with one another about what they have just observed. The family and therapist silently listen to the team, which reflects on the story of the family with positive and curious comments and questions. Questions often begin with "I seemed to notice" or "I couldn't help but wonder what would happen if." The team attempts to be sensitive, imaginative, and respectful, and to avoid any negative connotations, advice, or criticism. They introduce new ideas, bring out unnoticed exceptions, and expand the family's new story. This process usually lasts about five minutes, after which the family and therapist can reflect with each other on the reflecting team's conversation (Andersen, 1991).

15. *Certificates and Celebrations.* These acknowledgments can serve as a tangible affirmation of a defeat of the problem or a new description of an individual. Certificates punctuate celebrations of victories and actual celebrations—complete with balloons, cake, and punch—signify problems successfully challenged and defeated. These personal affirmations contribute to an individual's new story. To illustrate, Michael White (White & Epston, 1990) has a professionally printed certificate, complete with photo and logo, which reads, in part

> ***Monster Tamer & Fear Catcher Certificate***
>
> This is to certify that _____ has undergone a Complete Training Programme in Monster Taming and Fear Catching, is now a fully qualified Monster Tamer and Fear Catcher, and is available to offer help to other children who are bugged liars. (p. 193)

Another certificate, suitable for an adult, reads

> ***Escape From Guilt Certificate***
>
> _____ is over guilt. Now that guilt doesn't have such a priority in her life, she is able to give herself a priority of her self. This certificate will serve to remind _____ and others that she has resigned from the position of superresponsibility in the lives of others and that she is no longer vulnerable to invitations from others to live their life for them and to put her life to one side. (p. 199)

Evaluation of Effectiveness

Despite the impressive treatment effects noted in many case studies by Michael White and others, there continues to be a dearth of empirical research that examines the effectiveness of narrative methodology. This is most likely due to the narrativist conclusion that traditional quantitative investigatory methods with an emphasis on measurement and positivist thinking are at odds with the values espoused by the narrative and postmodern school. At the core of this dialogue is the issue of epistemology. With a different view of the nature of reality itself, reality and accompanying "normalcy" become moving targets, shifting with each family's differing narrative. Thus narrative therapists have mostly used the case study method to testify to the method's effectiveness and have been slow to experiment with ways of using quantitative methods to measure success. (See "Application" section for illustrations of problems for which case studies have been published.) However, as qualitative methodological approaches, perhaps more compatible with capturing the process of change in this approach, such as phenomenology (Moustakas, 1994), grounded theory (Glaser & Strauss, 1967; Strauss & Corbin, 1990) and the case study method (Merriam, 1988), continue to achieve higher credibility as vigorous methodological approaches, the literature will reflect more research. Although Neimeyer (1993b), suggests that the future of narrative therapy may rest in the hands of empirical investigators, who will further examine the effectiveness of the method using ideographic methods, it is also possible that the paradigm shift reflected in this approach may require alternative methods of evaluation to capture its true impact.

Application to Families at Other Levels of Need

The narrative approach has been used with a wide variety of individual and family problems, such as

- Couple/relationship therapy (Freedman & Combs, 2000; Neal, Zimmerman, & Dickerson, 1999; Snyder, 2000).
- Sexual offenders, adolescents (Jenkins, 1987).
- Children with disabilities (Goddard, Lehr, & Lapadat, 2000).
- Substance abuse (Anoretic & Anoretic, 1991; Winslade & Smith, 1997).
- Mental illness (White, 1987).
- Dissociative disorder (Gallant, Brownlee, & Vodde, 1995).
- AIDS (Dean, 1995; Rothschild, Brownlee, & Gallant, 2000; White & Epston, 1991).
- Male batterers (Jenkins, 1990).
- Gay/lesbian issues (O'Dell, 2000).
- Anorexia/bulimia (Epston, 1993a; Epston, Morris, & Maisel, 1995).
- Grief (McQuaide, 1995; White, 1989b).

Postscript

As Rob came to trust his therapist's commitment to partnering with him to fight alcohol, he felt empowered to stand up to the legacy of his biological mandate. He came to recognize the many ways that alcohol had seduced him into thinking he would gain more control when he drank, when, in fact, Al took control away from him. He also came to see how Al seemed to push him around the most when his stress level was high. One of the questions that Rob was asked to ponder was, "How am I different now?" Rob seemed to be able to reconnect with his creative talents when his therapist suggested that the multitalented Rob portray this question in artwork and song writing. His next big task was to fortify his energies in combating Al as he began slowly to explore dating again and to resume the high stress and accompanying temptations that were inherent in his career as a musician and artist. He felt comforted in knowing that he was not alone in this battle.

Summary

The narrative approach is an eclectic approach to individual and family therapy that uses the literary metaphors of story and writing and comes from a postmodern theoretical framework. It is rooted in social constructionism and sociological and linguistic epistemologies. A reaction against the normalizing and restraining effects of culture, the narrative model stresses that the therapeutic relationship should be collaborative, as the client and therapist co-create differences, new stories, and new realities. Problems are investigated in terms of their meanings, rather than their causes. Assessment and intervention occur through the enactment of stories, and strengths and exceptions emerge that actively deconstruct and challenge the problem-saturated story. Through a process of interventive interviewing involving questions, problems are externalized, and the relative influence of the problem on the person is examined. At this point, the influence of the person on the problem takes center stage. Exceptions to problematic situations are uncovered and their significance highlighted. Curious, gentle, respectful questions can be raised about these exceptions, involving the exception's history, significance, and spectators/audience ("How did you accomplish it, what does it mean, and who noticed?"). Setbacks can be anticipated and plans made to deal with them. If possible, a reflecting team can provide new descriptions and previously unnoticed exceptions. Letters, certificates, and celebrations can amplify the content of the sessions and provide continuity to what has been accomplished between and after sessions.

Discussion Questions _____

1. In the narrative perspective, what is reality assumed to be?
2. Why does narrative therapy emphasize the meaning of problems rather than their causes?
3. What is meant by the phrase "problem-saturated story"?
4. What is the role of assessment in narrative therapy?
5. What is meant by the phrase "the problem is the problem"?

6. What are some of the key ideas that narrative therapists rely on to increase the likelihood that therapy is a process of cocreation rather than therapist directed?

7. What roles do oppression and power play in the life of a person's problem?

8. What role can externalization of the problem play in deescalating the oppressive story of the problem?

9. What role can exceptions play in helping to reauthor a person's story?

10. What value do letters, celebrations, and reflecting teams have in narrative therapy?

11. How can the narrative approach be used with families that are perceived to be functioning at each of the four levels?

12. If you used the narrative perspective, how would the way in which you see yourself working with families be different from the way it is now?

Suggested Readings

Andersen, T. (Ed.). (1991). *The reflecting team: Dialogues and dialogues about the dialogues.* New York: Norton.
The development of a new strategy in therapy is presented, in which professionals and clients trade places, exchange conversations, and open up new possibilities for change. Dialogues are exchanged in collaborative discussions among family, therapist, and reflecting team, and result in the dissolving of traditional therapeutic boundaries.

Anoretic, M., & Epston, D. (1989). The taming of temper. *Dulwich Centre Newsletter* (Special ed.), 3–26.
Articles are included by Anoretic ("Temper taming: An approach to children's temper problems—Revisited") and Epston ("Temper tantrum parties: Saving face, losing face, or going off your face!"). Anoretic's article discusses temper and behavior problems from a narrative viewpoint and the development of his ideas in dealing with these issues. Epston's article presents a method for dealing with out-of-control temper in children or adults. The approach is simple, economical, and amusing for all concerned, as it teaches individuals to substitute self-control for the control of others.

Anoretic, M., & Kowalski, K. (1990). Overcoming the effects of sexual abuse: Developing a self-perception of competence. In M. Anoretic & C. White (Eds.), *Ideas for therapy with sexual abuse.* Adelaide, S. Australia: Dulwich Centre.
Drawing from both the narrative approach and the model of brief solution-focused therapy, the authors approach the issue of sexual abuse as qualitatively not unlike other issues in therapy. They propose a framework for enhancing the perception of self as competent rather than as victim.

Freedman, J., & Combs, G. (1996). *Narrative therapies: The special construction of preferred realities.* New York: Norton.
Drawing from the narrative approach, the authors present practical information to the clinician intent. Issues of practice power, sociocultural context, and ethics are addressed in this acclaimed book.

Gilligan, S., & Price, R. (Eds.). (1993). *Therapeutic conversations.* New York: Norton.
Emerging from a conference in Tulsa (June, 1992), the book's contributors are well known in the narrative family therapy tradition, the solution-focused tradition, and conversational therapies. Chapter authors respond to one another's positions and perspectives. Contributors include John Weakland, David Epston, Michael White, Steve de Shazer, Karl Tomm, and Michele Weiner-Davis.

Metcalf, L. (1991). Therapy with parent-adolescent conflict: Creating a climate in which clients can figure what to do differently. *Family Therapy Case Studies, 6*(2), 25–34.

Responsibility and protection are contrasted with freedom and independence as conflicting needs of parents and adolescents. As conflicts increase, guilt and blame often result. The case examples demonstrate a climate in which families can decide on alternative behaviors and resolve their conflicts. Ideas are used from both the brief solution-focused model and the narrative approach.

Monk, G., Winslade, J., Crockett, K., & Epston, D. (Eds.). 1997. *Narrative therapy in practice: The archaeology of hope.* San Francisco: Jossey-Bass.

This instructive book reflects a collaboration of practitioners who have applied narrative therapy to diverse populations. It is filled with instructive, illustrative examples that describe the application of this approach in creative and hope-filled ways.

Tomm, K. (1988). Interventive interviewing: Intending to ask lineal, circular, strategic, or reflexive questions? *Family Process, 27,* 1–15.

This article and the two preceding it (Interventive interviewing I and II, *Family Process, 26,* 3–13 and 167–183) discuss questions based on circular rather than linear assumptions. A framework is offered that distinguishes four major groups of questions with guidelines to their use. Linear assumptions lead to linear and strategic questions; circular assumptions lead to circular and reflexive questions. The categories of questions are discussed regarding their effects on families and on therapists.

White, M. (1991). Deconstruction and therapy. *Dulwich Centre Newsletter, 3,* 21–40.

White presents theory and case examples illustrating externalization of the problem and relative influence questioning. He explains deconstruction and the place of meaning in narrative. The article includes discussion of issues of power, the influence of Michel Foucault. It relates discussion of power back to case examples. White challenges therapists to question the notion of "expert power" in therapeutic situations.

White, M., & Epston, D. (1990). *Narrative means to therapeutic ends.* New York: Norton.

Letters, documents, and certificates become a respectful and often playful means to encourage the restorying of experience. The narrative approach is explained. Many examples are offered, suitable for children, adolescents, and adults. In addition, the restraints of power and the political implications inherent in therapy are discussed.

References

Abels, S. L. (2000). *Spirituality in social work practice: Narratives for professional helping.* Denver: Love Publishing Co.

American Psychiatric Association. (1994). *Diagnostic and statistical manual of mental disorders* (4th ed.). Washington, DC: American Psychiatric Association Press.

Andersen, T. (Ed.). (1991). *The reflecting team: Dialogues and dialogues about the dialogues.* New York: Norton.

Anoretic, M., & Anoretic, D. (1991). Michael White's cybernetic approach. In R. Todd & M. Selekman (Eds.), *Family therapy approaches with adolescent substance abusers.* Boston: Allyn and Bacon.

Anoretic, M., & Epston, D. (1989). Temper taming: An approach to children's temper problems revisited. *Dulwich Centre Newsletter,* 3–11.

Bateson, G. (1972). *Steps to an ecology of the mind.* New York: Ballantine.

Bateson, G. (1979). *Mind and nature: A necessary unity.* London: Wildwood House.

Besa, D. (1994). Narrative family therapy: A multiple baseline outcome study including collateral effects of verbal behavior. *Research on Social Work Practice, 4*(3), 309–325.

Bruner, E. (1986). Experience and its expression. In V. Turner & E. Bruner (Eds.), *The anthropology of experience.* Chicago: University of Illinois Press.

Bruner, J. (1990). *Acts of meaning*. Cambridge, MA: Harvard University Press.

Carlson, T. D., & Erickson, M., J. (2000). Re-authoring spiritual narratives: God in person's relational identity stories. *Journal of Systemic Therapies, 19*(2), 65–83.

Chang, J., & Phillips, M. (1993). Michael White and Steve de Shazer: New directions in family therapy. In S. Gilligan & R. Price (Eds.), *Therapeutic conversations*. New York: Norton.

Dean, R. G. (1995). Stories of AIDS: The use of the narrative as an approach to understanding in an AIDS support group. *Clinical Social Work Journal, 23*(3), 287–304.

Drewery, W., Winslade, J., & Monk, G. (2000). Resisting the dominating story: Towards a deeper understanding of narrative therapy In R. A. Neimeyer, & J. D. Raskin (Eds.), *Constructions of disorder: Meaning-making frameworks for psychotherapy*. Washington, DC: American Psychological Association.

Epston, D. (1984). Guest address: Fourth Australian family therapy conference, Brisbane, September 24th, 1983. *Australian Journal of Family Therapy, 5*, 11–16

Epston, D. (1992). "I am a Bear": Discovering discoveries. In D. Epston and M. White (Eds.), *Experience contradiction narrative and imagination* (pp. 173–188). Adelaide, S. Australia: Dulwich Centre Publications.

Epston, D. (1993a). Workshop on anorexia. Charter-Peachford Hospital, Atlanta, GA.

Epston, D. (1993b). *The approach of the Anti-Anorexia (Bulimia) League*. Auckland, New Zealand: Family Therapy Centre.

Epston, D., Morris, F., & Maisel, R. (1995). A narrative approach to so-called anorexia/ bulimia. *Journal of Feminist Family Therapy, 7*(1/2), 69–96.

Faiver, C., Ingersoll, R. E., O'Brien, E., & McNally, C. (2001). *Explorations in counseling and spirituality: Philosophical, practical and personal reflections*. Australia: Brooks/Cole.

Feinstein, D. (1997). Personal mythology and psychotherapy: Myth-making in psychological and spiritual development. *American Journal of Orthopsychiatry, 67*(4), 508–521.

Fish, V. (1993). Poststructuralism in family therapy: Interrogating the narrative/conversational mode. *Journal of Marital and Family Therapy, 19*(3), 221–232.

Foucault, M. (1965). *Madness and civilization: A history of insanity in the age of reason*. New York: Random House.

Foucault, M. (1979). *Discipline and punish: The birth of the prison*. London: Peregrine.

Foucault, M. (1980). *Power/knowledge: Selected interviews and other writings*. New York: Pantheon.

Freedman, J. H., & Combs, G. (1996). *Narrative therapies: The special construction of preferred realities*. New York: Norton.

Freedman, J. H., & Combs, G. (2000). Narrative therapy with couples In F. M. Dattilio & L. J. Bevilacqua (Eds.), *Comparative treatments for relationship dysfunction* (pp. 342–361). New York: Springer.

Gallant, J. P., Brownlee, K., & Vodde, R. (1995). "Not with me you don't!": A story of narrative practice and dissociative identity disorder. *Journal of Contemporary Family Therapy. Special Issue on The Story and Storytelling, 17*(1), 143–157.

Glaser, B., & Strauss, A. (1967). *The discovery of grounded theory*. Chicago: Aldine.

Goddard, J. A., Lehr, R., & Lapadat, J. C. (2000). Parents of children with disabilities: Telling a different story. *Canadian Journal of Counselling, 34*(4), 273–289.

Goldenberg, I., & Goldenberg, H. (2000). *Family therapy: An overview* (5th ed.). Australia: Brooks/Cole.

Hart, B. (1995). Re-authoring the stories we work by: Situating the narrative approach in the presence of the family of therapists. *Australian and New Zealand Journal of Family Therapy, 16*(4), 181–189.

Hewson, D. (1991). From laboratory to therapy room: Prediction questions for reconstructing the "new–old" story. *Dulwich Centre Newsletter 3*, 5–12.

Jenkins, A. (1987). Engaging the adolescent sexual abuser. Unpublished workshop notes.

Jenkins, A. (1990). *Invitations to responsibility: The therapeutic engagement of men who are violent and abusive*. Adelaide, S. Australia: Dulwich Centre Publications.

Laird, J. (2000). Culture and narrative as metaphors for clinical practice with families, In D. H. Demo, K. R. Allen, & M. A. Fine (Eds.), *Handbook of family diversity* (pp. 338–358). New York: Oxford University Press.

Madigan, S. (1991). Discursive restraints in therapist practice: Situating therapist questions in the presence of the family. *Dulwich Centre Newsletter, 3*, 13–20.

Markus, H., & Nurius, P. (1986). Possible selves. *American Psychologist, 41*, 954–969.

McLeod, J. (1999). A narrative social constructionist approach to therapeutic empathy. *Counseling and Psychology Quarterly, 12*(4), 377–394.

McQuaide, S. (1995). Storying the suicide of one's child. *Clinical Social Work Journal, 23*(4), 417–428.

McQuaide, S. (2000). Women's resilience at midlife: What is it? How do you mobilize it? In E. Norman, (Ed.), *Resiliency enhancement: Putting the strengths perspective into social work practice.* New York: Columbia University Press.

Merriam, S. (1988). *Case study research in education: A qualitative approach.* San Francisco: Jossey-Bass.

Monk, G., Winslade, J., Crockett, K., & Epston, D. (Eds.). (1997). *Narrative therapy in practice: The archaeology of hope.* San Francisco: Jossey-Bass.

Moustakas, C. (1994). *Phenomenological research methods.* Thousand Oaks, CA: Sage.

Neal, J. H., Zimmerman, J. L., & Dickerson, V. C. (1999). Couples, culture, and discourse. In J. M. Donovan (Ed.), *Short-term couple therapy.* New York: Guilford Press.

Neimeyer, R. A. (1993a). An appraisal of constructivist psychotherapies. *Journal of Consulting and Clinical Psychology, 61*(2), 221–234.

Neimeyer, R. A. (1993b). Constructivist psychotherapy. In K. T. Kuehlwein & H. Rosen (Eds.), *Cognitive therapies in action: Evolving innovative practice.* San Francisco: Jossey-Bass.

Nichols, M. P., & Schwartz, R. C. (2001*). Family therapy: Concepts and methods* (5th ed.). Boston: Allyn and Bacon.

O'Dell, S. (2000). Psychotherapy with gay and lesbian families: Opportunities for cultural inclusion and clinical challenge. *Clinical Social Work Journal, 28*(2), 171–182.

Parry, A., & Doan, R. E. (1994). *Story re-visions: Narrative therapy in the post-modern World.* New York: Guilford Press.

Ramsey, J. L., & Blieszner S., (2000). Transcending a lifetime of losses: The importance of spirituality in old age. In J. H. Harvey & E. D. Miller (Eds.), *Loss and trauma: General and close relationship perspectives.* Philadelphia: Brunner-Routledge.

Rothschild, P., Brownlee, K., & Gallant, J. P. (2000). Narrative interventions for working with persons with AIDS: A case study. *Journal of Family Psychotherapy, 34*(2) 1–13.

Semmler, P., & Williams, C. B. (2000). Narrative therapy: A storied context for multicultural counseling. *Journal of Multicultural Counseling and Development, 28*(1), 51–62.

Shuler, P., Gelberg, L., & Brown, M. (1994). The effects of spiritual/religious practices on psychological well being among inner city homeless women. *Nurse Practitioner Forum, 5*(2), 106–113.

Snyder, M. (2000). The loss and recovery of erotic intimacy in primary relationships: Narrative therapy and relationship enhancement therapy. *Family Journal—Counseling and Therapy for Couples and Families, 8*(1), 37–46.

Strauss, A., & Corbin, J. (1990). *Basics of qualitative research: Grounded theory procedures and techniques.* Newbury Park, CA: Sage.

Tomm, K. (1987). Interventive interviewing: Part I. Strategizing as a fourth guideline for the therapist. *Family Process, 26*, 3–13.

Tomm, K. (1993). The courage to protest: A commentary on Michael White's work. In S. Gilligan & R. Price (Eds.), *Therapeutic conversations.* New York: Norton.

Vodde, R., & Gallant, J. P. (1999). Bridging the gap between micro and macro practice: Large scale change and the work of Michael White and David Epston. Submitted for publication.

Waldgrave, C. (1998). The challenge of culture to psychology and postmodern thinking In M. McGoldrick (Ed.), *Re-visioning family therapy: Race, culture and gender in clinical practice* (pp. 404–413). New York: Guilford Press.

Walsh, F. (1998). *Strengthening family resilience.* New York: Guilford Press.

White, M. (1986). Family escape from trouble. *Family Therapy Case Studies, 1*, 29–33.

White, M. (1987, Spring). Family therapy and schizophrenia: Addressing the "in-the-corner" lifestyle. *Dulwich Centre Newsletter*, 14–21.

White, M. (1988/1989, Summer). The externalizing of the problem and the re-authoring of lives and relationships. *Dulwich Centre Newsletter*, 3–21.

White, M. (1989a, Summer). Family therapy training and supervision in a world of experience and narrative. *Dulwich Centre Newsletter, 27*–38.

White, M. (1989b, Spring). Saying hullo again: The reincorporation of the lost relationship in the resolution of grief. *Dulwich Centre Newsletter, 7*–11.

White, M. (1991). Deconstruction and therapy. *Dulwich Centre Newsletter, 3*, 21–40.

White, M. (1993). Deconstruction and therapy. In S. Gilligan & R. Price (Eds.), *Therapeutic conversations* (pp. 22–61). New York: Norton.

White, M., & Epston, D. (1990). *Narrative means to therapeutic ends.* New York: Norton.

White, M., & Epston, D. (1991). A conversation about AIDS and dying. *Dulwich Centre Newsletter, 2*, 5–16.

Winslade, J., & Smith, L. (1997). Countering alcoholic narratives. In G. Monk, J. Winslade, K. Crocket, & D. Epston (Eds.), *Narrative therapy in practice: The archaeology of hope.* San Francisco: Jossey-Bass.

12

Object Relations Family Interventions

Allie C. Kilpatrick, Ph.D.,
and Elizabeth O. Trawick, M.D.

Object relations family therapy is a relatively new model of family treatment. Its origins are in two separate schools of thought whose streams have merged into a dynamic body that is having a major impact on family therapy today. Not unlike the mighty, milky-white Amazon where it merges with the black waters of the Negro River, but remains separate before finally mingling, psychoanalysis and family therapy have run together and commingled before finally merging to form object relations family therapy.

Object relations theory is considered to be the bridge between psychoanalysis—the study of individuals—and family theory—the study of social relationships. It may be defined as

> the psychoanalytic study of the origin and nature of interpersonal relationships, and of the intrapsychic structures which grew out of past relationships and remain to influence present interpersonal relations. The emphasis is on those mental structures that preserve early interpersonal experiences in the form of *self and object-images*. (Nichols, 1984, p. 183)

Object relations theory is an existing general framework in psychoanalysis and psychiatry that provides the means for understanding the earliest developmental phases of childhood. Using this orientation, which gives primacy to the need for a human relationship even at birth, clinicians and researchers have studied the development of individuals in relation to the people around them from earliest infancy. In recognizing that the newborn baby has an ego, a part of the personality that copes with internal and external reality, object relations theorists have been able to understand early modes of mental functioning based on fantasies of splitting, projection, and introjection that occur in the processes of attaching to and differentiating from the family. These processes allow for the building up of an internal structure, the personality, which consists of condensations of the individual's own unique biopsychosomatic innate givens (the id) blended with experiences of others (resulting in a enriched ego and a superego). It is now recognized that this internal structure building, though most intense in the young, continues throughout life in response to ongoing relatedness. When positive, these early processes lead to a person's having a sense of his or her self as a valuable individual dependent on and working within an indispensable matrix. When negative, the person experiences little sense of self as differentiated from the matrix on which life is felt to absolutely depend and relies on primitive defense mechanisms such as projective identification to relieve emotional pain.

These processes, first described by psychoanalysts, have now been recognized in families and larger social groups. The lack of differentiation of family members has become one of the cornerstones of Murray Bowen's work (1978) in understanding families, as well as Helm Stierlin's work (1976) in studying larger social group functioning (Slipp, 1984). When personality structure does not develop, enmeshment within the family group interferes with recognition of individual needs, which then cannot receive attention. This leads to impoverishment of individuals and thus of the group.

Family Needs

Object relations concepts developed as a way to understand psychotic, borderline, and narcissistic conditions. They continue to provide the most useful tools for treatment of these conditions, in which mental functioning remains at an immature level, with massive use of defenses such as splitting and projective identification. With recognition that groups such as families may function in ways similar to immature individuals by joining to utilize early and immature defense mechanisms, the path was paved to develop interventions that interpret these processes within the family setting. Thus object relations family interventions (ORFI) are indicated whenever family patterns of resolving problems and relieving emotional pain rely on defensive functioning rather than on evaluation of reality with containment of emotional states followed by appropriate action. ORFI may be possible primarily in families functioning at Levels III or IV, where basic needs are met and family structure is stable enough for the family to meet regularly together. But ORFI may also be helpful in Level I and II families, when painful emotional states such as terror or depression are overwhelming the family's ability to maintain structural cohesiveness. At such times, the therapist's ability to know and modulate emotional states for the family may diminish actions that are damaging but is unlikely to lead to deeper change in the family system.

Within the family system, the modes of mental functioning discovered by psychoanalysts may promote or disrupt attachment, bonding, love, caring, development, and intimacy, depending on whether they are used as a means of communication with self and others or as a barrier against communication. To explain, projective identification was first described in 1946 by Melanie Klein, an English psychoanalyst, as a way of ridding the self of unwanted painful or terrifying experiences, which were projected onto the object who then came to be experienced as identical to the unwanted part. This was thought to be essential in early infancy, allowing the baby to nurture the growing ego by taking in good experiences while there was freedom from the bad. Overreliance on projective identification in infancy or its persistence after infancy was thought to be a sign of impaired ego development. As described by Grinberg, Sor, and Bianchedi (1977), Wilfred Bion, a student of Melanie Klein's, recognized that for the infant, projective identification is also the means of communicating with mother. Neuroscience researchers such as Schore (1994, 2000) have begun to describe the neural pathways through which the nonverbal infant seems to "give" to the mother emotional states representing needs for physical care and love. Through internal, neural processes of her own, the mother unconsciously and consciously considers the communication and responds. According to Bion, the infant introjects and internalizes the mother's response and attitude to the projection, thus learning early in life the meaning of its inner world and internalizing a listening attitude toward its self. When this process works "good enough," a term used by Donald Winnicott (1965), another English psychoanalyst, to describe adequate mothering, the stage is set for a lifelong process of intimate communication both verbally and nonverbally with projective processes. When the process does not work between the mother and the infant, the stage is set for a lifelong unconscious process of using projective processes to rid oneself of unwanted inner experiences. Because barriers are built against the unwanted parts that are felt to be in others, communication is interrupted. Carried to an extreme, reality may be so altered that an individual becomes psychotic. To a lesser extent, misperception of certain aspects of another person commonly occurs.

Within family units, systems of projective identifications develop and may persist throughout life. As with individuals, these projections may function as communications with both conscious and unconscious responsiveness to needs of individual members. Or the projections may function as a means of getting rid of the unwanted. In this case, the family develops collusive systems of projections, in which one member may carry a projection for another member in exchange for a need being met or a projection being accepted by the other. Carried to the extreme, families using a projective system become extremely poorly functioning, as reality testing is altered and action may be taken to protect against contact with the unwanted.

To a lesser extent, discommunicative projective systems are extremely common and cause a multitude of difficulties within families. These difficulties can often be addressed with ORFI when the family is able and willing to meet together. The three most common marital complaints—lack of communication, constant arguments, and unmet emotional needs—are understandable in this context. The remarkable and common experience of hearing two people describe one event with a totally different memory and emotional reaction can be comprehended with the recognition that each may be experiencing the other as an unwanted part of the self, thus altering reality of the interaction. Intimacy, emotional and sexual, is blocked by these processes. To make matters worse, because the family has become a system in which members depend on each other to carry projections, pursuit of individual goals is in conflict with relational goals and so are undermined (Finkelstein,1987). Enmeshment with unclear emotional boundaries results. To varying degrees, the family is experienced as a needed but hostile and controlling web.

As a result of these shared, unconscious, internalized object relations, children often develop symptoms and become the "identified patient" who is jealous, hyperactive, angry, or even ill. When children have illnesses or learning difficulties, families may respond inappropriately and with rejection, as the child may represent an unacceptable aspect of the parents or other siblings. At other times, parents may find ambivalent pleasure in allowing gratification of unacceptable desires by their children and then will be unable to limit behavior that is also disturbing. Thus children are confused by their parents' "double messages" and are truly in a bind as they sense their parents' pleased excitement with the unwanted behavior. Siblings may join parents in choosing one child as the recipient of projections. The child is then in the distressing position of accepting the role demanded by the projections in exchange for vital provisions. Not uncommonly, this child is unable to develop a sense of self and becomes depressed. ORFI in situations like this is necessary so that each family member can come to carry and be responsible for his or her own being, freeing each to develop.

Object relations family interventions deal with shared, unconscious, internalized object relations. Focusing on the interaction and interdependence of individual dynamics and family system functioning is crucial in the application of an integrated understanding to family interventions. The family is not perceived as a set of individuals, but as a system comprising sets of relationships that function in ways unique to that specific family. The immediate goal is not symptom resolution, but a progression through the current developmental phase of family life with an improved ability to work as a group and to differentiate among and meet the individual members' needs. Thus this model is especially relevant for Level IV families.

In regard to whether or not ORFI is indicated for a specific family, we must remember that psychological maturity is not necessarily related to socioeconomic status. Applegate (1990) explored aspects of object relations theory within the sociocultural context of family constellations, child-rearing practices, race, and ethnicity. The interrelationship of the internal world of object relations and the external world of multiculturalism is offered as a clinically useful way of examining issues arising from ethnic differences. Slipp (1988) observes that ethnicity alone has not been found to be an issue in ORFI's relevance. Although there are differences between ethnic and racial groups, if the clinician is sensitive and skilled, these can be worked through in treatment. In regard to sexual orientation, therapists generally use the same treatment methods with traditional and same-sex couples (Parker, 1996). One must remember, however, that lack of societal supports and resources, as well as societal sanctions imposed by the dominant culture, must be addressed within the therapeutic dialogue. Families that are functioning at Level IV may come to the clinician with problems described as internal or interpersonal conflicts, anger, blaming, lack of communication, desire for growth and greater intimacy, loss of confidence in self or spouse, depression, loneliness, or isolation. These families generally want an understanding of these situations and are reflective. The next section presents a case where ORFI is an effective explanatory and interventive method.

Family Case Assessment

Assessment of families for ORFI does not necessarily follow the common pattern of history taking, because, as with psychoanalysis, the way and order in which information is presented is essential to understanding the interactional difficulties. In other words, the mode of presentation is data to aid in diagnosis. Furthermore, as it is essential that the therapist be available to enter into the process as a recipient of projections of emotions, the therapist must remain nondirective and available from the beginning to hear the family. Though history is taken nondirectively, by the third to fourth interview the family's ability to use ORFI can be determined based on their cooperativeness in providing linked information and their response to a holding environment and interpretive interventions. The following case demonstrates this process:

At age 68, Al, a retired prosperous executive, called to seek treatment for his 61-year-old wife, who was in the midst of her fourth severe depression. He and his married children wished to bring her in, as she could not come herself. Indeed, when seen, Mary seemed barely functional: She spoke only in a whisper if at all, moved slowly, and had an extremely downcast, deadened expression. She said she saw no reason to live but had no suicidal plans. Al spoke for his wife, explaining that she had become depressed several weeks before during a trip to Europe with their son and daughter-in-law. He had a wonderful time, though it was somewhat difficult driving in strange countries, and he had depended on his competent son of whom he was proud. His wife however, had become more and more depressed as the trip went on, eventually withdrawing to hotel rooms and causing great discomfort in the group. All agreed that perhaps it was the rainy weather. As his wife sat motionless, the family explained that she had always been moody, especially so in the last seven to eight years, when she had begun to have severe episodes of depression. Al could not understand depression as he did not ever feel depressed. He had always worked and gotten along with people. He was a peacemaker, and it made his wife mad. He simply did not get angry. Since Al's retirement seven years before, Mary had become more depressed, wanting to be with him almost all the time. He, however, wanted time to golf with the boys and was troubled that she "punished" him by withdrawing to the back of the house after he spent a day away. On the trip, he had wanted to be with other people; she had wanted to be in the room with him at night and complained that her feet hurt and she would like to put them up on his lap and relax. As Al spoke, Mary sat motionless, and the children silently looked away, I became aware of a deep feeling of hurt, angry longing that seemed to be present, drawing them together and pushing them apart at the same time. And I was aware of my internal response, a wish to make peace as a mother might between two of her children, accompanied by an urge to tell them to knock it off, behave, and stop whining. On the surface, the consultation was about Mary's pain, but Al spoke for Mary, seeming to author the story of her depression as if he knew of it. The children seemed to agree that Al had the story right and wished their mother to be "corrected." I made a statement recognizing the longing each experienced without assigning it to any one person and was careful to avoid labeling Mary as the "ill patient." All wished to continue, and Mary seemed to move a little more freely. Al took her arm to help her as she left the room.

In assessing this original session, I thought that Mary was "holding" depression for all the family members and was overwhelmed. I was struck by the focus of the family on correcting the situation, not simply denying it. Mary seemed to accept the family's projections of emotional pain, and I wondered what the family accepted for her in return, why she was willing to engage in this painful collusion. I was aware that I had a mixed reaction of wishing to be helpful but feeling annoyed and critical at the same time. I was struck by the family's level of functioning, wish to work together, and positive response to my containing the emotional pain. Thus, despite Mary's deep depression, I elected to continue this approach.

In subsequent sessions, attended by Al and Mary and sometimes the grown children, Al focused on his frustration that their life was not happier since his retirement. He had thought there would be time to play golf with his friends and to travel. He wanted more time with his son and daughter and perhaps to go on a trip alone, something he had never done. Instead, he found that his children seemed more distant and he was tied to Mary. Mary, a housewife who had many artistic interests and volunteer activities, quietly whispered that she thought that they would finally be together. It emerged that, since their marriage 42 years before, Al had worked long hours, often getting home in time to read to the children and go to bed himself, only to be up at the crack of dawn and off to work. Weekends were devoted to church and children's activities when Al was not working at home. Mary had always felt lonely but had tolerated the situation because she felt it was for the family and the children were doing well. And she thought that some day "Al will retire and it will be my turn." Al had not noticed her loneliness or any emotional unhappiness in the family or himself. He had enjoyed the children, and Mary agreed that he was a wonderful father. The grand picture, re-created in interactions within the first few sessions and in their perceptions of their life together, was of Mary as frighteningly sensitive, demanding, and depressive; Al as happy, content, hard working, engaged, and devoid of unpleasant emotion other than criticism of Mary. The children had grown into competent adults, but with difficulties in tolerating feelings, seeming to agree with their father that their mother felt and demanded too much. In their own choice of partners, they had responded to dynamics within the family. Their daughter, always closest to her father, married a man who had not attended college but ran a blue-collar business and would always be home for dinner and weekends. Their son, perceived as sensitive and artistic like his mother, was highly successful at a business that he ran from his home while his wife worked long hours away from home. They had chosen to have no children. Mary's worry that this meant her son had been unhappy as a child angered Al, who said that they should not interfere.

Dialogue of retirement and the trip was associated with a feeling of depression, which Mary silently expressed by slumping more in the chair and which Al denied by turning the focus to curing Mary's depression, perhaps with medication. Rather than labeling Mary as the ill patient, interventions focused on depression as related to Al's retirement and aging. When these subjects were present, feelings of sadness and fear were present, but everyone turned to Mary and focused on her as depressed. As I interpreted the feelings of loss and fear for the future that arose in relationship to Al and Mary's aging, the family was able to shift the focus from Mary and began the human process of accepting losses. The process of projective identification was operative within the family, but when painful affects were contained in the therapeutic setting and identified by interpretation, the family responded, indicating that they were good candidates for ORFI.

As we explored the onset of Mary's depression, a similar process became apparent: Al had avoided feeling humiliated when he depended on his competent son to drive him around by focusing on his pride in his son; his son had focused on his joy at being with his kind father rather than on worry about his father; Mary felt more and more incapacitated by depression, showing the way in which she carried the painful affect. In return, Al complained but remained extremely dependent on her, never leaving her side, so Mary had a constant companion, which fulfilled strong lifelong needs of dependency, reinforcing the pattern. Furthermore, in the third session, Mary began to evoke criticism from the family rather than accepting sympathy instead of correction, indicating that she had a need to be criticized. She began to seem angry at me, as if I were taking something from her.

In this continuing assessment, I noted that the dynamics of the family were active and that I had become an observing participant. The family's ability to include me indicated the ego strength to relate and to form transferences with me. Even when unpleasant, the family members were able to consider my comments. I thus knew that the ability to tolerate good and bad was present, meaning that the family could consider their emotional states.

The collusive pattern that had been present throughout the couple's long and stable marriage had limited intimacy. Only over the course of several years of therapy were the underpinnings of this pattern understood as emotional states that could be identified and located in the rightful partner. Each partner fulfilled a function of containing or fulfilling longings for the other and of representing past objects. Both had grown up in large families during the Great Depression. Al was the fourth son, followed by a sister, brother, and another sister. Mary was the fifth child, preceded by four brothers, and followed by one younger sister. Al presented stories of an idealized view of childhood, such as of admiring his wonderful older brothers whom he watched run and play, and then criticized Mary's neediness.

Exploration revealed that, for Al, Mary represented the younger baby sister whom he, as a toddler, stayed home with while he watched his big brothers run off. Most significantly, he had to watch his sister be the baby, carried and held by his mother, in a way that he had still wanted. Originally, his neediness had been projected onto the baby sister, who was internalized by him as a resented representation of need. This internal representation had been reprojected (transferred) onto Mary throughout their relationship and had become more intense as he became more needy with aging. When his son became more competent than he, able to drive around easily in a strange country, his experience of his early life was strongly activated, as he again became the weak child left with baby sister and mother, who had no time for him. Mary became depressed, and he became annoyed with her, as he had felt toward his mother when she had no time to be with him.

As this picture of Al emerged, more of Mary's life experience became apparent. Her father was distant, often at work in the same blue-collar profession as their disappointing son-in-law. Mother, remembered as a well-respected, hard-working, self-reliant housewife, was dominant. She felt that her mother was not to be crossed and seemed to do little to oppose her, though she had often longed to go off with her brothers, who always left her. She also experienced her mother, a fantastic housekeeper, as focused on tasks and critical of any interferences. Even though she was the first girl, she did not feel she had been enjoyed by her parents. After high school, she had left home for a larger city and found employment as a secretary, where she met Al, already employed as a professional in the same company. From the beginning, his position paralleled that of admired older brothers, all of whom had left her. This experience primed Mary to accept the role of "wife at home waiting," but with the leftover pains of feeling that she was an unliked, bothersome baby, which were transferred into the marriage. A part of her internalized object world was a mother who did not deem feelings to be important but insisted on getting on with the tasks of maintaining a home and raising a family. For Mary, her mother had been internalized as so critical that she would have difficulty bearing the burden of it. Inducing her family to criticize her had thus allowed her to engage in a projective identification in which others carried the criticism. Resistance in therapy occurred when the family became less criticizing and more understanding. Then Mary had to accept responsibility for her internal sense of always feeling criticized and to work through her relationship with her mother.

A significant tension arose even in the beginning sessions—that of each of us waiting for another to speak or respond. Mary had said that she was was always waiting for Al, and this was re-created in the therapeutic setting. As I contained the painful tension and followed its lead, information arose that contributed to our understanding that this was a shared internal experience of both Mary and Al, as both had felt themselves to be always waiting for mother's attention. This common experience was dealt with in their habitual way of Al's taking actions that caused Mary to experience the feeling and then rejecting her if she expressed it. It could be seen that each of the children had internalized parts of this pattern which continued into the next generation. As we worked to follow the emotional states as they became alive, the patterns were altered in all family members. As pointed out by Thomas Ogden (1997), internal object relationships are not fixed, but are fluid sets of thoughts, feelings, and sensations that are continually in movement and always susceptible in newly experienced context. Thus even unconscious patterns can change as the intersubjective experience of the family is altered.

Treatment Goals

Safety of each family member is always a concern. In this case, the potential of suicide by Mary required evaluation. As the treatment progressed, the possibility that awareness of intense feelings that had been avoided throughout life could overwhelm Al, causing him to become suicidal, required ongoing assessment.

Once safety is established, in ORFI the goal is always to enable the family to engage so that the fundamental drive for relatedness will be met in the unique manner of each family. Interventions aim to support the family as a work group, so that impediments to relatedness can be identified and resolved. Impediments include family-of-origin issues, such as multigenerational transmission of conflicts and maladaptive roles, resistance to accepting and tolerating painful emotions, and attempts to control rather than to empower other members.

Goals directed toward specific symptom removal or achievement of desired behaviors are incompatible with ORFI, as they usually reflect attempts to manipulate or control the group and impede the family's being with the therapist in a way that reveals interactive projection–collusion processes. As the therapist identifies the collusive processes, a potentially destructive process is broken, allowing a more constructive relativeness in which individual and group development is supported.

Intervention Approach: Theory Base and Tenets

Object relations family intervention comes from the application of object relations theory to family systems. Object relations theory and its therapeutic approach regard the individual's inner world and external family as components of an open system. It can be used to develop typologies of family interaction and treatment that take into consideration the intrapsychic influences on family patterns, which in turn affect the client's personality. Thus psychoanalysis and family treatment complement each other to enhance the theoretical understanding in both fields and to foster an intervention approach that is dependent not on the theoretical orientation of the clinician but on the needs of the client family.

Historically, Freud is recognized as the father of psychoanalysis and contributed theories that are the foundation of object relations. As described by Hamilton (1989), in Freud's early biological theories infants were conceptualized as having drives directed toward an object (*Instincts and Their Vicissitudes*, 1915), so that the infant sought gratification from an object, usually the mother. Psychological growth occurs when drives are frustrated and the organism seeks increasingly effective means of energy discharge. The goal is maintenance of the organism, the infant, without recognition or focus on the object. Freud's later theories were the beginning of object relations theory. In *Mourning and Melancholia* (1917), he described introjection following the loss of a loved person as a means of maintaining a sense of continuing to be with the person receiving fantasied gratification. In his last work, *Splitting of the Ego in the Process of Defense* (1940b), he described splitting as a defense mechanism of the ego which resulted in a lifelong coexistence of two contradictory dispositions that do not influence each other. Splitting, projection, and introjection form the core concepts of all object relations theories in psychoanalysis and ORFI.

As described by Gomez (1997), object relations theory was a British development of psychoanalysis that arose in the mid-twentieth century with the recognition that relatedness is the core of all human interaction from the beginning of life. The need for others is not only biological, but is also the *need to be experienced by the other* in order to develop a sense of one's own existence. The term *object* shifts from a biological concept of functions that satisfy urges to an existential experience essential for development of mind and personality, in which a person lives a dual reality, internal and external. Working about the same time and comingling concepts, Melanie Klein (1935, 1936, 1937, 1940) and Ronald Fairbairn (1952) refined theories of splitting into good and bad objects and recognized the importance of introjection and projection for the buildup of personality structure, particularly the ego and superego. Continuing these theories, Winnicott (1965) developed the concept of the holding environment as an essential aspect of mother–infant relationship paralleled later in that of therapist–patient. Balint (1952, 1968), Guntrip (1968), and Bowlby (1953, 1969, 1973, 1980) extended these ideas to concepts of attachment theory. Wilfred Bion (1962a, 1962b, 1963), working in the late mid-twentieth century, extended knowledge of projective identification to recognize its importance as a normal means of communication operative in all groups. Object relations theory originally referred to internal objects but has been extended primarily by American analysts to include relations with external objects.

Although the basic tenets of ORFI are based on psychoanalysis, they continue to be modified. Specific historical tenets and concepts are now presented as they are currently used in assessment and interventions.

Freud (1940a) originally mentioned **splitting** as a defense mechanism of the ego and defined it as a lifelong coexistence of two contradictory dispositions that do not influence each other. Kernberg (1972), in tracing the process of splitting through developmental stages, states that splitting of the "all good" (organized around pleasurable mother–child interactions) and "all bad" (derived from painful and frustrating interactions) self-images, object images, and their affective links occurs from 2 to 8 months. The separation of the self from object representations occurs from 8 to 36 months. Splitting into good and bad persists, and this is seen as the fixation point for borderline patients. Following the splitting is the integration of the good and bad emotional images so that the separate self and object representations are each both good and bad. It is at this point that the ego, superego, and id become firmly established as intrapsychic structures and that the defenses of splitting are replaced by repression. Slipp (1984) sees this stage as the fixation point for neurotic pathology. In the last stage, internalized object representations are reshaped through actual current experiences with real people. A goal of ORFI is to assist in the development of this integration and reshaping.

Introjection is a crude, global form of taking in, as if those fragments of self–other interactions are swallowed whole. It is the earliest, most primitive form of the internalization of object relations, starting on a relatively crude level and becoming more sophisticated as the child grows (Nichols, 1984). The child reproduces and fixates its interactions with significant others by organizing memory traces that include images of the object, the self interacting with the object, and the associated affect. Good and bad internal objects are included, each with images of the object and the self. However, the resulting internal image does not completely parallel the actual external experience, which has been altered by projection of an already existent internal state. For example, a frustrated, enraged infant is likely to perceive mother as angry even when she is not and to store the image of her as an angry mother fused with itself as bad. To prevent this internalization, the mother must be able to provide a holding function, contain the anger, and respond in a way that alters the state of the infant and thus the perception of mother/self which is introjected.

Projective identification is a defense mechanism that operates unconsciously. Unwanted aspects of the self are attributed to another person, and that person is induced to behave in accordance with these projected attitudes and feelings (Nichols, 1984). For instance, in the case example, Al is unable to accept his sadness, anxiety, and longings to be held and supported, and projects them onto Mary. Mary, unable to tolerate the internal criticism of an introjected critical mother, projects this aspect of herself onto Al and her children. The concepts of transference (Freud, 1905), scapegoating (Vogel & Bell, 1960), symbiosis (Mahler, 1952), trading of dissociations (Wynne, 1965), merging (Boszormenyi-Nagy, 1967), irrational role assignments (Framo, 1970), and family projective process (Bowen, 1965) are all variants of Klein's (1946) concept of projective identification. The phenomena of projective identification as a life and clinical experience is most thoroughly described by Grotstein (1981) and Ogden (1982).

Collusion is an integral part of projective identification. The recipient of the split-off part of the partner does not disown the projection but acts on the conscious or unconscious message (Stewart, Peters, Marsh, & Peters, 1975). For example, the need for a "weak" woman requires that both partners agree to the assigned roles. Each spouse's ego identity (which includes both good and bad objects) is preserved by having one or more bad objects split off onto the partner. Thus each partner disowns his or her bad-object introjects and needs the other to accept the projection of these introjects in a collusive manner (Piercy et al., 1986). Dicks (1963) believes that this collusive process continues because both spouses hope for integration of lost introjects by finding them in each other. Clinicians using object relations theory attempt in various ways to help couples own their introjects and begin seeing their spouses for the people they really are, not projected parts of themselves.

Winnicott (1958) builds on his notion of *good enough mothering* to the idea of a holding environment. If the good enough mother (or primary nurturing person) provides a holding environment that is safe, secure, responsive, nurturing, nonretaliating, and supportive of separation-individuation, the child can achieve a firm sense of identity and a lifelong capacity for developing nonsymbiotic object relations.

Scharff and Scharff (1987) develop this concept further by defining the role of the father (or secondary nurturing person) as supporting the holding of the mother physically, financially, and emotionally; the father holds the mother as she holds the baby. This contextual holding provides an environmental extension of the mother's presence that later extends outward to grandparents and family, neighbors, and others. Feminist-informed object relations theory additionally considers the influence of gender on the holding environment. Sex role differentiation and shifting sex role mores are considered to affect the holding environment that is created within the couple, marital, and family settings (Juni & Grimm, 1994). Traditional concepts of masculine and feminine roles are challenged with the emergence of new realities that defy gender specification. A holding environment that typifies excessive power imbalances between partners may be understood within the context of early object relations (Silverstein, 1994). The need for dominance and power, particularly in the area of sexual arousal and pleasure, has been suggested to evolve from excessive control or coercion by a powerful parental object during early psychosexual development.

These concepts of the holding environment also apply to working with families. The clinician needs to provide a holding environment for the family by providing safety, competence, and concern for the whole family, and by engaging with the central issues of the family, being caring, interactive, and understanding. The concept of containment introduces a specifically mental ability of the therapist to allow unknown feelings, sensations, and thoughts of the family members to live within the boundaries of the therapist's being and so to be known, identified, and returned to the family in tolerable form and doses. Within this "therapeutic envelope," Al and Mary could tolerate their own experience and then accept the other as different, even if disagreeably so.

As to the current status of ORFI, there is no overall integrated theory. Various theorists have developed their own perspectives over the years, and others have made attempts at integration. One is Framo (1972), who calls his approach a "transactional" one. It leans heavily on the notion of projective identification as applied to a family system and offers a new way of presenting transference. He builds on Fairbairn's notion of the fundamental need for a satisfying object relationship. When a child interprets the parents' behavior as rejection or desertion and cannot give up the parent, it internalizes the loved but hated parent in the inner world of self as an introject (as if swallowed whole) or a psychological representation. In the course of time, as the person begins to force close relationships into fitting this internal role model, these split-off or divided introjects become important. Framo sees the introject of the parent as a critical issue in family therapy, and one that is much neglected. Framo tries to put together a basically intrapsychic concept, introjects, with a system concept. In doing so, he draws out the implications in Bowen's (1978) formulation of family theory for object relations theory.

Boszormenyi-Nagy and Spark (1973) are also concerned about introjects and object relations. They see family pathology as a specialized multiperson organization of shared fantasies and complementary need gratification patterns that are maintained for the purpose of handling past object loss experience.

Monumental groundbreaking work has been done by D. Scharff (1982), J. Scharff (1989), Scharff and Scharff (1987), and Slipp (1984, 1988). For Scharff and Scharff (1987), ORFI derives from the psychoanalytic principles of listening, responding to unconscious material, interpreting, developing insight, and working in the transference and countertransference toward understanding and growth. The immediate goal is not symptom resolution, but progression through the current developmental phase of family life with improved ability to work as a group and to differentiate among and meet the individual members' needs. Slipp (1984, 1988) studied diverse patient populations and their families to explore the interaction and interdependence of individual dynamics and family system functioning. His ultimate goal is to apply an integrated understanding to family treatment.

ORFI's basic tenet is that treatment of the individual and treatment of the family are theoretically and therapeutically consistent with each other, and both are parts of an open system. The two levels of the intrapersonal and the interpersonal are in a constantly dynamic relationship with each other. An assumption is that resolving problems in the relationships in the client's current family necessitates intrapsychic exploration and resolution of those unconscious object relationships that were internalized from early parent–child relationships. Another assumption is that these early influences affect and explain the nature of present interpersonal problems.

Application to Families on Level IV

Families who have needs on Level IV are generally introspective and reflective, and yearn to be more self-actualizing. There may be problems of inner conflict or difficulties with intimacy. Although we may still be treating symptomatic people, our goals have to do with the development of an inner "richness"—insight, more sensitive awareness of the relational world, an understanding of legacies and heritage. In all cases we would hope to deepen awareness of the inner world and to improve understanding of history, style, and unmet yearnings. A very important aspect is the spiritual therapies that help families discover the transcendent aspects of their beings. ORFI is a useful adjunct to all spiritual therapies because interventions that allow for a fuller experience of self, free of internal images or projections of others, supports an engagement with transcendence and assumption of responsibility for mature spiritual experience as described by Young-Eisendrath and Miller (2000).

In ORFI, the therapeutic environment is established by the therapist's encouragement of open dialogue in a safe, mutually helpful atmosphere. The family practitioner generally maintains a neutral stance that respects each member's autonomy. The practitioner avoids assuming a directive approach but attends to other material produced in the session as described by Slipp (1988). The past is linked to the present through interpretation of the transference, particularly the ways it is acted out interpersonally in the ongoing family relationships. In order to facilitate the acceptance of these interpretations, the therapist needs to join the family empathetically and to create a safe and secure holding environment where space for understanding is provided. In the research of Sampson and Weiss (1977), creating such a holding environment has been found to be the most crucial element for change and growth. The practitioner's stance with the family is one that reflects an awareness that he or she affects and is affected by the family (Slipp, 1988). ORFI fosters the kind of meaningful shared intimacy with respect for one another's individuality that the philosopher Martin Buber (1958) so aptly described as the "I–thou relationship."

These types of interventions are well suited for those families who have needs on Level IV. Their lives are in good enough order that this kind of finishing experience makes sense, and they are living in a stable enough way to benefit. Although many of our most highly valued interventions are appropriate for families whose needs are on Level IV, many, if not most, of the families seen by helping professionals such as social workers have more basic needs.

On the other hand, family practitioners who have not experienced Level IV work may be unprepared to deal with clients for whom meaning, awareness, and spiritual growth are issues. Some practitioners would not acknowledge the importance, or even the existence, of an inner world. If such practitioners encounter families who have Level IV needs, referral to a more existentially oriented practitioner would seem appropriate.

Interventions and Techniques

In ORFI, a vital part of the practitioner's role and function is assessment. Scharff and Scharff (1987, p. 155) cite six major tasks to achieve in the assessment phase to determine if ORFI would be effective.

1. The provision of therapeutic space, which includes trust and openness.
2. Assessment of developmental phase and level to determine tasks to be accomplished.
3. Demonstration of defensive functioning to determine ego strength.
4. Exploration of unconscious assumptions and underlying anxiety to determine intervention needs.
5. Testing of the response to interpretation and assessment format to see if they are ready for understanding and insight.
6. Making an assessment formulation, recommendation, and treatment plan.

These major tasks may be accomplished in a more structured assessment phase. Slipp (1984, pp. 204–205) reviews the steps in such an assessment process; see Table 12.1.

TABLE 12.1   Assessment Process in Object Relations Family Therapy

- **Explore the presenting problem** of patient and its background.
  1. Does it seem related to overall family functioning and/or to stress from a family life cycle stage?
  2. What has been done so far to remedy the problem?

- **Establish an individual diagnosis** for each family member including a judgment concerning the level of differentiation and the use of primitive or mature defenses.
  1. Gather data on the client and family development.
  2. Note any ethnic differences or conflicts.

- **Evaluate family constancy** to determine if parents can maintain their own narcissistic equilibrium, or if patient is needed to sustain their self-esteem and survival.
  1. Does a rigid homeostasis or defensive equilibrium exist that binds and prevents the patient from individuating and separating?
  2. Is there pressure for personality compliance within the family, or social achievement outside the family?
  3. What affiliative, oppositional, and alienated attitudes exist?

- **Explore precipitating stress** and its relation to a loss or other traumatic event (negative or positive) or a transitional point in the family life cycle that has disrupted homeostasis.

- **Define individual boundaries** for members. These may be rigidly too open (a symbiotically close relationship) or too closed (an emotionally divorced and distant relationship).
  1. Are **generational boundaries** intact, or are there parent–child coalitions?
  2. Are the parental coalition, the subsystems, and authority hierarchy intact?

- **Define the family boundary** to see if it is too open (symbiotic relations persist with family of origin) or too closed (family is isolated from community without social support system).

- **Determine the ability to negotiate differences and problem solve** through verbal dialogue involving respect for one's own and others' views, opinions, and motivations versus an egocentric controlling viewpoint resulting in coercion and manipulation.

- **Observe** communication patterns for evidence of spontaneous versus rigid stereotyping, distancing, or obfuscating; level of initiative versus passivity; rigidity of family rules; and the **power-role structure.**

- **Evaluate the loving and caring feelings** amongst members that allow for separateness (rather than acceptance only by conformity) and provide warmth, support, and comfort.

- **Define the treatment goals** in terms of difficulties that have been uncovered, and present the frame or boundaries of the treatment process.

Source: Slipp, 1984, pp. 204–205.

In addition to the ethnic differences or conflicts mentioned earlier, attention must also be given to other sociocultural–environmental factors that influence the family. Impacts of the entire ecosystem must be considered in the assessment process.

There are some specific techniques that ORFI uses in the beginning, middle, and last phases of treatment, which Slipp (1988, pp. 199–200) has outlined as a guide for clinicians; see Table 12.2.

Areas of Differentiation. There are specific techniques that differentiate the object relations approach from other treatment approaches. Stewart et al. (1975, pp. 176–177) give six areas of differentiation; see Table 12.3. These highlight overall techniques used in ORFI and discriminate this approach further.

Evaluation of Effectiveness

Because symptom reduction is not the goal of this model, it cannot serve as the measure of effectiveness. The presence or absence of unconscious conflict, because

---

TABLE 12.2 Phases of Treatment in Object Relations Family Therapy

- During the beginning phase of treatment the techniques are to
  1. Develop a safe holding environment through empathy, evenhandedness, and containment; an environment that facilitates trust, lowers defensiveness, and allows aggression to be worked with constructively.
  2. Interpret the circular positive or negative systemic interaction in a sequential non-blaming manner by
     a. Defining its origin.
     b. Defining what was hoped to be gained.
     c. Describing its effects.

- During the middle phase of treatment, the techniques are to
  1. Interpret projective identification by
     a. Reframing its purpose to give it a positive aim.
     b. Linking it with a genetic reconstruction.
     c. Clarifying why an aspect of the self needs to be disowned and projected. This process diminishes defensiveness, enhances the therapeutic alliance, and facilitates continued work with the reowned projective identification.
  2. Use the objective countertransference as a tool to understand the transferences and to provide material for interpreting projective identification.

- During the last phase of treatment, the techniques are to
  1. Work through individual conflicts and developmental arrests in the intrapsychic sphere. This process is gradual and may continue in individual therapy after the family treatment terminates.
  2. Terminate treatment.

Source: Slipp, 1988, pp. 199–200.

TABLE 12.3   Object Relations Therapy Approach Differentiated from Other Marital/Family Approaches

- While many marital partners may seem quite different, it soon becomes apparent that their psychic structures are very similar. Although they may behaviorally manifest these intrapsychic processes differently through collusion, projective identification, shared fantasy, etc., the similarities should be discussed and made explicit to the couple.

- The ORFI approach goes beyond countertransference usage in allowing the partner to "put into" the therapist disowned or split-off parts of himself. The more classical analytic approach considers the therapist's reactions as irrational countertransference phenomena. This approach regards such material as a valid, legitimate statement of issues with which the patient is struggling.

- When therapists split up a couple to see each of them individually, the emotional exchanges between the therapists will be similar to and/or mirror the affective transactions between the partners in the marital dyad.

- This ORFI approach provides a way of understanding family problems when a child is presented as the identified patient. The child becomes a carrier or container of the split-off, unacceptable impulses of the parent. The child may be idealized just as he may be denigrated.

- The more classical approach focuses on interpreting the patient's perception in terms of internal processes based on early experiences. This system considers the perception to be based on a need to solve an internal conflict through the use of external objects as carriers. There is an active invitation to other people to fulfill these roles.

- In classical analytical theory, the focus is upon individual psychotherapy and pathological involvement. Behaviorally oriented approaches also emphasize individual functioning. In contrast, object relations theory offers a perspective of the individual as a unit in which even the more pathological traits have a healthy reparative aspect. Consequently, the marital dyad continues to function in defiance of apparent breakdown and irreconcilable differences and conflicts. Awareness of the reciprocal, pathological, and subtle attempts to carry out ego repair generates a greater understanding in the therapist of the durability and maintenance of the marital dyad.

Source: Stewart, Peters, Marsh, & Peters, 1975, pp. 176–177. Reprinted by permission of *Family Process,* Inc.

it is not apparent to family members or outside observers, is difficult to measure. Therefore, assessment of effectiveness depends on the subjective clinical judgment of the therapist and on the family's reactions. With the current emphasis on scientific evidence and cost effectiveness, would these measures be considered sufficient? Clinicians would answer yes, as they consider the clinician's observations to be entirely valid as a means of evaluating theory and treatment. Blanck and Blanck (1972, 1987), discussing Mahler's methods and model, state that clinicians who employ Mahler's theories technically do not question the methodology or the findings, for they can confirm them clinically. This is a form of validation that meets as closely as possible the experimentalist's insistence on replication as a criterion of the scientific method. Along these same lines, Langs (1982) posits that the ultimate test of a therapist's formulation is in the use of these impressions as a basis for intervention. He states further that the patient's reactions, conscious and unconscious, constitute the ultimate litmus test of these interventions, and that true validation involves both cognitive and interpersonal responses from the patient.

The views held by current, eminent object relations family therapists are similar. Slipp (1988) holds that meeting the goals of treatment is the criterion that both the family and therapist use to consider ending treatment. These general goals do not lend themselves to empirical measurement, but to subjective assessments by therapists and families. Scharff and Scharff (1987) state that, at termination, the family can provide the holding environment for the members that is so necessary for attachment and growth. The family is able to return to or reach an appropriate developmental level so that they fit with the individuals' developmental needs for intimacy and autonomy. Slipp (1988) describes the end result as the restructuring of the internal world of object relations with resultant modification of the family's interpersonal relations. Each individual self is experienced as separate and less dependent on external objects to sustain self-esteem and identity. The family will be able to function as a group in a more intimate and adaptive fashion that meets each member's needs.

Although outcome studies have been, primarily, uncontrolled case studies, Dicks (1967) reported on a survey of the outcome of couples therapy at the Tavistock Clinic. He rated 73 percent of a random sample of cases as having been successfully treated. Others have investigated specific tenets of the ORFI theory and provided further empirical evidence of their existence (Slipp, 1984).

Application to Families Functioning at Other Levels

As discussed previously, object relations theory is very useful in understanding a vast array of needs behaviors, problem areas, and symptomatology. This understanding can be applied to families who have needs on any level. Although object relations theory has been utilized extensively to study and treat borderline and narcissistic personality disorders, it is now being used to understand and treat diverse populations and families.

As Slipp (1988) has stated, although ORFI is appropriate for families who desire and can tolerate intensity and closeness, it is certainly not restricted to only those families. As families develop trust and become closer in the intervention process, the treatment itself can serve as a model for more open and intimate relationships among family members. Thus the growth produced could enable the family to move to a higher level of relating.

A significant, though not the only, variable in selecting the most suitable type of family therapy for a specific family's level of need is the family's socioeconomic level. Clients who have Level I needs with overriding poverty and social problems want help that is more immediate and less abstract. Slipp's (1988) study showed that the ORFI approach is particularly fitting for and effective with middle-class families, as well as with a blue-collar population. These families would typically have Level II, III, and IV needs. On the basis of his study findings, ORFI with lower socioeconomic families is least effective and not recommended.

Scharff and Scharff (1987), however, caution clinicians that it should not be assumed that the poor or the culturally or intellectually disadvantaged cannot benefit from ORFI. Some families will fit cultural stereotypes of concrete thinking and dependency on directives and gratification, but others will take to a more reflective approach. Although this type of intervention is not for all families, it is for those that demonstrate an interest in understanding, not just in symptom relief.

Summary

Object relations family treatment can be effective with families who have their basic physical and nurturant needs met, are capable of abstract thinking and insight, and are interested in understanding and changing destructive patterns of behavior, achieving greater intimacy and commitment, reworking meanings, and rewriting their life stories. These patterns may involve poor communication, conflict, lack of differentiation, weak personal and intergenerational boundaries, inconsistent family structure, and rules. Therefore, ORFI is ideally suited for many Level IV families and can be very effective with Level II and III families. It is generally not recommended for Level I families.

Discussion Questions _____

1. What are ORFI's basic tenets, and how do they apply to the case example given?

2. What are the similarities and differences of introjection, projective identification, and collusion?

3. Do ethnicity and gender issues impact the use of ORFI?

4. How are family object relations interventions different from those of individual object relations interventions?

5. From your own practice, identify an individual or family that demonstrates "splitting." Briefly explain why the defense mechanism is evidenced in the person's behavior. Can you find projective identification and collusion as well?

6. What is the "holding environment," and how can it be developed and utilized in applying the techniques of ORFI?

7. How is the pain of Level IV families different from that of Level I, II, and III families in view of object relations theory?

Suggested Readings

Applegate, J. S. (1990). Theory, culture and behavior: Object relations in context. *Child and Adolescent Social Work Journal, 7*(2), 85–100.

Aspects of object relations theory are explored within the sociocultural context of family constellations, child-rearing practices, race, and ethnicity.

Fairbairn, W. R. D. (1954). *An object-relations theory of the personality.* New York: Basic Books.

A seminal work in object relations theory that has had a significant influence on the later work of Dicks, Bowen, Framo, and others. Required reading for those interested in the role of object relations in psychopathology.

Finkelstein, L. (1987). Toward an object relations approach in psychoanalytic marital therapy. *Journal of Marital and Family Therapy, 13*(3), 287–298.

Describes the features that distinguish psychoanalytic marital therapy from other forms of marital therapy, describes how object relations theories can be applied to psychoanalytic marital therapy, and indicates certain directions for further study.

Scharff, D. E., & Scharff, J. S. (1987). *Object relations family therapy.* Northvale, NJ: Jason Aronson.

Represents the Scharffs' efforts to develop a psychoanalytic object relations approach to families and family therapy. The Scharffs demonstrate that object relations theory provides the theoretical framework for understanding and the language for working with the dynamics of both the individual and the family system.

Silverstein, J. L. (1994). Power and sexuality: Influence of early object relations. *Psychoanalytic Psychology, 11,* 33-46.

This article challenges traditional concepts of masculine and feminine roles with the emergence of new realities that defy gender specification.

Slipp, S. (1988). *The technique and practice of object relations family therapy.* Northvale, NJ: Jason Aronson.

This book extends the clinical application of object relations family therapy that Slipp began in an earlier book. He further develops the application of his family typology to the treatment process with specific attention to techniques and process.

References

Applegate, J. S. (1990). Theory, culture and behavior: Object relations in context. *Child and Adolescent Social Work Journal, 7*(2), 85–100.

Baliant, M. (1952). *Primary love and psychoanalytic technique.* London: Hogarth.

Baliant, M. (1968). *The basic fault: Therapeutic aspects of regression.* London: Tavistock.

Bion, W. (1962a). *Learning from experience.* London: Heinemann.

Bion, W. (1962b). A theory of thinking. *International Journal of Psycho-analysis, 43,* 110–119.

Bion, W. (1963). *Elements of Psycho-analysis.* New York: Basic Books.

Blanck, G., & Blanck, R. (1972). Toward a psychoanalytic developmental psychology. *Journal of the American Psychoanalytic Association, 20,* 668–710.

Blanck, G., & Blanck, R. (1987). Developmental object relations theory. *Clinical Social Work Journal, 15,* 318–327.

Boszormenyi-Nagy, I. (1967). Relational modes and meaning. In G. H. Zuk & I. Boszormenyi-Nagy (Eds.), *Family therapy and disturbed families.* Palo Alto, CA: Science and Behavior Books.

Boszormenyi-Nagy, I., & Spark, G. (1973). *Invisible loyalties.* New York: Harper & Row.

Bowen, M. (1965). Family psychotherapy with schizophrenia in the hospital and in private practice. *Comprehensive Psychiatry, 7,* 345–374.

Bowen, M. (1978). *Family theory in clinical practice.* New York: Jason Aronson.

Bowlby, J. (1953). *Child care and the growth of love.* Harmondsworth: Penguin.

Bowlby, J. (1969). *Attachment and loss. Volume I: Attachment.* London: Hogarth.

Bowlby, J. (1973). *Attachment and loss. Volume II: Separation: anxiety and anger.* London: Hogarth.

Bowlby, J. (1980). *Attachment and loss. Volume III: Loss: Sadness and depression.* London: Hogarth.

Buber, M. (1958). *I and thou.* New York: Scribner.

Dicks, H. V. (1963). Object relations theory and marital studies. *British Journal of Medical Psychology, 36,* 125–129.

Dicks, H. V. (1967). *Marital tensions.* New York: Basic Books.

Fairbairn, R. (1952). *Psycho-analytic studies of the personality.* London: Routledge and Kegan Paul.

Finkelstein, L. (1987). Toward an object-relations approach in psychoanalytic marital therapy. *Journal of Marital and Family Therapy, 13*(3), 287–298.

Framo, J. L. (1970). Symptoms from a family transactional viewpoint. In N. W. Ackerman (Ed.), *Family therapy in transition.* Boston: Little, Brown.

Framo, J. L. (1972). Symptoms from a family transactional viewpoint. In N. W. Ackerman, N. Lielg, & J. Pearce (Eds.), *Family therapy in transition.* New York: Springer.

Freud, S. (1905). *Fragment of an analysis of a case of hysteria. Collected papers.* New York: Basic Books.

Freud, S. (1915). *Instincts and their vicissitudes.* Collected Works, Vol. 7.

Freud, S. (1917). *Mourning and melancholia.* Collected Works, Vol. 14.

Freud, S. (1940a). An outline of psychoanalysis. *Standard Edition, 23,* 139–171.

Freud, S. (1940b). *Splitting of the ego in the mechanism of defense,* Collected Works, Vol. 23.

Gomez, L. (1997). *An introduction to object relations.* New York: New York University Press.

Grinberg, L., Sor, D., & Tabak de Bianchedi, E. (1977). *Introduction to the work of Bion.* New York: Jason Aronson.

Grotstein, J. S. (1981). *Splitting and projective identification.* New York: Jason Aronson.

Guntrip, H. (1968). *Schizoid phenomena, object relations and the self.* London: Hogarth.

Hamilton, G. N. (1989). A critical review of object relations theory. *American Journal of Psychiatry, 146*(12), 1552–1560.

Juni, S., & Grimm, D. W. (1994). Sex roles as factors in defense mechanisms and object relations. *Journal of Genetic Psychology, 155,* 99–106.

Kernberg, O. F. (1972). Early ego integration and object relations. *Annals of the New York Academy of Science, 193,* 233–247.

Klein, M. (1935). A contribution to the psychogenesis of manic-depressive states. In *Love, guilt and reparation.* London: Hogarth.

Klein, M. (1936). Weaning. In *Love, guilt and reparation.* London: Hogarth.

Klein, M. (1937). Love, guilt and reparation. In *Love, guilt and reparation.* London: Hogarth.

Klein, M. (1940). Mourning and its relations to manic-depressive states. In *Love, guilt and reparation.* London: Hogarth.

Klein, M. (1946). Notes on some schizoid mechanisms. *International Journal of Psycho-Analysis, 27,* 99–110.

Langs, R. (1982). *Psychotherapy: A basic text.* New York: Jason Aronson.

Mahler, M. S. (1952). On child psychosis and schizophrenia: Autistic and symbiotic infantile psychoses. *Psychoanalytic Study of the Child,* Volume 7.

Nichols, M. (1984). *Family therapy: Concepts and methods.* New York: Gardner Press.

Ogden, T. H. (1982). *Projective identification and psychotherapeutic technique.* London: H. Karnac.

Ogden, T. H. (1997). *Reverie and interpretation, sensing something human.* Northvale, NJ: Jason Aronson.

Parker, G. (1996). Personal communication with A. Kilpatrick.

Piercy, F. P., Sprenkle, D. H., et al. (1986). *Family therapy sourcebook.* New York: Guilford Press.

Sampson, H., & Weiss, J. (1977). Research on the psychoanalytic process: An overview. *The Psychotherapy Research Group,* Bulletin No. 2 (March), Department of Psychiatry, Mt. Zion Hospital and Medical Center.

Scharff, D. E. (1982). *The sexual relationship: An object relations view of sex and the family.* Boston: Routledge & Kegan Paul.

Scharff, D. E., & Scharff, J. S. (1987). *Object relations family therapy.* Northvale, NJ: Jason Aronson.

Scharff, J. S. (Ed.). (1989). *Foundations of object relations family therapy.* Northvale, NJ: Jason Aronson.

Schore, A. N. (1994). *Affect regulation and the origin of the self: The neurobiology of emotional development.* Mahwah, NJ: Erlbaum.

Schore, A. N. (2000). Attachment and the regulation of the right brain. *Attachment and Human Development, 2,* 23–47.

Silverstein, J. L. (1994). Power and sexuality: Influence of early object relations. *Psychoanalytic Psychology, 11,* 33–46.

Slipp, S. (1984). *Object relations: A dynamic bridge between individual and family treatment.* New York: Jason Aronson.

Slipp, S. (1988). *The technique and practice of object relations family therapy.* Northvale, NJ: Jason Aronson.

Stewart, R. H., Peters, T. C., Marsh, S., & Peters, M. J. (1975). An object-relations approach to psychotherapy with marital couples, families and children. *Family Process, 14*(2), 161–178.

Stierlin, H. (1976). The dynamics of owning and disowning: Psychoanalytic and family perspectives. *Family Process, 15*(3), 277–288.

Vogel, E. F., & Bell, N. W. (1960). The emotionally disturbed as the family scapegoat. In N. W. Bell & E. F. Vogel (Eds.), *The family.* Glencoe, IL: Free Press.

Winnicott, D. W. (1958). *Collected papers: Through pediatrics to psycho-analysis.* London: Hogarth Press.

Winnicott, D. (1965). *The maturational processes and the facilitating environment.* London: Hogarth.

Wynne, L. C. (1965). Some indications and contraindications for exploratory family therapy. In I. Boszormenyi-Nagy & J. L. Franco (Eds.), *Intensive family therapy.* New York: Hoeber.

Young-Eisendrath, P. and Miller, M. (Eds.). (2000). *The psychology of mature spirituality, integrity, wisdom, transcendence.* London: Routledge.

13

The Family in the Community

John B. Turner, D.S.W., and Ray H. MacNair, Ph.D.

This chapter examines the community as the broader context in which families survive, thrive, or break down. The ecosystems perspective on the community touches on many aspects that affect families in crucial ways. Communities vary in the extent to which they meet the needs of their members. There needs to be a dual focus in family work—on the family system and its social environment. Emphasis is directed to a holistic and integrative analysis of patterns of human service networking which are intended to overcome the fragmentation found in many community service systems. Finally, a model of integrated family service networking systems is presented.

For many people, the term *community* connotes a place characterized by social warmth, common values, and economic and personal security. Perhaps most families would welcome such a haven in which to raise a family. Too often for some, the community is a place with social and physical risks that threaten the well-being of families. For many, especially the poor living in urban and rural neighborhoods, their social environment is not a healthy place for families. The movie *Boys in the Hood* dramatically illustrates the tension that can exist between families and neighborhoods. Either the family lacks the skills and resources needed for survival or it lacks the skills to negotiate with the community. Good or bad, the neighborhood community is where families live, and its impact on families must be considered (see Ewalt, Freeman, & Poole, 1998).

The family practitioner and agency may find that, in addition to interventions directed toward helping family members become more competent in performance of family functions, interventions in the neighborhood, community, and the larger society directed toward making them more supportive of families need to occur.

The Case of Mrs. Y.

Mrs. Y. wrote a letter to the local newspaper claiming that her rights and those of her family as citizens were being denied by her neighbors who wished to "run her off of the street." She claimed that her neighbors, and Mrs. X. in particular, actively discouraged other children from playing with her four children. The Y. family consisted of her husband, the four children, and her sister-in-law and brother-in-law. The sister-in-law was chronically ill. They lived in a four-room house. Mrs. Y. said that this house was a real improvement over the two-room house in which they had previously lived for 18 months. She told her family worker that where they had lived before there had been no outside space where the children could play. She stated that her husband sometimes held two jobs in order to make ends meet. The worker observed that the children were undisciplined. Managing the family seemed to be a bit too much for Mrs. Y., yet she clearly did not want to search for new housing.

The family worker learned that Mrs. X. was a black woman who was thought by Mrs. Y. to be 65 years old or older. She learned that Mrs. X. was a college graduate and that her father had founded a prominent church in the city. Mrs. Y. said that Mrs. X. thought of herself as belonging to the "elite." She had no children.

Later the worker spoke with Mrs. X., who readily admitted to applying pressures to force the Y. family to move. Mrs. X. indicated that several white and black families wanted the Y. family off the street and refused to allow their children to play with the Y.s' family children. They especially did not like the conduct of Mrs. Y.'s older boys. Conversation with a neighborhood club leader verified that strong social pressure was being directed against Mrs. Y. by some of her neighbors to isolate the family and pressure them to move from the street. It was also acknowledged that Mrs. X. was the leader in this effort.

What are the options for intervention in this situation? What objectives can the family worker seek with the Y. family? Should interventions be attempted with the neighborhood? If so, how might that be accomplished?

Dual Focus

The Y. family illustration highlights the dual focus needed in family work—the family system and its social environment of neighborhood, community and larger society. The need for the agency and family worker to pursue such a dual focus is critical in high risk neighborhoods and communities. This is especially required in the case of poor families. In such areas, even though some solid citizens reside in them, families are more likely to be confronted with violence, crime, poor quality housing, negative peer pressure on youth and adults, low school performance, social, political and physical isolation, poor air quality, racial, cultural and class differences. (See Chapter 3, "Contexts of Helping: Commonalities and Human Diversities."

Ideally, families could be encouraged and assisted in finding housing outside of high-risk living areas. In many cases this is not realistically possible. Intervention

in community situations that threaten families must be considered when relocation is not the answer.

To exercise the community intervention options, it is essential that the
agency understand and agree that community intervention is agency policy. Such
interventions where indicated are necessary for success in efforts to help families.
This means (1) training and supervision of the practice of community interventions and (2) acceptance of community action as a legitimate function by the
agency staff, administration, and board.

Definition of Community

The family is located in the center of a nest surrounding geopolitical systems:
(1) the neighborhood, (2) city and local community, (3) state and county, (4) regional, and (5) national. Within the boundary of each is the potential for providing support or harm to families (see Figure 13.1). Likewise, the agency and other
institutions, both private and public, are located in one or more of the concentric

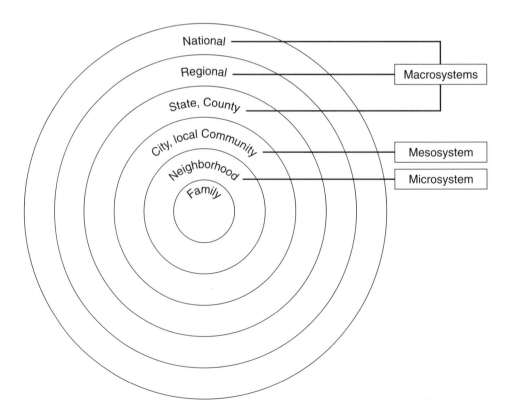

FIGURE 13.1   Levels of Community Systems

circles. Each may want and may possess some capacity to influence policy and actions regarding family policy.

Each community (geopolitical system) will possess to some extent the following general characteristics (Turner, 1968):

1. A constellation of social relationships and roles maintained over time.
2. An identifiable functional interdependence.
3. A specified locality.
4. A common value system.
5. Social stratification (distribution of power).
6. Communication channels.
7. Social control/normative behavior.
8. Production of goods and/or services.
9. Intercultural tolerance.

It is obvious that communities vary in the extent to which they meet each of these characteristics. In some cases, the variation is to such an extent that the community can be described as dysfunctional or disorganized. Also, families may be members of more than one community and, as members, are expected to conform to the requirements of more than one community that may be at odds with each other. This is frequently the case with youth gangs in urban neighborhoods and is often a source of problems for the family.

Family Practitioner and Agency Helping Function in Community

1. Helping Family Members Use Community Resources

It is not unusual to discover that family members are not using community resources that are available to them. Studies have shown that low-income families are reluctant to approach formal-looking institutions like schools, libraries, health centers, policy makers, city housing, inspection departments, and the like. Also, these services may be located outside of the immediate neighborhood. Transportation may be a deterrent in terms of both cost and convenience. The family worker needs to have a familiarity with such resources, including knowledge of key staff members in community institutions. In some instances, it will help to accompany family members to the resource on their first visit. It is also possible to have a volunteer accompany them on first visits in selected cases. In some neighborhoods, it may be unsafe for children and women to travel without someone accompanying them. It is also not unusual to find that parents are reluctant to attend or join groups such as street clubs, PTAs and civic groups, because they lack confidence in speaking at such groups or they are ashamed of their dress.

2. Documentation of Family Problems Related to Community Conditions

Negative or troublesome conditions faced by family clientele should be documented for prompt consideration by the agency for referral or some other course of action. It is important that such documentation and a means of determining how and when to act should be agency policy. Feedback to the practitioner is essential. Referrals to another human service agency, to city housing, to police, to the local school, or to legal aid are among the courses of action. The agency may also call for an interagency conference group on an ad hoc or continuing basis to plan a course of action.

3. Promoting a Community Development Program: Long-Range Planning

Finding adequate housing in a good neighborhood is a huge challenge to family programs. Of course, if housing could be found in quality neighborhoods, the effort involving documentation could be significantly downsized. Family programs need to urge city and county officials to a greater effort to maintain and improve neighborhoods.

In many communities, public and private groups are taking steps to redevelop neighborhoods and communities. These are multidiscipline and multiagency efforts designed to improve housing, streets, playgrounds, and police protection. They involve a large amount of citizen participation. Efforts like this could be called for by the boards of family programs.

Instead of thinking in terms of a multiplicity of so-called social problems, each demanding special attention and a different remedy, we can view them all as different symptoms of the same disease (Frank, 1948, pp. 1–2).

We now address patterns of human service networking as they reflect the community's optimism or pessimism and sense of collective efficacy.

Patterns of Human Service Networking

In the late 1940s, Bradley Buell (1952) observed the migrations of rural southerners into northern cities and the difficulties they experienced. They lacked the educational and organizational skills needed to understand what to do when family supports fell away as a result of the migration. They seemed to feel like aliens in a maze of human service and health agencies, and they distrusted the formality they encountered in bureaucracies that presumably had been designed to serve them. Buell conducted a tracking study in Minneapolis of families as they entered the network and stumbled through it in their efforts to survive.

Buell found (1) gaps in needed services; (2) duplication of services, each of which was inadequate by itself; (3) contradictory advice given by agencies, which should have been coordinated; (4) fragmentation, or the practitioner's view that one partial approach to a complex of problems would be sufficient to solve all problems; (5) bias against people in poverty as unworthy of the agency's time and energy; and (6) bureaucratic barriers to referral, including transportation, waiting lists, and repetitive paperwork. Much has been done nationwide in the ensuing years to address these problems and build coordinated networking systems. However, much resistance and inertia remain, and the problems of fragmentation persist. Many families today fail to wade through from one needed service to another. Much of the service that is rendered is wasted, because complementary services that would reinforce the gains made initially are not rendered.

The federal government, state governments, and foundations have taken up the banner of "integrated services" in a variety of ways. Resources and mandates for coordination have been offered and then revoked. Many pilot "integrated systems" have been tested, and that process continues in the 2000s.

Each community responds in its own way under varied state mandates and creative support by foundations. Within each community, a culture that engenders coordination emerges in varying degrees. A variety of styles can be identified, which result from and affect the optimism or pessimism of the agencies' collective network. They are (MacNair, 1981)

1. An authoritative style, which requires a command response to assigned coordinators. This style appears to result from a cynical view that providers will not consistently participate in networking systems unless they are commanded to participate. The command style invokes resentment and resistance by providers, with the result that a "turf-guarding" pattern emerges, sometimes with a vengeance. The pessimistic basis for the authoritarian style, in other words, provokes further pessimism.

2. A formalist style, based on the idea that providers do not have time and means to talk to each other and have established a paperwork system of referrals that avoids talking altogether. Again, much resistance and inertia are produced, related to the impersonal basis of the system. On the other hand, the possibility of generating highly efficient computerized networks is currently being pursued in some locations. We predict that they may produce a receptive provider response to the extent that providers feel the system is easy to operate and seems to be designed for their benefit.

3. The universalist style, based on an overly optimistic managerial assumption that *all* providers are equally able and willing to make *all* appropriate referrals for *all* clients who need them. Failing to recognize the thorough training and supervision such an assumption requires, this style generates confusion and a sense of inadequacy, resulting in cynicism.

4. The humanistic style, which relies on self-generated interpersonal networks and personalized connections. This style is grounded in an optimism about human relationships among providers. It can regenerate its own optimism if it is fostered carefully throughout the agency network. On the other hand, it may be biased and somewhat inconsistent.

5. The professional style, in which individual providers throughout the agency network are assigned to coordinating roles and trained accordingly. "Dedicated" case managers work with a professional level of knowledge of families with complex and intractable social problems. They have the knowledge of the agency network required to utilize it thoroughly. This approach is grounded in both optimism and realism. It can still lead to resentment by individual providers in agencies of the special status of professional case managers, unless it is tempered with a touch of humanism and guided teamwork. The result can be highly optimistic.

6. An inventive style, resulting from a sense that new, creative forms of networking and somewhat charismatic leadership will generate an enthusiasm for client change and an appreciation for coordinating roles which is contagious. Inventions are frequently sponsored by outside bodies and offer special resources. Hence they are born of optimism and are expected to generate optimism and a sense of efficacy within the network. Examples are (1) the historic "case-finding" programs that put outreach workers on the street to discover hidden but responsive clients and then connect them to available resources; (2) the evolving family preservation programs, which place practitioners in the home to render case management therapy, and guided family-building exercises (see Chapter 5); and (3) family resource centers, which combine interconnected social agencies with the resources of the school system and the mutual self-help resources of parenting groups. None of these styles addresses the problem of the midlevel managers who are frequently left out of the design and implementation of networking systems. Often, cynical by virtue of their position, middle managers are capable of undermining the best-designed system. Thus we suggest it is advisable to engage middle managers in the design and implementation of integrative systems. Teamwork at their level is just as vital as it is at the level of service provision.

Indeed, top managers, middle managers, service providers, and families themselves should all be involved in designing and implementing a networking system that engenders optimism and a sense of efficacy.

The next section proposes a model of a goal-directed community human services system.

A Model of a Community Human Services Networking System

This goal-directed model is based on the assumption that there are at least three types of human services: those directed at survival (Level I families), those focused on self-empowerment (Level II and III families), and those geared for self-realization and prevention (Level III and IV families). Examples of survival-oriented services are unemployment compensation, food stamps, Temporary Assistance to Needy Families (TANF, formerly AFDC), homeless shelters, psychiatric hospitals, youth detention centers, runaway shelters, and detoxification facilities. Corresponding self-empowerment services are training and job placement services, public housing in which rent is paid, outpatient mental health, youth home placement or family preservation service, and addiction treatment and support groups.

Self-realization and prevention services are career development programs, housing subsidies through Section 8 of the U.S. Housing Act, individual or family therapy, education for child rearing, and preventive action systems. The term *preventive actions systems* refers to inventive self-help organizing and empowerment activities that pull together at-risk populations prior to the outbreak of problems, such as teen pregnancy or teen drug addiction. For example, teen councils have been known to organize preventive actions systems of volunteers to mentor younger people, clean up neighborhoods, or offer community services.

For too long American society has been content to offer minimal survival services, or less, to Level I families. Self-empowerment has often been an espoused objective, but often the optimism and sense of professional efficacy required for success have been lacking. Limited resources and clearly documented effectiveness have been barriers to the development and maintenance of self-empowerment and self-realization/prevention services.

Nevertheless, an array of programs at all three levels is available in most urban communities. It is the goal-directed interconnection that is often missing. If survival, self-empowerment, and self-realization/prevention programs were clearly linked, a sense of effectiveness would be more likely. Each program should be designed to demonstrate achievement at one level, readiness to go to the next level, and preparation to receive families from previous levels. Practitioners should be prepared to guide families at Levels I and II from one set of goals to the other when their progress warrants the connection. A goal-directed human services networking system will demonstrate its eagerness to prepare families for the next level and receive them at the next. Documentation of progress should be used to account to the public for the achievements being made. A model of the three types of goals and their interconnections can be offered visually, as in Figure 13.2.

The model suggests that communitywide policies be established that encourage agencies to link with each other through information systems and goal setting with clients. Resources would be expected to follow clients through their connections within the networking system. Connections between programs are thus established that link TANF with child care, education, job training programs, and employment services. Finally, family practitioners will be primed for a networking practice through community workshops that focus on an awareness of the availability of program connections and the policies that guide those connections. A sense of optimism can thus be generated among families that the service system is set up to work for them.

The challenge for community human service networks is threefold: (1) to promote a culture among providers, middle managers, and top managers that they are part of a broader system of accountability; (2) to focus on the perception

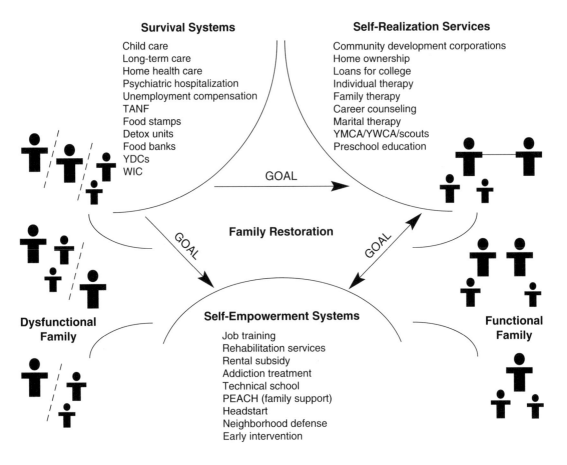

FIGURE 13.2 *Community Human Service Networking Systems, Linking Policies, Programs, and Practices*

of client family members of their own readiness for different kinds of services; and (3) to structure a networking system that honors the specialized problems of individual family members and at the same time integrates the service plan together with the family as a whole. Family practitioners could participate in such a system with a greater sense of confidence that their efforts will receive recognition as they move families forward.

Summary

The model of family practice that is suggested here is one that emphasizes the community as replete with opportunities for self-empowerment and enrichment. At the same time, it is fraught with dangers and with impediments to self-fulfillment. It recognizes the differences between communities in the level of positive and optimistic organizing that takes place among disadvantaged (Level I and II) families and on behalf of such families.

In addition to recognizing the variations in community attitudes and behavior, it is suggested that family practitioners participate in community development and prevention activities that have the potential for expanding opportunities and reducing self-defeating forms of pessimistic behavior. Individual family practice must be distinguished from group, neighborhood, or community-level activities. The social constructivist practitioner can, however, encourage individual participation when an assessment shows a readiness for it. This approach is consistent with the Family Empowerment and Social Justice model proposed by Haynes and Singh (1993).

The practitioner may also wish to refer to Gaudin's (1984) concept of "social work roles"; Kruzich's (1988) chapter in Chilman, Cox, and Nunnaly, "Helping Families with Income Problems"; and finally, Parsons, Hernandez, and Jorgensen's (1988) generalized practice model, "Integrated Practice: A Framework for Problem Solving." These models merge an individualistic model of family practice with models that focus on the collective activities of education groups, neighborhood organization, self-help, community planning, and legislative action. Clearly, these models reduce or eliminate the division and cleavage that are felt between clinical practitioners and macro-level practitioners. This is the major thrust of the multilevel view of families and family practice.

Discussion Questions

1. Explain why a dual focus is needed in family practice.

2. Discuss what the agency must be prepared to do in order to support practitioner efforts to ensure support form communities for families.

3. How does the cultural mix of a community affect the level of trust required in community building?

4. In performing an assessment of community human services networks, what features of network structure and function would you look for? What kinds of networks work best in the long run?

5. If you could design a community human services networking system for families, what would it look like?

Suggested Readings

Buell, B. (1952). *Community planning for human services.* New York: Columbia University Press. This research report is based on a tracking study of over 100 families with multiple problems and a sense of being lost in the community network of agencies. It is the first to document the fragmentation of services and establish the need for integrative practices among agencies. It is a landmark study.

Chilman, C., Cox, F., & Nunnaly, E. (Eds.). (1988). *Employment and economic problems: Families in trouble series, Volume I.* Beverly Hills, CA: Sage.
The editors present a compilation of articles on the issues families face with the threat of unemployment and loss of income, subjects that family practitioners must address if they are to deal with social justice issues on the individual and family levels. The articles are seminal.

Fraser, M., and Galinsky, M. (1997). Towards a resilience-based model of practice. In M. Fraser (Ed.), *Risk and resilience in childhood* (pp. 265–273). Washington, DC: NASW Press.
The authors discuss the person in an environment and the interplay of individual characteristics and contextual influences as determinants of human behavior.

Gans, H. J. (1962). *The urban villagers: Groups and class in the life of Italian-Americans.* New York: Free Press.
The author conducted an anthropology-style study of an Italian neighborhood in Boston that was scheduled for "removal" in an urban redevelopment project. Attention is given to family structure and culture, religion and politics, street-level recreational behavior, and relationships with the "caregivers" in social agencies. For the first time, a vivid portrayal is presented of the way a population of tenuous status views the people who pose as their guardians of social betterment.

Gaudin, J., Wodarski, J., Arkinson, N., & Avery, L. (1990–1991). Remedying child neglect: Effectiveness of social work interventions. *Journal of Applied Social Sciences, 15*(1), 97–123.
The author describes a networking intervention study with neglectful families. The intervention consisted of personal networking, volunteer linking, employing neighborhood helpers, and social skills training. A variety of measures were used to assess the results of the intervention.

Guitterez, L., Alvarez, A., Nemon, H., & Lewis, E. (1996). Multicultural organizing: A strategy for change. *Social Work, 41*(5), 501–508.
Concepts of community organizing are developed that take into account issues of cultural competence, social justice, family, and neighborhood empowerment. The role of the social worker is differentiated by virtue of degrees of identity with the ethnicities of the family and neighborhood.

Lassen, M. (1995). *Community-based family support in public housing.* Cambridge, MA: Harvard Family Research Project.
The author describes efforts in eight public housing communities to work with neighborhood and community factors in helping families to help themselves.

Nelson, G. M. (2000). *Self governance in communities and families.* San Francisco: Berrett-Koeler.
The author explains why partnerships between people and social institutions are essential to the well-being of both. The book describes how to work to achieve these partnerships.

Schorr, L. B. (1997). *Common purpose: strengthening families and neighborhoods to rebuild America.* New York: Anchor Books.
Inspiring tales and hard evidence of our social programs' success in helping disadvantaged children and families toward better lives, on a scale that is large enough to matter.

References

Buell, B. (1952). *Community planning for human services.* New York: Columbia University Press.

Ewalt, P. L., Freeman, E. M., & Poole, D. L. (Eds.). (1998). *Community building: Renewal, well-being, and shared responsibility.* Washington, DC: NASW Press.

Frank, L. K. (1948). *Society as the patient.* New Brunswick, NJ: Rutgers University Press.

Gaudin, J. (1984, May). Social work roles and tasks with incarcerated mothers. *Social Casework, 279–286.*

Gaudin, J., Wodarski, J., Arkinson, N., & Avery, L. (1990–1991). Remedying child neglect: Effectiveness of social work interventions. *Journal of Applied Social Sciences, 15*(1), 97–123.

Guitterez, L., Alvarez, A., Nemon, H., & Lewis, E. (1996). Multicultural organizing: A strategy for change. *Social Work, 41*(5), 501–508.

Haynes, A. W., & Singh, R. N. (1993). Helping families in developing countries: A model based on family empowerment and social justice. *Social Development Issues, 15*(1), 27–37.

Kruzich, J. (1988). Helping families with income problems. In C. Chilman, F. Cox, & E. Nunnaly (Eds.), *Employment and economic problems: Families in trouble series, Volume I.* Newbury Park, CA: Sage.

MacNair, R. (1981). *Case coordination: Designing interagency teamwork.* Athens: Institute of Community and Area Development, University of Georgia.

Parsons, R., Hernandez, S., & Jorgensen, J. (1988, September/October). Integrated practice: A framework for problem solving. *Social Work,* 417–421.

Turner, J. B. (1968). *Sociological theory and the concept of community as a client.* Unpublished manuscript.

Appendix A

The NASW Code of Ethics

Ethical Principles

The following broad ethical principles are based on social work's core values of service, social justice, dignity and worth of the person, importance of human relationships, integrity, and competence. These principles set forth ideals to which all social workers should aspire.

VALUE: *Service*
Ethical Principle: *Social workers' primary goal is to help people in need and to address social problems.*

Social workers elevate service to others above self-interest. Social workers draw on their knowledge, values, and skills to help people in need and to address social problems. Social workers are encouraged to volunteer some portion of their professional skills with no expectation of significant financial return (pro bono service).

VALUE: *Social Justice*
Ethical Principle: *Social workers challenge social injustice.*

Social workers pursue social change, particularly with and on behalf of vulnerable and oppressed individuals and groups of people. Social workers' social change efforts are focused primarily on issues of poverty, unemployment, discrimination, and other forms of social injustice. These activities seek to promote sensitivity to and knowledge about oppression and cultural and ethnic diversity. Social workers strive to ensure access to needed information, services, and resources; equality of opportunity; and meaningful participation in decision making for all people.

VALUE: *Dignity and Worth of the Person*
Ethical Principle: *Social workers respect the inherent dignity and worth of the person.*

Social workers treat each person in a caring and respectful fashion, mindful of individual differences and cultural and ethnic diversity. Social workers promote clients' socially responsible self-determination. Social workers seek to enhance clients' capacity and opportunity to change and to address their own needs. Social workers are cognizant of their dual responsibility to clients and to the broader society. They seek to resolve conflicts between clients' interests and the broader society's interests in a socially responsible manner consistent with the values, ethical principles, and ethical standards of the profession.

VALUE: *Importance of Human Relationships*
Ethical Principle: *Social workers recognize the central importance of human relationships.*

Social workers understand that relationships between and among people are an important vehicle for change. Social workers engage people as partners in the helping process. Social workers seek to strengthen relationships among people in a purposeful effort to promote, restore, maintain, and enhance the well-being of individuals, families, social groups, organizations, and communities.

VALUE: *Integrity*
Ethical Principle: *Social workers behave in a trustworthy manner.*

Social workers are continually aware of the profession's mission, values, ethical principles, and ethical standards and practice in a manner consistent with them. Social workers act honestly and responsibly and promote ethical practices on the part of the organizations with which they are affiliated.

VALUE: *Competence*
Ethical Principle: *Social workers practice within their areas of competence and develop and enhance their professional expertise.*

Social workers continually strive to increase their professional knowledge and skills and to apply them in practice. Social workers should aspire to contribute to the knowledge base of the profession.

Ethical Standards

The following ethical standards are relevant to the professional activities of all social workers. These standards concern (1) social workers' ethical responsibilities to clients, (2) social workers' ethical responsibilities to colleagues, (3) social workers' ethical responsibilities in practice settings, (4) social workers' ethical responsibilities as professionals, (5) social workers' ethical responsibilities to the social work profession, and (6) social workers' ethical responsibilities to the broader society.

Some of the standards that follow are enforceable guidelines for professional conduct, and some are aspirational. The extent to which each standard is enforceable is a matter of professional judgment to be exercised by those responsible for reviewing alleged violations of ethical standards.

1. Social Workers' Ethical Responsibilities to Clients

1.01 Commitment to Clients.   Social workers' primary responsibility is to promote the well-being of clients. In general, clients' interests are primary. However, social workers' responsibility to the larger society or specific legal obligations may on limited occasions supersede the loyalty owed clients, and clients should be so advised. (Examples include when a social worker is required by law to report that a client has abused a child or has threatened to harm self or others.)

1.02 Self-Determination.   Social workers respect and promote the right of clients to self-determination and assist clients in their efforts to identify and clarify their goals. Social workers may limit clients' right to self-determination when, in the social workers' professional judgment, clients' actions or potential actions pose a serious, foreseeable, and imminent risk to themselves or others.

1.03 Informed Consent.   (a) Social workers should provide services to clients only in the context of a professional relationship based, when appropriate, on valid informed consent. Social workers should use clear and understandable language to inform clients of the purpose of the services, risks related to the services, limits to services because of the requirements of a third-party payer, relevant costs, reasonable alternatives, clients' right to refuse or withdraw consent, and the time frame covered by the consent. Social workers should provide clients with an opportunity to ask questions.

(b) In instances when clients are not literate or have difficulty understanding the primary language used in the practice setting, social workers should take steps to ensure clients' comprehension. This may include providing clients with a detailed verbal explanation or arranging for a qualified interpreter or translator whenever possible.

(c) In instances when clients lack the capacity to provide informed consent, social workers should protect clients' interests by seeking permission from an appropriate third party, informing clients consistent with the clients' level of understanding. In such instances social workers should seek to ensure that the third party acts in a manner consistent with clients' wishes and interests. Social workers should take reasonable steps to enhance such clients' ability to give informed consent.

(d) In instances when clients are receiving services involuntarily, social workers should provide information about the nature and extent of services and about the extent of clients' right to refuse service.

(e) Social workers who provide services via electronic media (such as computer, telephone, radio, and television) should inform recipients of the limitations and risks associated with such services.

(f) Social workers should obtain clients' informed consent before audiotaping or videotaping clients or permitting observation of services to clients by a third party.

1.04 Competence.   (a) Social workers should provide services and represent themselves as competent only within the boundaries of their education, training, license, certification, consultation received, supervised experience, or other relevant professional experience.

(b) Social workers should provide services in substantive areas or use intervention techniques or approaches that are new to them only after engaging in appropriate study, training, consultation, and supervision from people who are competent in those interventions or techniques.

(c) When generally recognized standards do not exist with respect to an emerging area of practice, social workers should exercise careful judgment and take responsible steps (including appropriate education, research, training, consultation, and supervision) to ensure the competence of their work and to protect clients from harm.

1.05 Cultural Competence and Social Diversity.   (a) Social workers should understand culture and its function in human behavior and society, recognizing the strengths that exist in all cultures.

(b) Social workers should have a knowledge base of their clients' cultures and be able to demonstrate competence in the provision of services that are sensitive to clients' cultures and to differences among people and cultural groups.

(c) Social workers should obtain education about and seek to understand the nature of social diversity and oppression with respect to race, ethnicity, national origin, color, sex, sexual orientation, age, marital status, political belief, religion and mental or physical disability.

1.06 Conflicts of Interest.   (a) Social workers should be alert to and avoid conflicts of interest that interfere with the exercise of professional discretion and impartial judgment. Social workers should inform clients when a real or potential conflict of interest arises and take reasonable steps to resolve the issue in a manner that makes the clients' interests primary and protects clients' interests to the greatest extent possible. Occasionally, protecting clients' interests may require termination of the professional relationship with proper referral of the client.

(b) Social workers should not take unfair advantage of any professional relationship or exploit others to further their personal, religious, political, or business interests.

(c) Social workers should not engage in dual or multiple relationships with clients or former clients in which there is a risk of exploitation or potential harm to the client. In instances when dual or multiple relationships are unavoidable, social workers should take steps to protect clients and are responsible for setting clear, appropriate, and culturally sensitive boundaries. (Dual or multiple relationships occur when social workers relate to clients in more than one relationship, whether professional, social, or business. Dual or multiple relationships can occur simultaneously or consecutively.)

(d) When social workers provide services to two or more people who have a relationship with each other (for example, couples, family members), social workers should clarify with all parties which individuals will be considered clients and the nature of social workers' professional obligations to the various individuals who are receiving services. Social workers who anticipate a conflict of interest among the individuals receiving services or who anticipate having to perform in potentially conflicting roles (for example, when a social worker is asked to testify in a child custody dispute or divorce proceedings involving clients) should clarify their role with the parties involved and take appropriate action to minimize any conflict of interest.

1.07 Privacy and Confidentiality.   (a) Social workers should respect clients' right to privacy. Social workers should not solicit private information from clients unless it is essential to providing services or conducting social work evaluation or research. Once private information is shared, standards of confidentiality apply.

(b) Social workers may disclose confidential information when appropriate with a valid consent from a client, or a person legally authorized to consent on behalf of a client.

(c) Social workers should protect the confidentiality of all information obtained in the course of professional service, except for compelling professional reasons. The general expectation that social workers will keep information confidential does not apply when disclosure is necessary to prevent serious, foreseeable, and imminent harm to a client or other identifiable person or when laws or regulations require disclosure without a client's consent. In all instances, social workers should disclose the least amount of confidential information necessary to achieve the desired purpose; only information that is directly relevant to the purpose for which the disclosure is made should be revealed.

(d) Social workers should inform clients, to the extent possible, about the disclosure of confidential information and the potential consequences, when feasible, before the disclosure is made. This applies whether social workers disclose confidential information on the basis of a legal requirement or client consent.

(e) Social workers should discuss with clients and other interested parties the nature of confidentiality and limitations of clients' right to confidentiality. Social workers should review with clients circumstances where confidential information may be requested and where disclosure of confidential information may be legally required. This discussion should occur as soon as possible in the social worker–client relationship and as needed throughout the course of the relationship.

(f) When social workers provide counseling services to families, couples, or groups, social workers should seek agreement among the parties involved concerning each individual's right to confidentiality and obligation to preserve the confidentiality of information shared by others. Social workers should inform participants in family, couples, or group counseling that social workers cannot guarantee that all participants will honor such agreements.

(g) Social workers should inform clients involved in family, couples, marital, or group counseling of the social worker's, employer's, and agency's policy concerning the social worker's disclosure of confidential information among the parties involved in the counseling.

(h) Social workers should not disclose confidential information to third-party payers unless clients have authorized such disclosure.

(i) Social workers should not discuss confidential information in any setting unless privacy can be ensured. Social workers should not discuss confidential information in public or semipublic areas such as hallways, waiting rooms, elevators, and restaurants.

(j) Social workers should protect the confidentiality of clients during legal proceedings to the extent permitted by law. When a court of law or other legally authorized body orders social workers to disclose confidential or privileged information without a client's consent and such disclosure could cause harm to the client, social workers should request that the court withdraw the order or limit the order as narrowly as possible or maintain the records under seal, unavailable for public inspection.

(k) Social workers should protect the confidentiality of clients when responding to requests from members of the media.

(l) Social workers should protect the confidentiality of clients' written and electronic records and other sensitive information. Social workers should take reasonable steps to ensure that clients' records are stored in a secure location and that clients' records are not available to others who are not authorized to have access.

(m) Social workers should take precautions to ensure and maintain the confidentiality of information transmitted to other parties through the use of computers, electronic mail, facsimile machines, telephones and telephone answering machines, and other electronic or computer technology. Disclosure of identifying information should be avoided whenever possible.

(n) Social workers should transfer or dispose of clients' records in a manner that protects clients' confidentiality and is consistent with state statutes governing records and social work licensure.

(o) Social workers should take reasonable precautions to protect client confidentiality in the event of the social worker's termination of practice, incapacitation, or death.

(p) Social workers should not disclose identifying information when discussing clients for teaching or training purposes unless the client has consented to disclosure of confidential information.

(q) Social workers should not disclose identifying information when discussing clients with consultants unless the client has consented to disclosure of confidential information or there is a compelling need for such disclosure.

(r) Social workers should protect the confidentiality of deceased clients consistent with the preceding standards.

1.08 Access to Records.   (a) Social workers should provide clients with reasonable access to records concerning the clients. Social workers who are concerned that clients' access to their records could cause serious misunderstanding or harm to the client should provide assistance in interpreting the records and consultation with the client regarding the records. Social workers should limit clients' access to their records, or portions of their records, only in exceptional circumstances when there is compelling evidence that such access would cause serious harm to the client. Both clients' requests and the rationale for withholding some or all of the record should be documented in clients' files.

(b) When providing clients with access to their records, social workers should take steps to protect the confidentiality of other individuals identified or discussed in such records.

1.09 Sexual Relationships.   (a) Social workers should under no circumstances engage in sexual activities or sexual contact with current clients, whether such contact is consensual or forced.

(b) Social workers should not engage in sexual activities or sexual contact with clients' relatives or other individuals with whom clients maintain a close personal relationship when there is a risk of exploitation or potential harm to the client. Sexual activity or sexual contact with clients' relatives or other individuals with whom clients maintain a personal relationship has the potential to be harmful to the client and may make it difficult for the social worker and client to maintain appropriate professional boundaries. Social workers—not their clients, their clients' relatives, or other individuals with whom the client maintains a personal relationship—assume the full burden for setting clear, appropriate, and culturally sensitive boundaries.

(c) Social workers should not engage in sexual activities or sexual contact with former clients because of the potential for harm to the client. If social workers engage in conduct contrary to this prohibition or claim that an exception to this prohibition is warranted because of extraordinary circumstances, it is social workers—not their clients—who assume the full burden of demonstrating that the former client has not been exploited, coerced, or manipulated, intentionally or unintentionally.

(d) Social workers should not provide clinical services to individuals with whom they have had a prior sexual relationship. Providing clinical services to a former sexual partner has the potential to be harmful to the individual and is likely to make it difficult for the social worker and individual to maintain appropriate professional boundaries.

1.10 Physical Contact.   Social workers should not engage in physical contact with clients when there is a possibility of psychological harm to the client as a result of the contact (such as cradling or caressing clients). Social workers who engage in appropriate physical contact with clients are responsible for setting clear, appropriate, and culturally sensitive boundaries that govern such physical contact.

1.11 Sexual Harassment.   Social workers should not sexually harass clients. Sexual harassment includes advances, sexual solicitation, requests for sexual favors, and other verbal or physical conduct of a sexual nature.

1.12 Derogatory Language. Social workers should not use derogatory language in their written or verbal communications to or about clients. Social workers should use accurate and respectful language in all communications to and about clients.

1.13 Payment for Services. (a) When setting fees, social workers should ensure that the fees are fair, reasonable, and commensurate with the service performed. Consideration should be given to the client's ability to pay.

(b) Social workers should avoid accepting goods or services from clients as payment for professional services. Bartering arrangements, particularly involving services, create the potential for conflicts of interest, exploitation, and inappropriate boundaries in social workers' relationships with clients. Social workers should explore and may participate in bartering only in very limited circumstances when it can be demonstrated that such arrangements are an accepted practice among professionals in the local community, considered to be essential for the provision of services, negotiated without coercion, and entered into at the client's initiative and with the client's informed consent. Social workers who accept goods or services from clients as payment for professional services assume the full burden of demonstrating that this arrangement will not be detrimental to the client or the professional relationship.

(c) Social workers should not solicit a private fee or other remuneration for providing services to clients who are entitled to such available services through the social workers' employer or agency.

1.14 Clients Who Lack Decision-Making Capacity. When social workers act on behalf of clients who lack the capacity to make informed decisions, social workers should take reasonable steps to safeguard the interests and rights of those clients.

1.15 Interruption of Services. Social workers should make reasonable efforts to ensure continuity of services in the event that services are interrupted by factors such as unavailability, relocation, illness, disability, or death.

1.16 Termination of Services. (a) Social workers should terminate services to clients, and professional relationships with them, when such services and relationships are no longer required or no longer serve the clients' needs or interests.

(b) Social workers should take reasonable steps to avoid abandoning clients who are still in need of services. Social workers should withdraw services precipitously only under unusual circumstances, giving careful consideration to all factors in the situation and taking care to minimize possible adverse effects. Social workers should assist in making appropriate arrangements for continuation of services when necessary.

(c) Social workers in fee-for-service settings may terminate services to clients who are not paying an overdue balance if the financial contractual arrangements have been made clear to the client, if the client does not pose an imminent danger to self or others, and if the clinical and other consequences of the current nonpayment have been addressed and discussed with the client.

(d) Social workers should not terminate services to pursue a social, financial, or sexual relationship with a client.

(e) Social workers who anticipate the termination or interruption of services to clients should notify clients promptly and seek the transfer, referral, or continuation of services in relation to the clients' needs and preferences.

(f) Social workers who are leaving an employment setting should inform clients of appropriate options for the continuation of services and of the benefits and risks of the options.

2. Social Workers' Ethical Responsibilities to Colleagues

2.01 Respect.   (a) Social workers should treat colleagues with respect and represent accurately and fairly the qualifications, views, and obligations of colleagues.

(b) Social workers should avoid unwarranted negative criticism of colleagues in communications with clients or with other professionals. Unwarranted negative criticism may include demeaning comments that refer to colleagues' level of competence or to individuals' attributes such as race, ethnicity, national origin, color, sex, sexual orientation, age, marital status, political belief, religion and mental or physical disability.

(c) Social workers should cooperate with social work colleagues and with colleagues of other professions when such cooperation services the well-being of clients.

2.02 Confidentiality.   Social workers should respect confidential information shared by colleagues in the course of their professional relationships and transactions. Social workers should ensure that such colleagues understand social workers' obligation to respect confidentiality and any exceptions related to it.

2.03 Interdisciplinary Collaboration.   (a) Social workers who are members of an interdisciplinary team should participate in and contribute to decisions that affect the well-being of clients by drawing on the perspectives, values, and experiences of the social work profession. Professional and ethical obligations of the interdisciplinary team as a whole and of its individual members should be clearly established.

(b) Social workers for whom a team decision raises ethical concerns should attempt to resolve the disagreement through appropriate channels. If the disagreement cannot be resolved, social workers should pursue other avenues to address their concerns, consistent with client well-being.

2.04 Disputes Involving Colleagues.   (a) Social workers should not take advantage of a dispute between a colleague and employer to obtain a position or otherwise advance the social workers' own interests.

(b) Social workers should not exploit clients in disputes with colleagues or engage clients in any inappropriate discussion of conflicts between social workers and their colleagues.

2.05 Consultation.   (a) Social workers should seek advice and counsel of colleagues whenever such consultation is in the best interests of clients.

(b) Social workers should keep informed of colleagues' areas of expertise and competencies. Social workers should seek consultation only from colleagues who have demonstrated knowledge, expertise, and competence related to the subject of the consultation.

(c) When consulting with colleagues about clients, social workers should disclose the least amount of information necessary to achieve the purposes of the consultation.

2.06 Referral for Services.   (a) Social workers should refer clients to other professionals when other professionals' specialized knowledge or expertise is needed to serve clients fully, or when social workers believe they are not being effective or making reasonable progress with clients and additional service is required.

(b) Social workers who refer clients to other professionals should take appropriate steps to facilitate an orderly transfer of responsibility. Social workers who refer clients to other professionals should disclose, with clients' consent, all pertinent information to the new service providers.

(c) Social workers are prohibited from giving or receiving payment for a referral when no professional service is provided by the referring social worker.

2.07 Sexual Relationships.   (a) Social workers who function as supervisors or educators should not engage in sexual activities or contact with current supervisees, students, trainees, or other colleagues over whom they exercise professional authority.

(b) Social workers should avoid engaging in sexual relationships with colleagues where there is potential for a conflict of interest. Social workers who become involved in, or anticipate becoming involved in, a sexual relationship with a colleague have a duty to transfer professional responsibilities, when necessary, to avoid a conflict of interest.

2.08 Sexual Harassment.   Social workers should not sexually harass supervisees, students, trainees, or colleagues. Sexual harassment includes sexual advances, sexual solicitation, requests for sexual favors, and other verbal or physical conduct of a sexual nature.

2.09 Impairment of Colleagues.   (a) Social workers who have direct knowledge of a social work colleague's impairment which is due to personal problems, psychosocial distress, substance abuse, or mental health difficulties, and that interferes with practice effectiveness should consult with that colleague when feasible and assist the colleague in taking remedial action.

(b) Social workers who believe that a social work colleague's impairment interferes with practice effectiveness and that the colleague has not taken adequate steps to address the impairment should take action through appropriate channels established by employers, agencies, NASW, licensing and regulatory bodies, and other professional organizations.

2.10 Incompetence of Colleagues.   (a) Social workers who have direct knowledge of a social work colleague's incompetence should consult with that colleague when feasible and assist the colleague in taking remedial action.

(b) Social workers who believe that a social work colleague is incompetent and has not taken adequate steps to address the incompetence should take action through appropriate channels established by employers, agencies, NASW, licensing and regulatory bodies, and other professional organizations.

2.11 Unethical Conduct of Colleagues.   (a) Social workers should take adequate measures to discourage, prevent, expose, and correct the unethical conduct of colleagues.

(b) Social workers should be knowledgeable about established policies and procedures for handling concerns about colleagues' unethical behavior. Social workers should be familiar with national, state, and local procedures for handling ethics complaints. These include policies and procedures created by NASW, licensing and regulatory bodies, employers, agencies, and other professional organizations.

(c) Social workers who believe that a colleague has acted unethically should seek resolution by discussing their concerns with the colleague when feasible and when such discussion is likely to be productive.

(d) When necessary, social workers who believe that a colleague has acted unethically should take action through appropriate formal channels (such as contacting a state licensing board or regulatory body, an NASW committee on inquiry, or other professional ethics committees).

(e) Social workers should defend and assist colleagues who are unjustly charged with unethical conduct.

3. Social Workers' Ethical Responsibilities in Practice Settings

3.01 Supervision and Consultation.   (a) Social workers who provide supervision or consultation should have the necessary knowledge and skill to supervise or consult appropriately and should do so only within their areas of knowledge and competence.

(b) Social workers who provide supervision or consultation are responsible for setting clear, appropriate, and culturally sensitive boundaries.

(c) Social workers should not engage in any dual or multiple relationships with supervisees in which there is a risk of exploitation of or potential harm to the supervisee.

(d) Social workers who provide supervision should evaluate supervisees' performance in a manner that is fair and respectful.

3.02 Education and Training.   (a) Social workers who function as educators, field instructors for students, or trainers should provide instruction only within their areas of knowledge and competence and should provide instruction based on the most current information and knowledge available in the profession.

(b) Social workers who function as educators or field instructors for students should evaluate students' performance in a manner that is fair and respectful.

(c) Social workers who function as educators or field instructors for students should take reasonable steps to ensure that clients are routinely informed when services are being provided by students.

(d) Social workers who function as educators or field instructors for students should not engage in any dual or multiple relationships with students in which there is a risk of exploitation or potential harm to the student. Social work educators and field instructors are responsible for setting clear, appropriate, and culturally sensitive boundaries.

3.03 Performance Evaluation.   Social workers who have responsibility for evaluating the performance of others should fulfill such responsibility in a fair and considerate manner and on the basis of clearly stated criteria.

3.04 Client Records.   (a) Social workers should take reasonable steps to ensure that documentation in records is accurate and reflects the services provided.

(b) Social workers should include sufficient and timely documentation in records to facilitate the delivery of services and to ensure continuity of services provided to clients in the future.

(c) Social workers' documentation should protect clients' privacy to the extent that is possible and appropriate and should include only information that is directly relevant to the delivery of services.

(d) Social workers should store records following the termination of service to ensure reasonable future access. Records should be maintained for the number of years required by state statutes or relevant contracts.

3.05 Billing.   Social workers should establish and maintain billing practices that accurately reflect the nature and extent of services provided, and that identify who provided the service in the practice setting.

3.06 Client Transfer.   (a) When an individual who is receiving services from another agency or colleague contacts a social worker for services, the social worker should carefully consider the client's needs before agreeing to provide services. To minimize possible confusion and conflict, social workers should discuss with potential clients the nature of the clients' current relationship with other service providers and the implications, including possible benefits or risks, of entering into a relationship with a new service provider.

(b) If a new client has been served by another agency or colleague, social workers should discuss with the client whether consultation with the previous service provider is in the client's best interest.

3.07 Administration.   (a) Social work administrators should advocate within and outside their agencies for adequate resources to meet clients' needs.

(b) Social workers should advocate for resource allocation procedures that are open and fair. When not all clients' needs can be met, an allocation procedure should be developed that is nondiscriminatory and based on appropriate and consistently applied principles.

(c) Social workers who are administrators should take reasonable steps to ensure that adequate agency or organizational resources are available to provide appropriate staff supervision.

(d) Social work administrators should take reasonable steps to ensure that the working environment for which they are responsible is consistent with and encourages compliance with the NASW Code of Ethics. Social work administrators should take reasonable steps to eliminate any conditions in their organizations that violate, interfere with, or discourage compliance with the Code.

3.08 Continuing Education and Staff Development.   Social work administrators and supervisors should take reasonable steps to provide or arrange for continuing education and staff development for all staff for whom they are responsible. Continuing education and staff development should address current knowledge and emerging developments related to social work practice and ethics.

3.09 Commitments to Employers.   (a) Social workers generally should adhere to commitments made to employers and employing organizations.

(b) Social workers should work to improve employing agencies' policies and procedures, and the efficiency and effectiveness of their services.

(c) Social workers should take reasonable steps to ensure that employers are aware of social workers' ethical obligations as set forth in the NASW Code of Ethics and of the implications of those obligations for social work practice.

(d) Social workers should not allow an employing organization's policies, procedures, regulations, or administrative orders to interfere with their ethical practice of social work. Social workers should take reasonable steps to ensure that their employing organizations' practices are consistent with the NASW Code of Ethics.

(e) Social workers should act to prevent and eliminate discrimination in the employing organization's work assignments and in its employment policies and practices.

(f) Social workers should accept employment or arrange student field placements only in organizations that exercise fair personnel practices.

(g) Social workers should be diligent stewards of the resources of their employing organizations, wisely conserving funds where appropriate and never misappropriating funds or using them for unintended purposes.

3.10 Labor–Management Disputes.   (a) Social workers may engage in organized action, including the formation of and participation in labor unions, to improve services to clients and working conditions.

(b) The actions of social workers who are involved in labor–management disputes, job actions, or labor strikes should be guided by the profession's values, ethical principles, and ethical standards. Reasonable differences of opinion exist among social workers concerning their primary obligation as professionals during an actual or threatened labor strike or job action. Social workers should carefully examine relevant issues and their possible impact on clients before deciding on a course of action.

4. Social Workers' Ethical Responsibilities as Professionals

4.01 Competence.   (a) Social workers should accept responsibility or employment only on the basis of existing competence or the intention to acquire the necessary competence.

(b) Social workers should strive to become and remain proficient in professional practice and the performance of professional functions. Social workers should critically examine and keep current with emerging knowledge relevant to social work. Social workers should routinely review the professional literature and participate in continuing education relevant to social work practice and social work ethics.

(c) Social workers should base practice on recognized knowledge, including empirically based knowledge, relevant to social work and social work ethics.

4.02 Discrimination.   Social workers should not practice, condone, facilitate, or collaborate with any form of discrimination on the basis of race, ethnicity, national origin, color, age, religion, sex, sexual orientation, marital status, political belief, or mental or physical disability.

4.03 Private Conduct.   Social workers should not permit their private conduct to interfere with their ability to fulfill their professional responsibilities.

4.04 Dishonesty, Fraud, and Deception.   Social workers should not participate in, condone, or be associated with dishonesty, fraud, or deception.

4.05 Impairment.   (a) Social workers should not allow their own personal problems, psychosocial distress, legal problems, substance abuse, or mental health difficulties to interfere with their professional judgment and performance or to jeopardize the best interests of people for whom they have a professional responsibility.

(b) Social workers whose personal problems, psychosocial distress, legal problems, substance abuse, or mental health difficulties interfere with their professional judgment and performance should immediately seek consultation and take appropriate remedial action by seeking professional help, making adjustments in workload, terminating practice, or taking any other steps necessary to protect clients and others.

4.06 Misrepresentation.   (a) Social workers should make clear distinctions between statements made and actions engaged in as a private individual and as a representative of the social work profession, a professional social work organization, or the social worker's employing agency.

(b) Social workers who speak on behalf of professional social work organizations should accurately represent the official and authorized positions of the organizations.

(c) Social workers should ensure that their representations to clients, agencies, and the public of professional qualifications, credentials, education, competence, affiliations, services provided, or results to be achieved are accurate. Social workers should claim only those relevant professional credentials they actually possess and take steps to correct any inaccuracies or misrepresentations of their credentials by others.

4.07 Solicitations.   (a) Social workers should not engage in uninvited solicitation of potential clients who, because of their circumstances, are vulnerable to undue influence, manipulation, or coercion.

(b) Social workers should not engage in solicitation of testimonial endorsements (including solicitation of consent to use a client's prior statement as a testimonial endorsement) from current clients or other persons who, because of their particular circumstances, are vulnerable to undue influence.

4.08 Acknowledging Credit.   (a) Social workers should take responsibility and credit, including authorship credit, only for work they have actually performed and to which they have contributed.

(b) Social workers should honestly acknowledge the work of and the contributions made by others.

5. Social Workers' Ethical Responsibilities to the Social Work Profession

5.01 Integrity of the Profession.   (a) Social workers should work toward the maintenance and promotion of high standards of practice.

(b) Social workers should uphold and advance the values, ethics, knowledge, and mission of the profession. Social workers should protect, enhance, and improve the integrity of the profession through appropriate study and research, active discussion, and responsible criticism of the profession.

(c) Social workers should contribute time and professional expertise to activities that promote respect for the value, integrity, and competence of the social work profession. These activities may include teaching, research, consultations, service, legislative testimony, presentations in the community, and participation in their professional organizations.

(d) Social workers should contribute to the knowledge base of social work and share with colleagues their knowledge related to practice, research, and ethics.

Social workers should seek to contribute to the profession's literature and to share their knowledge at professional meetings and conferences.

(e) Social workers should act to prevent the unauthorized and unqualified practice of social work.

5.02 Evaluation and Research.   (a) Social workers should monitor and evaluate policies, the implementation of programs, and practice interventions.

(b) Social workers should promote and facilitate evaluation and research to contribute to the development of knowledge.

(c) Social workers should critically examine and keep current with emerging knowledge relevant to social work and fully use evaluation and research evidence in their professional practice.

(d) Social workers engaged in evaluation or research should carefully consider possible consequences and should follow guidelines developed for the protection of evaluation and research participants. Appropriate institutional review boards should be consulted.

(e) Social workers engaged in evaluation or research should obtain voluntary and written informed consent from participants, when appropriate, without any implied or actual deprivation or penalty for refusal to participate; without undue inducement to participate; and with due regard for participants' well-being, privacy, and dignity. Informed consent should include information about the nature, extent, and duration of the participation requested and disclosure of the risks and benefits of participation in the research.

(f) When evaluation or research participants are incapable of giving informed consent, social workers should provide an appropriate explanation to the participants, obtain the participants' assent to the extent they are able, and obtain written consent from an appropriate proxy.

(g) Social workers should never design or conduct evaluation or research that does not use consent procedures, such as certain forms of naturalistic observation and archival research, unless rigorous and responsible review of the research has found it to be justified because of its prospective scientific, educational, or applied value and unless equally effective alternative procedures that do not involve waiver of consent are not feasible.

(h) Social workers should inform participants of their right to withdraw from evaluation and research at any time without penalty.

(i) Social workers should take appropriate steps to ensure that participants in evaluation and research have access to appropriate supportive services.

(j) Social workers engaged in evaluation or research should protect participants from unwarranted physical or mental distress, harm, danger, or deprivation.

(k) Social workers engaged in the evaluation of services should discuss collected information only for professional purposes and only with people professionally concerned with this information.

(l) Social workers engaged in evaluation or research should ensure the anonymity or confidentiality of participants and of the data obtained from them. Social workers should inform participants of any limits of confidentiality, the measures that will be taken to ensure confidentiality, and when any records containing research data will be destroyed.

(m) Social workers who report evaluation and research results should protect participants' confidentiality by omitting identifying information unless proper consent has been obtained authorizing disclosure.

(n) Social workers should report evaluation and research findings accurately. They should not fabricate or falsify results and should take steps to correct any errors later found in published data using standard publication methods.

(o) Social workers engaged in evaluation or research should be alert to and avoid conflicts of interest and dual relationships with participants, should inform participants when a real or potential conflict of interest arises, and should take steps to resolve the issue in a manner that makes participants' interests primary.

(p) Social workers should educate themselves, their students, and their colleagues about responsible research practices.

6. Social Workers' Ethical Responsibilities to the Broader Society

6.01 Social Welfare.   Social workers should promote the general welfare of society, from local to global levels, and the development of people, their communities, and their environments. Social workers should advocate for living conditions conducive to the fulfillment of basic human needs and should promote social, economic, political, and cultural values and institutions that are compatible with the realization of social justice.

6.02 Public Participation.   Social workers should facilitate informed participation by the public in shaping social policies and institutions.

6.03 Public Emergencies.   Social workers should provide appropriate professional services in public emergencies, to the greatest extent possible.

6.04 Social and Political Action.   (a) Social workers should engage in social and political action that seeks to ensure that all people have equal access to the resources, employment, services, and opportunities they require to meet their basic human needs and to develop fully. Social workers should be aware of the impact of the political arena on practice and should advocate for changes in policy and legislation to improve social conditions in order to meet basic human needs and promote social justice.

(b) Social workers should act to expand choice and opportunity for all persons, with special regard for vulnerable, disadvantaged, oppressed, and exploited persons and groups.

(c) Social workers should promote conditions that encourage respect for cultural and social diversity within the United States and globally. Social workers should promote policies and practices that demonstrate respect for difference, support the expansion of cultural knowledge and resources, advocate for programs and institutions that demonstrate cultural competence, and promote policies that safeguard the rights of and confirm equity and social justice for all people.

(d) Social workers should act to prevent and eliminate domination of, exploitation of, and discrimination against any person, group, or class on the basis of race, ethnicity, national origin, color, sex, sexual orientation, age, marital status, political belief, religion, or mental or physical disability.

Appendix B

Ethics Cases and Commentaries

The ethics cases and commentaries in this appendix are taken from NASW, (1998). *Current Controversies in Social Work Ethics: Case Examples* (1998). Each example first lists the primary relevant citation of a standard of the NASW Code of Ethics (1996). Other applicable standards are listed in chronological order and are not ranked.

Case 1

An undocumented Mexican woman lives in southern California with her husband and two school-age children. Her husband is frequently physically and verbally abusive to her. She cannot drive and has little facility with English. She is completely dependent on her husband for transportation and assistance with English. She loves her husband and wishes he would not abuse her but fears he may abuse the children if she is not at home. Because she feels she has few options, she rarely seeks medical help. A friend insisted she seek help from the local shelter for battered women, and when she went there, she met with a social worker, who is feeling caught between the shelter's philosophy of encouraging women to leave abusive homes and her client's desire to return home. The social worker understands that through occasional stays at the shelter, her client may become more self-determining and assertive and eventually find safe alternatives for herself and her children. The shelter's board of directors is considering a policy that women must leave abusive situations to receive ongoing services.

NASW Code of Ethics: 1.01; 1.02; 1.05; 1.15; 2.06a; 3.09b

Commentary

Surely the social worker's understanding of cultural factors in this situation is essential to inform her work with and understand the behavior of this client. It is her responsibility to help the client identify and clarify her goals and perhaps develop their priority. The social worker may need to develop a long-range strategy that ensures some continuity of service, despite the interruptions. If the shelter can offer counseling services to clients who are not residing in the shelter, she could work with the client toward strengthening her resolve to change factors in her life and toward obtaining help for the husband. The social worker should initiate a legitimate study of clients' real needs in the context of agency resources and guide the policy and program development of the agency accordingly. If there is not a resolution of the conflicting factors, the social worker should explore other community resources that could better serve the client on an ongoing basis.

Case 2

A child protective services worker must present recommendations to the court regarding placement for the 10- and 12-year-old daughters of a recently deceased lesbian mother. Since their separation five years ago, the mother's former lesbian partner has paid monthly child support and all medical and dental costs for the girls. She has also maintained positive relationships with the girls and their mother, visiting regularly and taking the children on vacations. She and the mother had an unwritten understanding that the former partner would become the guardian for the children should something happen to the mother. The biological father maintains only occasional contact with the girls and has arranged for a few visits to his mother and sisters. The father and mother were never married. The social worker favors placing the girls with their father because of her religious convictions in which homosexuality is considered immoral.

NASW Code of Ethics: 1.02; 1.01; 1.03c; 1.05b,c; 1.14; 4.02; 4.06a; 5.01 b; 6.01

Commentary

Although the children are not of an age to make a final decision regarding with whom they will reside, their preferences still must be sought and weighed. Limitations in their self-determination should not relate to a social worker's preferences for heterosexual environments, a value she may hold as a private individual but which should be distinguished from her professional position. The girls have grown up with lesbian parental figures, and the social worker's competence should encompass an understanding of such. Social justice issues are inherent in the development of a plan for these youngsters and an optimal environment for them. The social worker's recommendation to the judge is likely to be a significant factor in the outcome for the young clients.

Case 3

A first-year MSW student has a field placement at a city psychiatric hospital. Her first unsupervised intake interview is with the wife of a well-known physician, who has published many articles. During the intake, the student learns that the client has been treated over many years at various mental health facilities. Believing that all other possible forms of treatment have been exhausted without lasting success, the client's husband has recommended hospitalization, and the client has agreed. During the intake interview, the client reveals that her husband has been involved in romantic affairs with other women. The social work student completes the interview, makes a provisional diagnosis, and decides against recording specific assertions made by the woman.

NASW Code of Ethics: 1.07a; 2.05a,c; 3.04a,c

Commentary

This is the MSW student's first unsupervised intake interview, which may mean it is the first interview the student has conducted alone. She has access to a field instructor, however, and the case should be discussed carefully with the instructor. Is there anything to argue that because the client's information has not been verified and the information conveyed relates to a prominent person that extra care should be taken to protect the physician's privacy? The competence of the student to make a decision regarding what should be included in the record and to make a provisional diagnosis is questionable. The field instructor and the agency-based supervisor of the student bear ultimate responsibility for case decisions and should be involved in determining the significance of information.

The *Code of Ethics* states that social workers should not solicit private information from clients unless it is essential to the provision of service. Furthermore, information included in the record should be directly relevant to the care and treatment of the client. At the same time, social workers should keep accurate records and include sufficient information to facilitate delivery of services and ensure continuity of services. Is the wife's perception of her husband's behavior based on fact? Is her perception significant to her condition? The student should discuss the case carefully with the field instructor and consult with the agency supervisor to determine the recording procedure that is required and the usual information that is recorded. Every effort should be made to protect the rights of the client, the privacy of her husband, and the policies of the hospital.

Case 4

A clinical social worker meets weekly for therapy with a 15-year-old female client. During a session, the client reports that she is dealing drugs and has begun seeing a boyfriend who just completed a six-month jail sentence for selling drugs. The client's parents have forbidden contact between their daughter and her boyfriend and have asked the social worker to inform them if their daughter reported that she is seeing the boy again. The social worker believes that her client trusted her not to pass on this information to anyone else and that disclosure might permanently impair the trust in their relationship. However, the social worker told her client when they first began their sessions that she could not promise to keep confidential any statements that indicate a threat to harm self or others. The social worker is concerned for her client's safety with the boyfriend but also is far more concerned about her illegal involvement in the sale of drugs and the dangers she may face from the drug trade.

NASW Code of Ethics: 1.07a,c,d; 1.01; 1.02; 1.03a

Commentary

The social worker must struggle among obligations to her primary client, a minor; to her parents, who are inevitably part of the client system; and to society, whose laws are intended to protect. She can seek to work with the client toward the goal of achieving consent to bring the parents into active work as a family unit. The social worker would endeavor to support the client and work toward accomplishing consent to reveal the relationship but with the goal of establishing a growing alliance with her parents. Or she can weigh the dangers to the client of the renewed relationship with her boyfriend plus the betrayal of the collateral clients' (the parents) expectations for the protection of their daughter and decide that revealing the information to them constitutes a compelling exception to confidentiality. If she decides on the latter course of action, the primary client (the daughter) must be informed in advance of the disclosure.

Case 5

Social workers regularly discuss client progress and receive supervision at a community mental health center's weekly case review. In the case review, a social worker reports that her client has recently discovered that he is HIV positive, and she requests help in considering changes in his treatment plan in light of this information. Another social worker, who is treating the wife of the recently diagnosed HIV positive client, learns of her client's husband's HIV status because she attends the same case review. She knows that the couple is having unprotected sex and that the wife is unaware of her husband's HIV status.

NASW Code of Ethics: 1.07c,d,q; 2.05a

Commentary

The value of confidentiality is frequently challenged in providing services to clients. Although social workers should protect the confidentiality of a client, there are limitations, and the possibility of an exception should be addressed with the male client. The social workers participating in the case review are obligated to keep confidential all cases discussed, yet there may exist sufficient compelling reason to breach a client's confidence. The exception that requires a disclosure to prevent serious, foreseeable, and imminent harm to the client's wife must be considered as a basis of the social worker's decision making. The client's wife is at high risk of becoming HIV positive, thus providing a compelling reason to breach confidentiality. In working with the husband, the social worker needs to provide information, incentive, and details about her obligation to breach his confidentiality if the client takes no steps to inform and protect his wife.

Case 6

A social worker who specializes in marriage and family counseling sometimes works with couples who decide to divorce. In one such case, the social worker receives a subpoena to provide testimony regarding his sessions with the divorcing couple. The husband's lawyer has recommended that the social worker be asked to give a deposition, and the wife and her attorney have agreed; both have provided signed consents for release of information. In his sessions with the husband, the social worker learned that the husband had had an affair that his attorney is unaware of. Although the social worker does not believe it is in the husband's interest that he testify, he considers that he is being ordered "by a court of law or other legally authorized body" to disclose "confidential or privileged information."

NASW Code of Ethics: 1.07d,e,f,g,j; 1.06d

Commentary

It is not unusual for social workers to be subpoenaed to testify about their contact with clients. As in this case, social workers may be subpoenaed in conjunction with divorce proceedings. As a general rule, social workers should not disclose confidential information without their clients' consent or unless they have been ordered to do so by a court of law. If a court of law or other legally authorized body orders social workers to disclose confidential or privileged information without a client's consent and such disclosure could cause harm to the client, social workers should request that the court withdraw or limit the order.

In this particular case, the social worker should have discussed with the husband the possibility that the social worker's knowledge of the husband's affair, if disclosed during the deposition, could be harmful to the husband's legal interests. The social worker should have given the husband an opportunity to consider this possible consequence when the social worker obtained the husband's informed consent for the social worker to testify. The requirement to inform clients of the limitations of confidentiality applies whether social workers disclose confidential information on the basis of a legal requirement or with client consent. In addition, social workers who provide services to two or more people who have a relationship with each other, such as couples, should clarify with all parties which individuals will be considered clients and the possibility of conflicts of interest among them.

Case 7

A social worker employed in a well-respected sectarian mental health agency met with his supervisor to discuss treatment of an HIV-positive adolescent client's disclosure that he has anonymous sex with men. The following week the social worker's supervisor, espousing agency policy—whether formal or informal—advised him that his client's case must be closed because he poses a safety risk to the other adolescents in the program and because the agency's reputation could be tarnished for serving gay boys with AIDS.

NASW Code of Ethics: 1.16b; 3.07d; 3.09c,d; 4.02; 6.04b

Commentary

The central conflict is the client's right to treatment regardless of sexual orientation and the social worker's obligation to the agency. A sectarian agency has a legal right to develop policies according to its religious beliefs. However, the social worker has a professional obligation not to discriminate against a client based on sexual orientation. In terms of the mission of a mental health agency that employs social workers and other mental health professionals, how the agency could morally justify discrimination by refusing services to this client should be questioned. The manner in which it is doing so amounts to a requirement that the social worker abandon the client. This has both ethical and legal implications. The sectarian organization, by the nature of its mission grounded both in social work values and religious values, should be helped to recognize its moral responsibility to this client. The *Code of Ethics* requires that social workers, as a part of their commitment to employers, inform them of their ethical obligation as prescribed by the *Code.* Moreover, the social worker has the responsibility to help administrators create a work environment that helps their employees carry out their ethical responsibilities.

In situations such as these, the social worker may have to consider whether he or she can continue employment with an agency where there is a conflict between one's professional values and an agency's prerogatives. Religious agencies should make their policies based on religious values and how these are expected to be carried out in practice clear at the time of contracting with an employee. All of the relevant facts are needed to determine one's ethical action; the situation suggests the need for consultation.

Glossary

Note: These definitions are based on how the terms are used in this book.

accommodation The process of adjustment of family members to each other in order to coordinate their functioning, or a therapeutic tactic used by practitioners, especially in structural family interventions, to adapt to the family style in order to create a therapeutic alliance.

alignment Who is with or against the other in the transaction generating the problem.

amplification Used by a solution-focused therapist when a client mentions positive changes. The therapist asks numerous questions to help the client expound on these changes.

attachment theory Concepts about the stages that children go through in developing social relationships and the influence of this development on relationships in later life.

behavior rehearsal A technique used in social learning family interventions, in which the practitioner suggests desired behavior and then encourages the person or family to behave similarly through demonstrations, role plays, or descriptions.

boundary What defines who is in or out of a family relationship vis-à-vis the focal issue, as well as what their roles are in this interaction.

brief family therapy Short-term interventions that are usually goal oriented, active, and focused. They emphasize resolving the presenting problem rather than seeing it as a symptom of underlying dysfunction.

brokerage A function of case managers to identify, locate, and obtain needed community resources for individuals and families.

case management A procedure for planning, securing, and monitoring services on behalf of a person or family from a variety of relevant agencies and resources.

circular causality The recursive nature of interactions of the family and other systems where the behavior of one component affects the behavior of all others.

circular question Used by a solution-focused therapist to assist family members in understanding the motivation for their behaviors; namely, "What do you think she thinks?"

coaching In Bowen's family theory, the practitioner's role is to be both a role model for individual family members in the differentiation of self-process and a facilitator or coach as they explore their families of origin.

cognitive restructuring Procedures that attempt to modify or restructure disruptive or maladaptive thought patterns that may result in maladaptive behaviors by changing feelings and actions.

collusion An integral part of projective identification in object relations theory, where the recipient of the split-off part of the partner does not disown the projection but acts on the conscious or unconscious message.

confidentiality A principle of ethics where the family practitioner or other professional may not disclose any information about the individual or family without that person's or family's consent. This includes identity, content of verbalizations, or opinions.

consulting break A break taken by a solution-focused therapist to consult with or without a team regarding recommendations to make to a client following a session.

coping question Used by a solution-focused therapist to switch the client from problem-talk to solution-talk; namely, "Given all of these problems, how do you cope?"

cultural pluralism The coexistence and mutual respect for differences and strengths of cultures and groups other than one's own.

customer   The person in solution-focused therapy who is the most motivated to effect change.

detriangulate   In Bowen's family theory, this intervention consists of pointing out the triangulation process in order to withdraw a person from the buffer or go-between role, usually with parents so as not to be drawn into alliances with one against the other. This is many times more helpful than dealing with the presenting issues.

developmental transitions   The movement of persons or families from one life stage to another. This is a time of greater stresses, problems, and conflicts, as tasks from the previous stage are consolidated and progress toward the tasks of the next stage is begun.

differentiation   In family systems theory, this is the psychological separation of intellect and emotion in the differentiation of self, and also the ability of family members to separate their identities, emotions, and thoughts from other family members' in terms of autonomy and independence. This is the opposite of fusion or enmeshment.

eclecticism   The use of many theories together or in sequence, or selected parts of them used in combination. Caution is urged in the selection of theories to use together.

ecological systems perspective   A metatheory that shows the systemic relatedness of family variables and the environment, and allows for multiple intervention methods and practitioner roles.

ecology   A science that studies the relationships that exist between organisms and their environment. In human ecology, it relates to how humans adapt or achieve goodness of fit with the environment.

ecomap   A diagram used to show reciprocal influences between a family and their environment. It would include extended family members, relevant social institutions, and environmental influences.

ecosystem   A concept pertaining to the physical, biological, and social environments of family members and the interaction between every relevant component contained therein.

effectiveness   Producing a definite or desired result. Research into the effectiveness of different theories can help us determine their validity; however, because many theories are not pre-scriptions for actions but are about ideas and interpretations, the research findings do not give us all the answers about usefulness.

empowerment   The process of helping a person or family increase their influence and strength over their own lives and circumstances.

enactment   Where a family lives out its focal struggle in a therapy session that approximates its experience at home.

encopresis   The inability to control one's bowel functions; an elimination disorder.

enmeshment   In structural family theory, this is where boundaries are blurred between family members, so that there is little autonomy or independent functioning.

environment   The conditions, circumstances, and influences of ecological or situational forces that affect the development and behavior of individuals or groups in a particular setting.

equifinality   The premise that the same result may be reached from different beginning points.

Eriksonian theory   Erik Erikson's conceptualization of human psychosocial development through eight stages of life. Each stage has a task to be accomplished before the next stage can be reached. There are conflicts or danger at each stage that could interfere with development.

ethnic competence   The ability to behave in a manner that is congruent with expectations of various ethnic groups, thus demonstrating respect for the family's cultural integrity.

ethnocentrism   The belief that one's own culture or ethnic group is superior to others.

ethnographic interviewing   Learning about specific cultures or groups by going into their natural settings, as is done when family preservation workers go into a family's home and community to provide services.

exceptions to the rule   Instances where a problem behavior did not exist or was successfully overcome; used in solution-focused therapy.

exosystem   This system represents the social structures, both formal and informal, that influence, limit, or constrain what happens there. Exosystem practice would focus on community-level factors that have an impact on the way people function.

externalizing problems   A technique in the narrative approach of getting families to view problems as external to them, thus motivating them to strengthen exceptions to the problems and control them.

family preservation Intensive services based on family strengths which are provided to families whose children are at imminent risk of out-of-home placement.

family structure The pattern of organization underlying family interactions.

first-order change In systems theory, this is a temporary and superficial change in the family system and the way it functions which leaves the basic structure and functioning of the system unchanged.

formula tasks Very general tasks that are scripted by the solution-focused therapist for use with any client regardless of the presenting problem.

fusion Fusion occurs when blurred intellectual and emotional functioning within an individual parallels the degree to which that person loses autonomy and differentiation with other family members.

generic Relating to more basic universal characteristics or patterns like those commonly found in all families, such as boundaries and authority.

genogram A graphic presentation of a multigenerational relationship system where recurring behavior patterns within the family system can be traced.

habitat The place where a person or family lives, including the physical and social setting within cultural contexts.

hedging words Words used by a solution-focused therapist to suggest to a client movement or change in a positive direction (*might, seems, could*).

holistic An individual or family is seen as more than the sum of all its parts, and problems are more than specific symptoms. Physical, social, psychological, spiritual, and cultural influences are integrated.

homeostasis A dynamic balance or equilibrium in a family or other system where one or more variables are very stable.

hypnotic situations Nontrance-induced situations developed by the solution-focused therapist that result in the client becoming more susceptible to a therapeutic suggestion.

idiographic research The study of an individual, couple, or family where baselines are established and repeated measures are used to deter-

mine results of interventions. The results may be replicated with other individuals, couples, or groups.

idiosyncratic Characteristics that are unique to a particular family with their own expectations, meanings, interactions, and behaviors that would not be representative of other families.

indigenous workers Members of a community who work with helping professionals in providing services such as those used in family preservation.

introjection In object relations theory, a primitive form of identification involving a process where an individual takes in the characteristics of other people, which then become part of the individual's own self-image.

joining A process whereby the practitioner enters the family system and relates to all members individually and to subsystems, thus developing a therapeutic alliance so that treatment goals may be reached.

levels of need Used specifically in this book to refer to families' specific needs, where lower-level needs must be met before higher-level needs are addressed.

life stage theory The idea that every period of life, including that of an individual, couple, or family, has certain goals and dangers inherent in it that serve to modify behavior and order priorities. Each higher stage builds on the accomplishments of the previous stage or may be hampered by unfinished tasks.

macrosystem The larger system that includes the overall broader context and culture. Macrosystem practice would work toward improvements in the general society through such means as political action or community organization.

maintenance An accommodation technique that is supportive of a family's structure as it is. The practitioner may relate to other family members through this structure, as, for example, a parent as the central figure.

mental research institute (MRI) The original developer of "brief therapy," this institute is in Palo Alto, California, and the model is based on the work of Gregory Bateson. MRI involves a cybernetic systems approach to working with families which focuses on observable behavioral interactions and the interventions that alter the system.

mesosystem The system that incorporates the interactions of individuals, families, and groups within the person's microsystem. Mesosystem practice would focus on interpersonal relationships within these systems.

metaphor   A figure of speech containing an implied comparison, where a word or phrase ordinarily used for one thing is applied to another to express feelings, imagination, or objective reality.

metatheory   A comprehensive system of thought that covers a wide area of practice and that would accept the inclusion of other perspectives and methods.

microsystem   This system represents the individual in family and group settings that incorporate the day-to-day environment. Microsystem practice would focus on interventions on a case-by-case basis to deal with the problems faced by individuals and families.

mimesis   A therapeutic tactic used especially by structural family practitioners as an accommodation technique, where the practitioner imitates or mirrors a family's style and communication and behavioral patterns in order to gain acceptance and accomplish goals.

miracle question   A future reality coconstructed between the solution-focused therapist and client, in which the present problems do not exist; namely, "If a miracle happened and your problems no longer existed, what would you be doing differently?"

modeling   Used in social learning theory to encourage the imitation and acquisition of behaviors observed in others that have led to more desirable outcomes.

multiculturalism   Understanding, appreciating, and valuing cultures other than one's own with their own uniquenesses and strengths.

narrative   A story created by a person or family where objective and subjective experiences are selectively arranged, which serve to organize and give meaning to the person or family.

niche   The particular role or status of an individual or family in its community and environment resulting from accommodation to this environment.

normalizing   A therapeutic technique that depathologizes problems in a way that changes perceptions of the situation, gives relief to the family, and deemphasizes the problem.

object relations theory   An interactional systems theory that views the basic human motivation

as the search for satisfying interpersonal relationships. It is based on early parent–child interpersonal relationships, which the child internalizes and which become the model for later interpersonal relations in the family of origin, mate selection, family of procreation, and other intimate relationships.

oppression   When a group, institution, or government places severe restrictions on or withholds power from other groups or institutions.

power   The relative or comparative influence of the participants upon one another in the interactions.

Premack principle   A social learning principle that requires the completion of a desired activity or low-probability behavior before doing a preferred activity or high-probability behavior; also known as "Grandma's law."

prescription   Recommendations made to a family by a solution-focused therapist following a consulting break with or without a team. Generally consists of compliments, reframes, and a task.

presuppositional questioning   In solution-focused interventions, a family is led to believe that a solution will be achieved by implying the occurrence of a specific event or selecting a specific verb tense. For example, saying, "What good things happened since last session?" instead of "Did anything good happen since last session?"

projective identification   An unconscious defense mechanism and interactional style of families where unwanted aspects of the self are attributed to another person, thus inducing that person to act according to these projected feelings and attitudes in an act of collusion.

relabeling   A therapeutic intervention that involves reframing a problem in more positive terms so that it is perceived differently and so that the person or family can respond to it differently and in a healthier way.

resilience   The ability to withstand and rebound from crises and adversities.

restructuring   The process of producing change in a family system through changing its structure; for example, strengthening the boundaries around the spousal subsystem.

scaling question   Used by the solution-focused therapist to gauge the severity of a problem; namely, "On a scale from 1 to 10, with 1 being terrible and 10 being good, how would you rate your problem?"

second-order change   In systems theory, this is a basic and lasting change in the structure and functioning of a family.

self-help organizations   These are formally structured groups, such as Parents Without Partners or Alcoholics Anonymous, that provide mutual assistance for group participants who have a common problem with which some of the members have coped successfully.

service networks   The linking of formal or informal persons, agencies, or organizations on behalf of a person or family in order to make the services available, accessible, and need-satisfying.

shaping   A procedure used especially in behavioral therapy where an area of competence or desired behavior is acknowledged and reinforced.

social constructionism   A metatheory where behaviors and relationships are seen in terms of organized efforts to create meaning out of personal experiences. Reality is seen as constructed by the person or family, family functioning is based on shared meanings, and the family practitioner becomes a coauthor of a living story with them.

social learning theory   This theory focuses on reciprocal relationships and uses principles from social and developmental psychology and learning theory for understanding and treating behavior.

solution-focused intervention   A style of intervention that emphasizes solutions or exceptions that families have already developed for their problems rather than the problems themselves.

spirituality   The dimension of life that contains the meaning people give to their lives, their standards of morality, and their definition of the social context within which they practice their beliefs.

splitting   In object relations theory, a primitive defense process where a person separates the good from the bad in an external object and then internalizes this split perception. These splits can then be projected upon other people.

strategic family interventions   A therapeutic approach where the practitioner designs interventions to resolve specific problems that will, at the same time, require the family system to modify other interactions. The focus is on second-order change and breaking the recursive sequence that seems to be maintaining the problem.

structural family therapy   A model of therapy that works through immediate experience to solve present-day key issues by altering the underlying structure of people's relationships.

symbiosis   An intense emotional attachment where the boundaries between individuals become indistinct, and they react as one as in an undifferentiated ego mass.

Tarasoff decision   A 1976 ruling by the Supreme Court of California in the case of *Tarasoff* v. *Regents of the University of California,* stating that, under certain circumstances, psychotherapists whose clients tell them that they intend to harm someone are obliged to warn the intended victim.

therapeutic alliance   The capacity of the practitioner and family systems to mutually invest in and work together toward their goals.

therapeutic contract   The agreement that the family and the practitioner have worked out together concerning what the problem is and how they will work on it. Goals, methods, mutual obligations, and timetables may be a part of the formal or informal agreement.

triangle   In family systems theory, this is a three-person system that results when a dyad under stress pulls in a third person to dilute the stress and maintain the system. The triangle is considered to be the smallest stable emotional system.

triangulation   In family systems theory, it can refer to any triangle where the conflict of two persons pulls in a third person and immobilizes this third person in a loyalty conflict. Most commonly it involves two parents and a child.

underorganization   Family structures that have not achieved the constancy, differentiation, and flexibility they need to meet the demands of family functioning.

yes-set   A hypnotic situation developed by the solution-focused therapist, in which the therapist manages to elicit affirmative responses from the client generally during the delivery of the prescription. This yes-set is meant to make the client more susceptible to a therapeutic suggestion.

Name Index

Subject Index

Page numbers followed by *f* or *t* indicate figures and tables.